CW01035093

The Real Mozart

The Real Mozart

THE ORIGINAL KING OF POP

Judith Grohmann

PEN & SWORD
HISTORY

AN IMPRINT OF PEN & SWORD BOOKS LTD.
YORKSHIRE – PHILADELPHIA

First published in Great Britain in 2023 by
Pen & Sword History
An imprint of
Pen & Sword Books Ltd
Yorkshire - Philadelphia

ISBN 978 1 39901 696 4

Printed and bound in England by CPI (UK) Ltd.

Pen & Sword Books Ltd incorporates the Imprints of Pen & Sword Archaeology,
Atlas, Aviation, Battleground, Discovery, Family History, History, Maritime,
Military, Naval, Politics, Railways, Select, Transport, True Crime, Fiction,
Frontline Books, Leo Cooper, Praetorian Press, Seaforth Publishing,
Wharncliffe and White Owl.

For a complete list of Pen & Sword titles please contact

PEN & SWORD BOOKS LIMITED
47 Church Street, Barnsley, South Yorkshire, S70 2AS, England
E-mail: enquiries@pen-and-sword.co.uk
Website: www.pen-and-sword.co.uk

or

PEN AND SWORD BOOKS
1950 Lawrence Rd, Havertown, PA 19083, USA
E-mail: uspen-and-sword@casematepublishers.com
Website: www.penandswordbooks.com

Without music, life would be a mistake.

Friedrich Nietzsche

Music is the vapour of art. It is to poetry what reverie is to thought, what fluid is to solid, what the ocean of clouds is to the ocean of waves.

Victor Hugo

Rhythm and harmony find their way into the inward places of the soul.

Plato

Contents

Acknowledgements

With this book, a dream of mine comes true. That is why I would like to thank – with all my heart – the following people who helped me to find a path in this charming, very Austrian topic:

First, my father Karl, who was a music enthusiast and who went with his family to the Wiener Staatsoper, the Konzerthaus or the Musikverein regularly and as often as he could. He was the person who brought my attention to this genius from a very tender age. *The Magic Flute* was my first opera. Then followed more of Wolfgang Amadeus Mozart's operas, but also his symphonies, piano, violin, horn, flute and wind instrument concerts that we played at home at disco volume-level – which, by the way, amused our neighbours very much.

Second, my journalistic mentor, the investigative reporter Mr Alfred Worm, who offered me many oeuvres of Mozart back in the 1980s, 1990s and, till his death, on 'old-fashioned' cassettes, and who liked to discuss music composers, styles and singers with me.

Third, my 'partner in crime' at Pen & Sword, if I am allowed to say so, Miss Heather Williams, who loves both Austria and Mozart. She gave me the big chance to discover many, many unknown sides of this magical composer and Austrian artist and to describe him here in this book.

Fourth, I would like to thank my dear and best friend, Mrs Anne-Marie le Claire, who painted a new and cool version of Wolfgang Amadeus Mozart. I must confess that I am absolutely in love with her painting.

Fifth, I would like to thank the team of the Mozarthaus in Vienna, especially Mrs Constanze Hell, a historian who told me many impressive and fascinating stories about Wolfgang Amadeus' life and eighteenth-century Vienna, as well as her colleague, Mrs Stefanie Höller, who, as the head of the Mozarthaus shop, has a very sharp mind and told me several incredible, but very funny stories about that time and the man himself.

Sixth, my absolutely gorgeous editor, the female James Bond of editing books, Mrs Carol Trow. Thank you for your strong perception and your 'sharp eyes of a Lynx'.

Seventh, I would like to thank the International Mozarteum Foundation in Salzburg and especially the head of the scientific department, Dr Ulrich Leissinger, for allowing me to look behind the curtain of this wonderful artist.

And last, but by no means least, I also want to thank Dr Gernot Gruber, an Austrian musicologist, as well as all the international Mozart experts whose books in German and in English have inspired me and who gave me the important viewpoint into a more scientific approach.

Prologue

A man was sitting at a table in his apartment in Vienna's old town. From his window on the first floor of the corner wing of his house, he could watch the passers-by as they strolled into the next street. In downtown Vienna, every street and every house had a story, like in a fairytale, and he loved that. He lived on Rauhensteingasse. Much to the amusement of his friends, his house was called the Little Imperial House, which is *Kleines Kaiserhaus* in German. But in fact, this nickname referred to the former owners of the house, the Keyser family, while the name of the street was derived from 'on the rough stone' and had an interesting Freemason connotation, because Freemasons see people as 'undressed ashlar [rough stone]', which means 'as human beings with an imperfect character, but which can be improved'.

Like most respectable men of his generation and position, he wore a brightly coloured three-piece suit, consisting of a long-sleeved jacket with large cuffs, a waist-length waistcoat, and breeches. It was basically the same cut for all classes, but you could tell from the materials exactly to what status the respective wearer belonged. On his business travels across Europe, he always stocked up on accessories and fabrics; silk, cotton, calico and wool. His profession demanded that, and he was a very vain man and he valued perfection.

But today, he was concentrating on another important topic of his life; he was writing a letter. The culture of letters had flourished, especially in the century in which he lived, the eighteenth. This era of sensitivity was characterized by a retreat into the private sphere and sentimental cultivation of feelings.

On his table he had positioned his inkwell with black ink and a whole stack of paper. In his left hand he was holding a quill pen, made from a flight feather of a swan. Again and again he mechanically dipped this pen into the inkwell; in front of him lay a coarse-grained, yellowish sheet of paper, which he held gently. His hand trembled towards the sheet, while in his head the most diverse images were combined into a whole. Then, finally, his quill pen simply flew with a great swing over the lines of the letter, which he was writing with great enthusiasm.

He was extremely focused right now, because the letter he wrote was for his wife, who he missed very much. But she had decided to stay in Baden, a suburb of Vienna around 31 kilometres away, to relax and to be free of him. After she had estranged him from his father and sister, ruined him and socially isolated him, the woman with the beautiful name of Constanze now, for the third summer and autumn, sought her amusement in the elegant little city of Baden, while he tormented himself in Vienna to get the money for her pleasures.

Of the approximately sixty letters that he wrote to her in Baden in the summer and autumn of 1791, only twenty-one have survived today. He was so full of love for her, that he wrote to her at least once a day. She, on the other hand, didn't really do anything on her own, but always wanted to be asked by him to do it.

The letters he wrote to her were heart-breaking. He spoke of increasing loneliness, the longing for her and the constant effort to make money. In his last letters to her, the topics were the same; the permanent search for money and his unfulfilled need for love. He seemed to have come to terms with the fact that not only Viennese society, friends and colleagues were avoiding him, but now his wife was too. It is said that she had an affair with a much younger man at a time when she was pregnant – officially, of course, by her husband.

In his letters, her husband only found mockery of the crudest kind for her young companion, Franz Xaver Süssmayr. He was a 25-year-old man, who she used to refer to as 'his student'. However, according to legend, this man was introduced to everybody as a music copyist and a family friend. Süssmayr also prepared the voice excerpts and copies of a composition for his master that was about to be created in Vienna.

In his letters he mostly started with a salutation in French, before unexpectedly switching into German; even if sometimes he used a combination of other languages like Italian, his writing had more a narrative character and was, in fact, full of love.

Ma très chère Epouse!   Vienna, 11th June, 1791

I cannot tell you how much I would give, if I could be sitting with you in Baden. – For no other reason than pure boredom I composed an aria for the opera today – I was already up at half past 4 this morning – now be astonished! – I managed to open my watch; – but – because I did not have a key, I unfortunately could not wind it up; isn't that sad? – shlumbla! – that is another word to think about – instead, I wound up the big clock. – Adieu – Love! – Today I dine at Puchberg's – I kiss you 1000 times and, in thought, join with you in saying: Death and Despair were his wages! – Your husband who loves you eternally.[1]

It seems surprising that the man whose beloved wife was currently staying in Baden and who wrote in his letter about 'composing an aria for the opera today' was in fact Austria's most distinguished artist and he reigned as one of the finest composers, conductors and musicians of his time. With over 600 works in many styles – like symphony, concerto, opera, vocal, piano – the man whose name was Wolfgang Amadeus Mozart gave in his very short life to all lovers of classical music the most treasured music ever written.

In June 1791 he was composing his masterpiece *The Magic Flute*, an opera which followed the tradition of Singspiel, a style that featured both music and dialogue and which binds fantastic fairy-tale creatures, crazy buffoonery, touching ideas of humanity and enlightenment with Wolfgang Amadeus Mozart's heavenly melodies.

The libretto of *The Magic Flute*, written by the German impresario and dramatist Emanuel Schikaneder, centred on the Queen of the Night, who sends Prince Tamino to free her daughter Pamina, who was being held captive in Sarastro's Realm of Light. Along the way, the prince realizes that not everything is as it seems. Accompanied and supported by his magic flute and his loyal companion, the bird catcher Papageno, they search for truth, love and enlightenment. Tamino is enlightened in Sarastro's kingdom and the kingdom of darkness has to step back. Papageno passes all the tests to become worthy of Sarastro's kingdom, and, most importantly, wins Papagena's heart and hand at the end of the opera.

His last stage work is extremely sophisticated. It brings together some of the composer's most beautiful and beloved melodies in an elegant allegory whose wicked queens and noble princes are just the beginning of a true story. The story of the real Wolfgang Amadeus Mozart, the original King of Pop.

This book is a look behind the curtain of the career and the real personality of the composer, who was born in Salzburg in 1756 as a music child prodigy. He played different instruments from a tender age and eventually created his own style by blending the traditional with the contemporary. He was beloved and hyped, but he was also a controversial personality. In his short life, Wolfgang Amadeus anticipated almost everything that makes a star today; international tours, hysterical fans, success, big hits, sex and addiction. He wrote obsessively and composed till the end of his life. As far as we know today, his oeuvre contains around 1,060 titles. Nowadays he would be showered with Grammys and platinum discs. Instead of that, the Pope knighted him, which was at that time the greatest award for an artist.

Chapter 1

Mozart's Childhood – Born as a Prodigy

It all started with a letter dated 9 February 1756, when Leopold Mozart wrote quite demurely to his publisher from the German city of Augsburg, Johann Jakob Lotter, that 'on January 27th at 8 o'clock in the evening mine had delivered a boy, but the afterbirth had to be taken away from her. So she was amazingly weak. But now, thank God, child and mother are doing well. She takes her leave on both sides.'[2] The same year, Leopold Mozart, who was originally from Augsburg in Germany and who had moved to Salzburg to study Law at the Benedictine University, before switching to a more 'profane life' and to music, beginning in 1743 as the fourth violin player at the Salzburg Court Orchestra, had published his book *The attempt of a thorough violin school*. Though Leopold Mozart came from a family of eight children, he received a thorough education, which included excellent music lessons from the Jesuits of St. Salvator. Before compulsory education became the norm, education by monks in monastery schools was a great opportunity for gifted children from low-income families.

He found his first safe job as a valet for the Salzburg canon, Johann Baptist Graf zu Thurn-Valsassina und Taxis, to whom he dedicated his first printed work in 1740. This position made it possible for him to establish himself in Salzburg and then to marry his childhood sweetheart, Anna Maria Pertl. At the time, the city of Salzburg was a carefree paradise. The idyllically pastoral beauty of the region, with heavenly mountains trailing off into the green riverbanks of the Salzach River completed this impression. Here you could indeed find people who excelled in their profound knowledge of their chosen professions. It was also a place for talents and Leopold Mozart was a favoured employee at the Imperial court.

Leopold Mozart worked professionally as a violinist, composer, theoretician and teacher. Reasonableness and following his principles characterized the musician in him. He always gave due diligence to each of his individual fields of work.

His wife Anna Maria was born in the picturesque village of Sankt Gilgen, situated on the northwest shore of Lake Wolfgang, near Strobl and the Upper Austrian municipality of St. Wolfgang. The village belonged to the Salzkammergut region in the Alpine Republic, where salt was mined. This 'white gold' used to be so precious that the region north of the Alps was managed directly by the Hofkammer in Vienna, which was responsible of the imperial finances and Vienna kept a close watch on this region. Its inhabitants needed, for example, written permission to leave and strangers were not welcomed with open arms. Over time, it seemed as if this seclusion also led to the emergence of a collective 'Salzkammergut-DNA'. People from this region were very self-confident and demonstrated a strong sense of community, as well as a touch of rebelliousness against many of the measures that had been passed in Vienna and affected their beautiful home. During the time of Emperor Franz-Joseph I, the Salzkammergut area was also an enchanting hub of cultural life.

Anna Maria Mozart's father was a senior official in charge of the administration and jurisdiction of Sankt Gilgen am Wolfgangsee, but he had not got much money. That is why Anna Maria, as a bride, was without a dowry. But what was more important to her husband Leopold was that she was a warm-hearted, lively, cheerful and musical woman. It is said that she and Leopold were the 'most beautiful married couple in Salzburg' back then. She had learned to deal with hardship from an early age and grew into a modest and thrifty woman and corresponded therefore perfectly to the image of an exemplary wife and mother who appeared inconspicuous outwardly. Most of all, she endured everything with a certain 'mother wit', for which she was known.

Leopold and Anna Maria had seven children, but only two survived. One of them was her daughter Maria Anna Walburga Ignatia, called Marianne and affectionately nicknamed Nannerl by the whole family. Maria Anna was not like her mother; the mother-wit was lost in her and what remained was the bitterness of renunciation. The reason was that although she loved music and culture so much, in her time it was simply impossible for a woman to become a professional artist. So, Maria Anna gave up, because she didn't want to protest either. Her brother's genius cast a shadow over her life, even though she was also extremely gifted.

The second child who survived in this family was the one born on 27 January 1756 at 8 o'clock in the evening in a three-room apartment in the Getreidegasse 9 in Salzburg. He was christened the next morning with the name of Joannes Chrisostomus Wolfgangus Theophilus Mozart at the Salzburg Cathedral by the city chaplain, Leopold Lamprecht. The first name, Theophilus, is Greek and is *Gottlieb* in German – 'beloved of God'. It was chosen in honour of his godfather Johann Gottlieb Pergmayr, who was a Salzburg merchant and friend of the Mozarts and who had already acted as godfather to their second child. Between 1769 and 1772 Mozart went to Italy three times with his father and renamed himself during this time to the Italian version of his name, Wolfgango Amadeo.

But what is particularly exciting and amazing is that Wolfgang Amadeus Mozart, as he called himself later, was born to an impressive family, each member having a character of his or her own.

With his own compositions, the hardworking Leopold Mozart provided his family with an additional income on top of his annual salary as deputy conductor of 500 guilders. He also gave stunning piano, singing and violin lessons, educating his children himself, which was considered extremely progressive for the time.

Concerning his working activities, Leopold Mozart achieved more international prestige with his violin instruction book, published in Augsburg by Johann Jakob Lotter, than with his compositions. Even today, it stands out as one of the most distinguished instrumental teaching school books of the eighteenth century. It testified to the popular violinist's thorough knowledge of performance practice, to his didactic skill and ability to systematize, but also to his broad educational horizon.

All these abilities were to be challenged in an incomparable way by his new born son. It seems interesting that musicians very often feel compelled to support their children's musical education. Leopold Mozart did so with his daughter Nannerl, and indeed, little Wolfgang Amadeus, who was a brave and interested child, followed his sister and found himself interfering in her music classes. He was, as it seems, a very brave boy, never got spanked and always ate well. Maybe he even was a spoiled little child. His beloved sister Nannerl told, years later, that he was 'never forced to compose or to play, on the contrary one always had to stop him, because if not, he would sit day and night at the piano or compose'.

In this very ordinary process, during the music lessons with Nannerl, Wolfgang Amadeus's extraordinary talent came into play, which his father immediately recognized in the then four-year-old child. Leopold tried to make a sober estimate of the apparent situation and the chances and possibilities associated with it, which he staked out. Leopold Mozart noted in Nannerl's music book some pieces that 'Wolfgang Amadeus started to learn at the age of 4 years'. At this age, his father started with his music lessons.

Leopold Mozart's educational principles were love, patience and being a role model, combined with an enormous teaching workload, in which the Mozart children grew up, to later concert tours that took the whole family across Europe in their own carriage, when the two siblings and child prodigies got to know, later on, princes, emperors and kings. But they knew that they were also going to amaze and be admired – and would attract increasing attention in the music world.

Childlike obedience to parents was in this time just as normal as it was to rulers and to God. For the deeply religious father, this current situation in the family must have been a pure revelation, or even a great gift, to be able to follow, live, every single day. What a great talent was currently growing up in his family.

His son became more and more the centre of Leopold Mozart's life. Meticulously, he trained him in all the core subject areas. Mankind's entire experience was contained in this young and extraordinary musical spirit, just waiting to be awakened – for example by engaging with the works of other great artists or by improvising on the piano. Wolfgang Amadeus grasped sounds, techniques and entire systems during these episodes with his beloved father, in which he immediately began to become creative, experiencing self-realization. It was a very special process, taking place in front of the eyes of his father and his sister. At the tender age of six, he received a small violin and – without the slightest instruction – he started to play, like a professional musician.

From later letters, it is known that the father had become so involved in his son's musical education, that he took the upbringing of the talented child upon himself and completely limited the influence of his mother, Anna Maria. Her desperate attempts to curb the various naughtinesses of the young musician – that every child has at this age – remained, much to her annoyance, most of the time fruitless. Instead, mother and daughter were allowed to serve and to love the little boy – that became their main job. Meanwhile, his father worked hard on him and became his great mentor.

This led Andreas Schachtner, trumpeter to the Archbishop of Salzburg and an old family friend, to report even after Mozart's death, to his sister Nannerl:

> Mozart was a very bright and affectionate child. He was full of fire and was very attached to every object. Before he started his interest in music, he was so extremely receptive to any

childishness spiced with a little wit, that he could forget about eating and drinking and everything else. I became so fond of him because I ... was so outwardly so receptive of him, that he often asked me ten times in a day whether I'd loved him.

This early childhood receptivity found its fascinating topic in classical music, and 'as soon as he has started to deal with music, all his senses for all other businesses were as much as dead, that even the children's eyes and flirtation had to be accompanied by music, if they were to be of interest to him.'

Leopold Mozart's sense of reality reflected the ideological and social mood of the time, with the liberal thinking and the enlightened despotism in Europe. Feudalism and clericalism in an *ancien régime* versus the rise of a bourgeoisie striving for freedom; hierarchical thinking and loyalty to Christian dogma versus a spirit of criticism, that turned against bare guidelines and the system. Exploitation versus the fight for human rights, belief in miracles versus the cult of the intellectual, old versus new in business and industry or in the academic pursuit of science. Many of the progressive critics came from privileged classes themselves. They had a strong urge to help their ideas to public effectiveness and therefore consequently sought the proximity of the powerful.

In this world and time, Leopold Mozart became the strategist, promoting the child prodigy glory of his two children. With a fine intuition for local circumstances, he used his contacts with nobility – princes and kings, as well as churches, prominent musicians and intellectuals – or the emerging new possibilities of a musical market and the media of the time, in a very targeted manner for his family.

For artists, but especially for the performance practitioners among them, such as people from theatres, singers or musicians, it was – and will always be – extremely important that their performance is preceded by fame, that when we talk about them, a potential audience of whatever social class has already a vividly illustrated expectation of their appearance. Of course, most of the known prodigies also unfold part of their well-known power of fascination in exactly this way.

Something had to move forward for the Mozart family and their talented children. That is why they had to go on a journey and this would unfortunately cause different problems. First of all, they had to be allowed to travel, because no employer feels happy when his employee (at that time they were called 'subordinates') moves abroad with his whole family but still wants to keep his job. In the case of Leopold Mozart, the man was lucky again, because his employer, Prince Archbishop Siegmund Christoph Graf Schrattenbach, was a very compassionate man. Nonetheless, the second problem was a financial one. Of course, you can care for seed capital, but you then need to allow more money for the travelling, the accommodation and the meals for your family. In this phase, you are already dependent on an income, which in turn is much more difficult to calculate. Another risk involved maintaining constant good health for the whole time of the concert tour. All these uncertainties could only be guaranteed through continuous success. Therefore, Leopold Mozart needed the right strategy for his concert tour with his children. But he was a smart man and so two aspects shaped his actions; first he planned to do a concert in a geographically close, familiar and well-known place with the help of personal contacts he already had, planned with little effort and in a short period of time for the stay. If this first project was successful, then nothing stood in the way for another journey to a larger city and a less familiar audience. Glory and risk would grow equally, he thought realistically.

The first step was completely clear for Leopold Mozart and therefore he targeted the residence of Maximilian III Joseph, Elector of Bavaria in Munich, a city that was only two days journey from Salzburg in those days, and the nearest place to start the tour. Because

Wolfgang Amadeus, at the age of 5½, had successfully accomplished a theatre performance as a dancer in front of a huge audience in Salzburg, his father decided to take the whole family on a trip on 12 January 1762 to Munich, somewhere that he already had visited before.

The Elector was considered a party-loving man who enjoyed going to the opera and who was enthusiastic about theatre and hunting. The fact that the Elector, who himself was a musician and composer, received the Mozarts, can be interpreted as positive. But due to a need for strict frugality, no post could be offered; in the end, it turned out that Elector Maximilian III Joseph had limited resources.

Leopold Mozart was now trying to take the next step towards success as quickly as possible and feverishly considered what he could do. So on 18 September 1762, he decided to travel from Salzburg to Vienna with his family for an appearance at the Imperial court. The journey lasted exactly three months and they came back to Salzburg on 5 January 1763.

On the outward journey, Wolfgang Amadeus gave demonstrations of his skills at various places along the Danube river. He did this to let the move to Vienna precede a sort of 'fame', a good recognition by many people because of his skills and probably to be able to show this good reputation in front of the Viennese.

On 13 October 1762, the Holy Roman Emperor Francis Stephen I and his wife, Holy Roman Empress Maria Theresa, received the Mozart family. It was a memorable day. Ten-year-old Maria Anna and six-year-old Wolfgang Amadeus played for the imperial family in the Hall of Mirrors at Schönbrunn Palace. Maria Theresa, Francis Stephen I and twelve archdukes and archduchesses listened attentively to their recital on the piano and on the violin. Anecdotes say that the Mozart children played with the imperial children after the concert and romped through the Hall of Mirrors. Wolfgang Amadeus slipped, was caught by Archduchess Marie Antoinette and allegedly announced that he would marry her when he grew up!

Wolfgang Amadeus's father described the first scene of this meeting in a letter:

> Wolferl jumped onto the Empress' lap, got hold of her round the neck and kissed her roundly. In brief, we were with her from 3 o'clock to 6 o'clock and the Emperor himself came out into the other room to fetch me in order to hear the Infanta playing the violin.[3]

After that, the Mozart family was passed around in the aristocratic houses in Vienna, where the performances took between one and three hours each time. The recommendation by the Empress Maria Theresa was the best gift for the family to get and a wonderful promotion too. Wolfgang Amadeus and Nannerl not only received 100 gold ducats (450 guilders – to get a feeling for the currency of the time; a horse cost about 10 guilders, a simple travelling carriage about 60 guilders) as a fee for their performance, but also preciously embroidered gala dresses that had previously belonged to the children of Maria Theresa – because at the Imperial court it was common at that time to give away children's clothes to subordinates.

However, the happiness of the Mozart family did unfortunately not remain undisturbed. Even after this tremendous first success, enormous problems suddenly arose during this kind of child prodigy trips. On one hand, the income from these sorts of performances in front of the aristocracy remained low and on the other hand, Wolfgang Amadeus suddenly started to fight against a skin condition, because of the stress of the concert tour. This illness was called *Erythema nodosum*, which was an inflammatory skin condition. The first signs were flu-like symptoms such as a fever, cough, malaise, and aching joints. Because of this illness, the second concert in Schönbrunn Palace was affected.

Before the family travelled home from Vienna on 15 December, the philanthropist Count Thomas Vinciguerra Collalto gave them a written verse during an evening gathering, delivered in high praise, *On the little six-year-old Clarinettist from Salzburg*. This was certainly a wonderful and promotionally effective gift for the family and especially for the little Wolfgang Amadeus.

As soon as the family was back in Salzburg in January 1763, Leopold Mozart, in order not to lose time, started the planning of the next concert tour with his children. What needs to be said is that there was also a political influence at that time. Notably because of the treaty of Hubertusburg on 15 February 1763, the Seven Years War between Austria and Prussia ended. Finally there was peace and this had a calming effect on the whole of Europe. Leopold Mozart thought that he could benefit from this situation and so he started, slowly but surely, to organize and plan meticulously the next steps for the touring of his child prodigies.

On 6 June 1763, the Mozart family started a new trip that led them to cities like Paris and London, taking more than three years. This journey was certainly a peak in intensity and spread of prodigy fame, but also for the family a possibility to experience this world of talent and of a musical career growing each day. After all, it was a time where the family members could observe the inner change of the child prodigy Wolfgang Amadeus Mozart and his developing compositional creativity.

This trip cost a total of 20,000 guilders and credits had to be paid and be redeemable quickly at various locations along the way. A friend of the Mozart family, the entrepreneur Johann Lorenz Hagemauer, helped and supported the family during this journey, to ensure that everything was perfect. The stay in Paris was extremely long and the journey took a long time too.

Quite the perfect music agent of his time, Leopold chose the travel destinations and stations in such a way that they gave the best opportunities for performances and were crowned with success. This worked particularly well in the German-speaking countries and also in the Habsburg Netherlands. But things changed as soon as the family went to France. The French were not yet informed about the talented little Wolfgang Amadeus.

The most important stops planned by Leopold Mozart included Munich, Augsburg, Ulm, Ludwigsburg, Schwetzingen, Mainz, Frankfurt, Cologne, Aachen, then Brussels and Paris. In Munich it was primarily about contacts with princes; the Mozart family was received and encouraged by Prince Maximilian III Joseph, Elector of Bavaria, Duke Clemens of Bavaria and Prince Karl August Christian of Zweibrücken. They received letters of recommendation and sums of money, but also important contacts were made with other people, who were met again at the next stop and who helped with financial transactions.

But when the family finally arrived in Paris on 18 November, they entered a new cultural and artistic territory. France was a centralized state whose main focus was on the residential city of Paris. Under different circumstances, Austria's Empress Maria Theresa had begun to thoroughly organize and reform her territory, which particularly increased the value of Vienna. But one could not compare Vienna with Paris.

What also happened was that all the letters of recommendation from Brussels and Vienna that Leopold Mozart got for Wolfgang Amadeus were worthless in Paris. But with the help of good contacts, the Mozart family found accommodation in the famous Hôtel de Beauvais, a palace which was the residence of the Bavarian ambassador, the Count Maximilian Emanuel Franz von Eyck, whose wife Maria Anna Felicitas, Countess van Eyck, came from the family of the Counts of Arco. And so, the Mozarts lived at this palace for five months.

The court of King Louis XV and his royal household in Versailles outshone everything and the Mozarts experienced at first hand how the cultural life of the city of Paris had a special vibrant autonomy. That is why they decided to immerse themselves in the seductive French artist life, which was full of salons, meetings of intellectuals, with aristocrats who were interested in the zeitgeist.

The family Mozart eventually discovered that there was indeed an interest in artists from other countries, whose activities already stretched across Europe like a huge spider's web. But it was clear that in order to gain access to this artistic structure, the Mozart family needed the help of beneficial contacts, who would spin a thread between the aristocratic bourgeoisie and the court sphere. To find the right person to realize this took the Mozarts more than five weeks. Finally, Leopold Mozart got in touch with the assistant of the Duke of Orléans, Baron Friedrich Melchior Grimm, through a businessman from Frankfurt. And he was fortunate, because Grimm became extremely enthusiastic about Nannerl and Wolfgang Amadeus. More help came also from Grimm's mistress, the writer Louise Florence Pétronille Tardieu d'Esclavelles d'Épinay, a woman known in the Parisian society under the name of Madame d'Épinay. She was surrounded by scandals, but thanks to her good liaisons in all artistic and intellectual fields in the city, the Grande Dame de Salon – as they called her in Paris – was present everywhere. Thanks to her, the Mozart family was taken to the noble Palace of Versailles by a contact, Louis de Noailles Duc d'Ayen, a French peer and Marshal of France.

The letter that Grimm himself published on 1 December 1763 in his magazine *La Correspondance littéraire, philosophique et critique* is the liveliest:

> The true wonders are rare enough to speak of when one has an opportunity to see one. A conductor from Salzburg named Mozart has just arrived with two children of the prettiest appearance in the world. His daughter, eleven years old [she had been 12 in July], plays the piano at its most brilliant, performing the largest and most difficult pieces with astonishing precision. Her brother, who will be seven next February [actually he was eight in January 1764], is such an extraordinary phenomenon that what one sees with one's eyes and hears with one's ears is hard to believe. It is not only easy for the child to play the most difficult pieces with

the greatest accuracy and with little hands that can hardly grasp the sixth; nay, it is incredible to see him fantasize for a whole hour, giving himself up to the enthusiasm of his genius and to a wealth of delightful ideas, which he succeeds in following one another with taste and without confusion. It is impossible for the most practiced *Kapellmeister* to have such a deep knowledge of harmony and modulations that he knows how to carry them out in the least known but always correct way. He has such dexterity on the keyboard, that if you take it away from him by putting a napkin over it, he will play it on the napkin with the same speed and precision. It is easy for him to decipher everything that is presented to him; it writes and composes with an admirable ease, without approaching the piano and looking for its chords on it [thus even then complete independence from sensual support]. I set him a minuet and asked him to write the bass below it; the child took hold of the pen and, without going near the piano, put the bass under it. You may well imagine that it does not take him the slightest trouble to transpose any aria that is put before him and play whatever note it is asked for. Just what I have seen is no less incomprehensible. A woman asked him the other day: would he accompany an Italian cavatina, which she knew by heart, by ear and without looking at her? She started singing. The child tried a bass that wasn't strictly correct, because it's impossible to predict exactly the accompaniment of an unfamiliar song! But as soon as the song was over, he asked the lady to start again, and now he not only played the whole thing with his right hand, but also added the bass with his left without the slightest embarrassment; whereupon he asked her ten times in a row to start again, and with each repetition he changed the character of his companion. He would have had it repeated twenty more times had he not been asked to stop. I can really see it coming, that this child will turn my head if I hear it one more time; and it makes me understand how hard it must be to keep yourself from madness when you experience miracles. Herr Mozart's children aroused the admiration of all who saw them, and the Emperor and Empress showered them with kindness. They experienced the same reception in Munich and Mannheim. It's a pity that people in this country understand so little about music![4]

A little later, in the middle of December, the two Mozart children performed in front of the powerful mistress of King Louis XV, Madame de Pompadour. Leopold found her very attractive, but full of pride; in his view, she already looked like an empress. He smiled as Wolfgang Amadeus whispered to him, that she looked like Threzel, who was their cook in Salzburg.

After the performance, 6-year-old Wolfgang Amadeus is said to have tried to give the lady what Austrians call a *Busserl* (a sweet kiss), with which he had delighted many distinguished ladies. But this time it didn't work out. Madame Pompadour reacted defensively. And instead of walking silently away from her, apparently not used to such rejection, Wolfgang Amadeus is said to have announced in German (which Madame Pompadour did not understand), 'Who is she that doesn't want to kiss me? The Austrian Empress kissed me after all.'

In December 1763, the Mozarts assisted at the Christmas mass in the Royal chapel, close to the royal family. And on New Year's Day, Leopold Mozart narrated a scene similar to that in Vienna as he was a guest of the Empress Maria Theresa, to his friends in Salzburg, the Hagenauers. The Mozarts were invited to the King's *Grand Couvert* and little Wolfgang Amadeus stood next to the French Queen Marie Leszczynska, the wife of Louis XV, Leopold near the king and Nannerl between the Dauphin and Madame Adélaïde:

The most extraordinary thing in the eyes of the worthy French gentlemen, however, was at the grand couvert held on New Year's Day. Here, not only did a way have to be made free for all of us as far as the royal table, but it was also granted to my Master Wolfgangus to stand beside the Queen the whole time, to speak to her constantly and to kiss her hand frequently, and to eat at her side the food which she gave him from the table. The Queen speaks German as well as we do. But, as the King has no grasp of it, the queen interpreted for him everything that our heroic Wolfgang said.[5]

At the end of the meal, Louis XV asked to hear little Wolfgang Amadeus play the organ. A time was agreed for the next day. But the impatient king got up and went straight to the royal chapel. Everyone followed him. The child struck a prolonged note, then another, followed by a deluge of harmony. Louis was amazed. Leopold Mozart found the music of the Royal Chapel both good and bad. According to him, the choirs were excellent, but the vocal music 'too cold' and 'too French'.

Everything in Paris was expensive; logs to keep warm, black clothes to look good, sedan chairs to move around. Costs were fortunately offset by the luxurious presents that the two little musicians received – for example snuffboxes, watches and precious boxes, all made of solid gold – and by a special gift of 1,200 pounds that Louis XV granted the Mozarts by the *Menus-Plaisirs* (the service in charge of the French king) as soon as they left France.

Nevertheless, the performance in Versailles and the royal audience made an impact and invitations from French nobility flooded in. It is interesting to observe that, again, noblewomen became the first French mentors of the young Mozart. The French salon holder and letter writer Adrienne Catherine de Noailles, Comtesse de Tessé was one of them, as was Victoire-Marie-Anna de Savoie, Princess of Carignan, who lived a scandalous life at the Hôtel de Soisson, turning it into a most dangerous place for gambling and acting herself as a spy in Paris for her Italian father and influencing the politics of

Louis XV. The Mozart family stayed at the court of the king for more than fifteen days.

One of the economic highlights of the time the Mozart family spent in Paris was a concert organized by Baron Grimm on 10 March 1764 in the theatre of Mr. Félix on the Rue et Porte Saint Honoré. The takings that day were a staggering 112 Louis d'Or. In newspapers in Germany and in Austria, journalists wrote about the success of this concert. From then on, printed matter became increasingly important as a means of attracting attention – whether in the form of a feuilleton or of reports that were obviously initiated primarily by Baron Melchior Grimm or even written by himself, or in the form of Wolfgang Amadeus's first published compositions.

As a sign of gratitude, in March Wolfgang Amadeus dedicated his first two harpsichord sonatas published in Paris to Princess Victoire of France, the fifth daughter and seventh child of Louis XV and Marie Leszczinska. At the end of their stay in Paris, Leopold Mozart was so delighted that he wrote joyfully in a letter to his friends in Salzburg, 'Now we are acquainted with all the envoys of foreign powers here.'

But the next travel destination on their epic first long trip approached all too soon; it was England on 23 April 1764. The Mozart family discovered the beautiful city of London, with a thoroughly self-confident and wealthy aristocracy and an equally self-confident bourgeoisie, so to speak, for whom culture was an important element in their life; therefore their musical life was very intense. The city had a respectfully nurtured tradition of instrumental and choral music. Maybe this was the reason why the Mozarts stayed there more than a year.

Leopold Mozart originally wanted to organize this stay in the same way as the one in Paris. However, the family lived in London without any connection to the nobility and initially moved into an apartment belonging to a hairdresser. Through contact with Claude-Adrien Helvetius, who was a French philosopher, freemason and *littérateur*, the Mozarts were received at the court of George III, who was married to Charlotte of Mecklenburg-Strelitz from Germany. Both of them were highly interested in music. Queen Charlotte even played the harpsichord.

The Mozart children were seen in public much more in London than they had been in Paris. Here they played in concert halls and at charity events. The venues included famous places in the city, like the Haymarket Theatre, the rotunda in Ranelagh Gardens near Chelsea or the Great Room in Spring Garden. An article in the *Niederlandsch Mengel-Nieuws* from 16 February 1765 described the first impressions that the British public had of the young Wolfgang Amadeus:

Among the wonders of the arts and sciences may surely be placed the case of a certain High German boy named Wolfgang Mozart, who is only around 8 years old and is a composer and master of music the like of which no one has ever seen. This boy, who recently arrived in England, not only plays by heart on the harpsichord with incredible precision and skill the concertos and sonatas of various masters, but also improvises in a wonderful way the most difficult Fantasias, worthy of the greatest masters. If one presents him with a piece, he will vary it and even play it in another key. If one presents him with an aria to sing, he will do so while simultaneously playing an accompaniment, without having seen it beforehand. If one gives him something without a bass, he will play it, adding bass and middle voices without effort. If, on the contrary, one gives him a simple bass part, he will play it while adding the required melody. He will execute the most demanding compositions on the organ; in short, no matter how he is put to the test, people always become convinced of his superior and almost incomprehensible talent. In addition, he composes his pieces without touching the keyboard; this musical wonder submits himself boldly to the judgment of all masters of music and connoisseurs, expecting them to do him justice on account of his abilities, and the whole world, thus informed, to agree that he is an example without equal, and that one has to see and hear him in order to be properly convinced of his astonishing prowess in music. Thus one sees that diligence and desire are capable of raising someone from childhood to great ability and that it is not always the mature years that bring forth great men.[6]

But these successes were again torpedoed by illnesses, first of the young Wolfgang Amadeus, who fell ill for about ten days in May, followed by his father, who was sick for a whole month. After that, it was very difficult to get back the old success. One reason may be that, looking back, the Mozart family simply stayed in England for far too long. Nothing changed when they again approached George III.

In spring 1766, the family was invited to make a trip to Den Haag and to meet the Dutch envoy there. They stayed about a year in Den Haag and then moved to Amsterdam. Wolfgang Amadeus performed again in front of royals, this time Prince Wilhelm V from the House of Orange-Nassau and his sister Princess Carolina. Both were huge music enthusiasts. But here again, the augurs had other plans for the Mozart family.

It all started with a drama, because this time it was Wolfgang Amadeus's sister Nannerl who fell ill with the highly dangerous abdominal typhus. She was even given the last rites in October 1765, but fortunately survived the illness. Then, in November it was Wolfgang Amadeus who became ill with the same disease, but he recovered in December. And at the end of January 1766, it was finally possible for the children to give a concert – once again, the family had an income. This concern about their livelihood threatened the Mozart family whenever they were on a concert tour. It was always possible that one of the children – or one of the adults – could become sick and then it became a struggle every day for an income for four people.

After the death of his father and an interregnum under his mother Anne of Hanover, his grand-mother Marie-Louise of Hesse-Cassel and his sister Princess Carolina of Orange-Nassau, William V assumed the position of stadtholder and Captain-General of the Dutch States Army at the age of 18 on 11 March 1766. Wolfgang Amadeus was invited to give a concert during the celebrations for the official introduction of the Prince. Wolfgang Amadeus's quodlibet, a musical composition in which several well-known melodies are combined, either simultaneously or, less frequently, sequentially, for humorous effect, which he called *Galmathias Musicum* (KV 32), was probably performed as table music on this occasion.

Successful and honoured, the family travelled to Amsterdam, then on to Haarlem, Utrecht and Rotterdam, before continuing their trip to Antwerp and Brussels before they finally drove to Paris. But before that, there was a trip to Valenciennes, which was a commune in the Nord department in northern France, to meet Marie-Thérèse Geoffrin, whose salon in Paris was one of the most famous meeting places for intellectuals.

In mid-May, the Mozarts were back in the French capital, Paris. Leopold Mozart's great goal for his son of gaining fame as a child prodigy in the major centres of Europe was achieved. The family stayed in Paris for two more months and was received again at the court in Versailles. The Mozarts had now acquired an important status in Parisian high society; they were considered as highly important, they had attracted important acquaintances in different places, but they also had cultivated, so to speak, a noble fan base. As was common during the eighteenth century, reports in newspapers, pictures and word of mouth did the rest to keep the curious public of this time up to date about this young musical prodigy.

And from that moment on, Leopold Mozart no longer had to develop strategies to find a personality who could help him to promote his son, and suddenly everything was crystal clear. The Mozarts were received with respect and invited to the best events in the city, so that they could network with intellectuals and musicians. Everybody became interested in coming into contact with the Mozart family.

These invitations were not as spectacular as those in the Netherlands, but honourable and above all they opened up new, additional performance options for the Mozart family. Last but not least, the Mozart family did not return to Salzburg with a fortune worth millions, but with many extremely valuable gifts. These gifts could easily be monetized. As soon as the family had returned to Austria, Leopold made new plans for the next concerts, even cherishing a plan based on the many letters he and his family received and wrote, including those he wrote to his friend Johann Lorenz Hagenauer; he would write a new book based on these letters, which were memoirs of their experiences.

The children grew older. Wolfgang Amadeus was now 11 and his sister Nannerl was 15 years old. But something important changed; at the beginning, when Wolfgang Amadeus was only 7, he had the 'prodigy bonus', but now, at the age of 11, he was a young composer who had thrived with works in a wide variety of genres and on a larger scale in Paris, London, Amsterdam, Germany and Switzerland. And Leopold Mozart was obviously the best music manager one could imagine at that time, because he skilfully wove a career for his 11-year-old son, knowing that one could make a very good name for oneself in church and theatre.

Shortly after the family had returned to Salzburg, Wolfgang Amadeus composed an aria in homage to Prince Archbishop Schrattenbach, which was officially performed at the end of a play given by an Italian theatre company.

In March 1767, the first part of an oratorio by Wolfgang Amadeus was then performed in the Salzburg Residence. It was called *The Obligation of the First Commandment* (KV 35), with the second and the third parts composed by Joseph Haydn and Anton Kajetan Adlgasser. On Good Friday, his *Grave Music* (KV 42) was performed in the Salzburg Cathedral and the young prodigy's first bigger piece of musical theatre was *Apollo et Hyacinthus* (KV 38), performed in the auditorium of the Salzburg University in May as an interlude of a Latin tragedy.

Finally, on 11 September, the Mozart family travelled to Vienna to give a concert at the wedding of the young Archduchess Josepha, who was about to marry Ferdinand IV of Naples. But while the Mozarts were still on their way, the young aristocrat died in the smallpox epidemic. Leopold Mozart tried to avoid the illness for him and his family by taking a detour via Olomouc and Brno. Nevertheless, his two children fell ill, but survived the illness well and were able to return to their music events in December. At the beginning of the next year, the Mozarts were finally back in fashionable Vienna and were again received in audience on 19 January by Empress Maria Theresa. During the audience, King Joseph II, who genuinely appreciated Mozart's music and greatly admired his operas, asked Wolfgang Amadeus if he wanted to compose and conduct an opera. Of course, he and his father accepted and chose as a style the *opera buffa* with libretto by Carlo Goldoni. It was originally planned to finish the opera in the autumn, but the people from the theatre business were not satisfied with the king's choice. Their concern was whether it was really possible to expect such a task from a child prodigy? Because of these special worries, they had a plan and decided to delay the opera's performance. They did this until Leopold Mozart wrote the emperor a letter complaining about the hopeless situation. Specifically, he complained about the scheming impresario Giuseppe Affligio. The emperor reacted quickly and ordered an investigation, but this came to nothing. For this reason, Mozart's first opera, *La Finta Simplices*, was not performed in Vienna.

However, Empress Maria Theresa got Wolfgang Amadeus a new job in the field of church music and so the 11-year-old worked diligently on his next composition commissions. One of these concerned the celebration of the consecration of the church of the orphanage on

Rennweg. And so the *Orphanage Mass* (KV 139) was developed by him, as well as an offertory and a trumpet concerto, which Wolfgang Amadeus Mozart himself was to conduct. These were so-called compensation orders. A Viennese doctor, Dr Franz Anton Mesmer, who later went down in the history of Viennese medicine as the founder of hypnosis and of music therapy, paid the young composer for his next work which was performed in 1767/68. In Mesmer's palace with a huge garden in the Rasumofskygasse 29, in Vienna's third district, the Singspiel *Bastien and Bastienne*, about the love story of a man and a woman and how a village fortune teller helps deepen that love, was performed by the young Mozart.

While still in Vienna, Leopold Mozart was already planning the future of his prodigy-son and he considered organizing a trip to Italy, because he saw and he also understood how fast the time ran. Although Wolfgang Amadeus was already 14 years old when this trip to Italy took place, his compositional development was progressing incredibly quickly. That is why even his own father took it upon himself to write a biography of the young man, that contained a list of all of his compositions since he was 7 years old. But first, Leopold Mozart wanted to write the second edition of his successful book, *The attempt of a thorough violin school.*

Chapter 2

Becoming a Star in the Music Industry
of the Time

Wolfgang Amadeus Mozart was obviously the child musical prodigy par excellence of the eighteenth century, if not for all time. He played songs on the harpsichord by the age of four and started already to compose simple pieces of music by the age of five. After he turned seven, the family embarked on a first series of tours to showcase the amazing musical abilities of the young prodigy and of his equally remarkably gifted older sister. There is also no lack of numerous anecdotes about the astonishing musical ability, the memory, as well as the great creativity of the young composer Mozart.

Of course, the prodigy fame of his son and daughter was not only due to the success of the clever strategist Leopold Mozart. In reality, both of his children were talented and therefore prodigies. But there was a difference between men's and women's career at this time, with the promotion and treatment of women being completely different to that of men. As a child and later also as a woman of the eighteenth century, Maria Anna had a much harder time making a career than her little brother did. This applied not only to the daring step from child prodigy to professional composer, but rather to all decision-making situations in which the young woman had to defy her father's will. It is interesting to note that even today, everyone calls her by her nickname Nannerl, and not by her real name Maria Anna. But it would seem absurd to call the composer of *The Magic Flute* by a nickname, like Wolfgangerl. Although his father Leopold did sometimes use the nickname "Woferl" in letters to his friends. It is all the more tragic to observe how early the younger brother of Maria Anna started a music career with such ease, before he rushed ahead in his development.

At this point it is interesting to mention how various, later well-known artists of the twentieth century commented on Wolfgang Amadeus Mozart, for example the provocative Canadian pianist Glenn Gould, who commented that only the early Mozart was brilliant, but not that of the generally recognized masterpieces.

However, not all of Gould's admirers were so tolerant of his unorthodox views. In 1968 he hosted a segment of the weekly public television series *Public Broadcast Library*. The topic of the thirty-seven-minute-program, which features Gould talking and playing music, was 'How Mozart became a bad composer'. This was, perhaps suffice to say, a very unpopular opinion, but it was significant in several respects and showed his ambivalent feelings toward Mozart's music. The program outraged viewers in the United States and Canada, including formerly sympathetic fans and critics. Gould opened his programme, dressed in a dark blue suit, seated at the piano – presumably his beloved Steinway concert grand, CD 318 – and started with a selection from Mozart's *Piano Concerto in C minor*, then claimed in his critical commentary that the piece had:

> a rather better press than it deserves, I think. Despite its gently swooning melodies, its meticulously balanced cadences, despite its stable and architecturally sound form, I will offer it as a good example of why I believe Mozart, particularly in his later years, was not a very good composer.[7]

Later Gould casually compared Mozart's 'dependent' craftsmanship to 'the way an accountant sends out an internal memo.'[8]

It was no coincidence that the programme appeared in April 1968. The reason behind this was simple; the same month, the record label Columbia Masterworks Records released the first album in Gould's cycle of Mozart's sonatas, which would ultimately comprise five volumes, the last released in 1975. The first album included the five sonatas, KV 279 through KV 283, that Mozart composed in Munich early in 1775, around the time he turned nineteen. Gould wrote no liner notes for any of his Mozart albums but would make his case about Mozart's music in other forums over the years. His PBL appearance was his first major effort in that campaign. Gould's Mozart albums received a great deal of attention, much of it unflattering; his lean, fleet-footed, insistently contrapuntal and unsentimental readings of the sonatas startled many listeners.

By contrast, the famed American composer, pianist, music lecturer and conductor Leonard Bernstein said in a lecture, entitled 'The Ageless Mozart', that he gave together with the New York Philharmonic Orchestra on 22 November 1959, the exact opposite:

> Mozart is all music; there is nothing you can ask from music that he cannot supply. I wish we could perform for you enough of Mozart's music to give you the range of his emotional palette – such works as the *C Minor Mass*, the *Requiem*, *Cosi Fan Tutte*, the *E Flat Symphony*, the *G Minor Quintet*, and so on.[9]

And to explain the admiration for the young Austrian composer, Bernstein continued to describe the artist, who in his opinion was a grand master of 'serious' music. 'The key to the mystery of a great artist is that for reasons unknown, he will give away his energies and his life just to make sure that one note follows another ... and leaves us with the feeling that something is right in the world.' Aside, obviously, from his capacity as a composer, having written one of the great musicals of our time in *West Side Story*, Bernstein saw the importance of helping those who are otherwise non-musical to understand why it is that someone like Mozart is great and why, exactly, Mozart's music is foundational and intriguing. He knew, too, that the conducting profession entailed something far greater than merely touring around the world with an accomplished orchestra in order to offer respectable interpretations of the great pieces.

In his fourth televised Young People's Concert in 1958, Leonard Bernstein added an explanation of the term 'development in Arts', by saying to his audience, 'Development is really the main thing in life, just as it is in music; because development means change, growing, blossoming out; and these things are life itself.'[10] Bernstein then continued, during this fourth concert to explore the techniques of music composers.

> But what does development mean in music? The same thing as it means in life; great pieces of music have a lifetime of their own from the beginning to the end of any piece; and in that period all the themes and melodies and musical ideas the composer had, no matter how small they are, grow and develop into full-grown works, just as babies grow into big, grown-up people.

Bernstein goes on to describe how musical ideas – such as four simple notes – blossom into a beautiful symphony, using the example of Mozart's *Jupiter* Symphony Number 41 in C Major KV 551. For Bernstein, the last movement of this symphony was 'one of the greatest examples of development in the whole history of music'. And this is mesmerizing, because this beautiful piece of music developed only from four interesting notes, as Bernstein analyzes for his audience. What makes the art of Mozart so extraordinary, in Bernstein's opinion, is that the music of the composer and 'greatest creative spirit' Wolfgang Amadeus Mozart cannot be put in a cage, or a frame of its time, the eighteenth century, which was an era of manners, of conformism, a time of great formality, a huge amount of attention being paid to style, courtly gestures, to modes of dress, to elegance and behaviour and to forms of address. 'Mozart's music is constantly escaping from its frame, because it cannot be contained in it. No matter how clearly every bar of it is labeled 1779 or 1784, the music is essentially timeless. It is classical music by a great romantic.'[11]

Bernstein suggests that this may come as a surprise to some of those, who are interested in music and who have the habit of 'equating Mozart with aristocratic delicacy' and nothing more. 'It's the ornament that makes the excitement. So, it turns out, that Mozart has actually used the ornament itself for deep musical values and not only for eighteenth century icing. But these ornaments.'[12]. And then Leonard Bernstein goes deeper and gives an in-depth analysis, 'Mozart combines serenity, melancholy, and tragic intensity into one great lyric improvisation. Over it all hovers the greater spirit that is Mozart's – the spirit of compassion, of universal love, even of suffering – a spirit that knows no age, that belongs to all ages.' The creativity of a real artist in music has in Leonard Bernstein's opinion no boundaries:

> You can see again how Mozart has transcended the limitations of the formula by the power and depth of his own invention. So, we begin to discern what this eighteenth-century frame is made of: cadence formulas, accompaniment formulas like Alberti basses, or repeated figurations, or triplet figures. I don't know if you are familiar with the great *C Major Piano Concerto*, whose second movement begins with just those triplets. But when an unbelievable melodic line begins to soar above it, the mechanical little accompaniment becomes in itself a thing of a rare beauty, especially orchestrated as it is with delicious pizzicato basses and subtle woodwind reinforcement. I find it one of the special treasures of all music history.[13]

That both children of Leopold Mozart were talented is not a myth. But the reality behind the curtain can surprise, because an achievement that arouses astonishment must not always be creative from the outset. The performances of the young Mozart children definitely had some circus-like elements, which could only be achieved through a lot of practice, even with regular training. A certain astonishment was already triggered by the high dexterity of Maria Anna and Wolfgang Amadeus when the two were playing the 'piano', which at this time was more a harpsichord, a fortepiano or a clavichord.

Many concertgoers could not explain how Wolfgang Amadeus performed demanding piano movements with his small hands, which could hardly span more than – as some music experts note – the interval of a sixth. But the young Austrian seemed to be just very clever. His sister Maria Anna mainly played the piano and occasionally sang. Wolfgang Amadeus also played piano and sang with his sister and with their father. But compared to his sister, Wolfgang Amadeus was constantly expanding his repertoire of musical activities. One can read this in the numerous letters from his father, for example here from 1762, to Johann Hagenauer:

Monsieur mon très cher ami,

On the feast of Saint Francis we set out from Linz at 4:30 in the afternoon with the socalled Wasser-ordinaire, and reached Matthausen the same day by dark night at half past. The following Tuesday, we came to Ips in the afternoon, where Minorites and a Benedictine, who were with us on the ship, read Holy Mass, during which our Woferl so cavorted around on the organ and played so well that the Franciscan fathers, who were at that moment sitting with some guests at their midday meal, left their food, took the guests with them, ran to the choir and almost died of astonishment.[14]

In this letter Leopold Mozart explains that his little son embarked on genuine 'music adventures' with great pleasure and under no pressure from adults.

Wolfgang Amadeus not only dedicated himself to the piano, but also explored other instruments, such as the violin, which he began to play at the very early age of five years. He might have inherited his enthusiasm for this instrument, which has the ability to evoke almost any mood, whether sounding sweet or sad, playful or sombre, from his father, who was a violinist and who earned his first money with violin lessons, before writing his book *The attempt of a thorough violin school*. At some of Wolfgang Amadeus's concerts, he appeared as a violinist, but he was also able to play the organ. It is important to mention here that anyone coming from the piano has only trained his hands to that instrument and it requires a complete rethink to play an organ. The brain has extreme problems dividing concentration between hands and feet. In addition, unlike the hands, pedalling works blind, making it much more difficult to learn. The organ is an instrument mentioned in a letter that Leopold Mozart wrote on 29 June 1764 to his good friend Johann Hagenauer:

> I will have Wolfgang play a concerto on the organ there and thus take part in the project of an English patriot who seeks in every way he can to further the usefulness of this hospital erected *pro bono publico*. You see, this is a way to win the love of this quite special nation...[15].

In revisiting purpose and vision for the Higher Music Education of the twenty-first century, questions cannot therefore be ignored about the ways in which the creative process of making and mastering music are indeed of value in societies and the degrees to which these are realized, the roles musical practices may play within rapidly changing situations, and how they may be part of nurturing flourishing and inclusive societies for the long term. As the violinist Yehudi Menuhin once said, 'Practicing is not forced labour; it is a refined art that partakes of intuition, of inspiration, patience, elegance, clarity, balance, and, above all, the search for ever greater joy in movement and expression.'[16]

In many ways, a contemporary zeitgeist is crying out for the creativity and humanity of music and the arts, with their unique potential to uplift, heal, and engage people in expressing themselves, to help make sense of experience and challenge perspectives, and to contribute to building and sustaining communities.

A social, moral and political core to music-making may not, however, always sit comfortably with the directions that music has taken since the eighteenth century, becoming over the years more and more a global industry. Perceptions of excellence have easily tended to focus on attributions of artistic skills and creativity distanced from local or societal orientation. In Western classical music, for example, the ideal of the virtuoso soloist as the pinnacle of achievement has long been prominent, accompanied by growing craft specialization and technical standards.

The twentieth century also saw an exponential rise in an international 'star' culture, with considerable economic value being derived from it. Tensions between the priorities of global star performance and locally-oriented music traditions are evident. Besides that, public venues are being more and more challenged over accessibility, elitism and cultural reproduction of economic, race and gender inequalities within their methods. With some large concert halls increasingly hard to fill and struggling to serve the diversity of their communities, calls to widen access and evolve more inclusive processes are set to grow.

During the eighteenth century, the best way for a musician to get in contact with his audience was with a bit of theatrics, like a good actor, some even wanted to see a magician on the podium, who appeared and asked the audience to 'please be very actively involved in the musical happenings' – for example by singing something. Wolfgang Amadeus then performed their musical lines with his instrument. Or a member of the audience sang his favourite song and Wolfgang Amadeus accompanied the singing with his piano. Often, however, the sheet music he had brought with him was placed on the music desk and then he had to implement the notated composition on the respective instrument as soon as he read the sheet music for the first time without prior practice – 'sight-reading', a skill some otherwise great musicians never completely master.

Sight reading and improvising were a great strength of the young Wolfgang Amadeus Mozart. Presumably the young boy already had the desire – some musical theorists even spoke of 'pleasure' – from a young age to master every requirement placed on him with a certain degree of perfection. It was interesting to observe that as soon as Wolfgang Amadeus felt a certain tension, which quickly developed into the child being overwhelmed, a certain naivety emerged, which freed him from the wishes of his fans and brought the evening to a close.

But with that prodigy status, not only did a standing ovation come, but also questions from some sceptics. Was this boy really that young? Was he really that talented? One person eager to examine the truth was Englishman Daines Barrington. He was a solicitor, antiquarian, naturalist and a friend of the Royal Society of London, England. During the young musician's year-long London trip, he stayed in the city with his family. Londoners were fascinated by his talent, which he displayed in public concerts and in private audiences with King George III and Queen Charlotte. On a few visits to the Mozart family's London lodgings, Barrington endeavoured to 'scientifically' verify, whether or not this young Mozart was the Real Deal. Barrington's findings were even presented in a separate report to the Royal Society.[17] So, how did Barrington find out the truth about this young and talented Austrian boy? Barrington took a totally new score with him when he visited the Mozart lodgings. He brought with him a manuscript which the 8-year-old had never seen before. In reality it was a new opera by a London composer. To compound the problem, two of the five lines were in the offbeat contralto clef.

No sooner had he placed it on the young Mozart's desk that the boy began to play it so perfectly, 'in a most masterly manner', wrote Barrington, 'and in the time and style which corresponded to the composer's intention'. This was indeed a very tough test, and Mozart not only played it flawlessly but he also captured the composer's tempos, dynamics and musical intentions. Barrington goes on for two pages explaining the complexity of the feat to the non-musician readership of the Royal Society.

This was not enough for Barrington and so the test continued. Next, he asked young Wolfgang Amadeus if he'd be good enough to improvise a love song. The child gave him an arch look, as though to say 'ask me something harder', and he proceeded to create a complete piece with recitative and two movements.

'Could you then,' asked Barrington, 'compose me a song of anger?' This time, Mozart tore into the keyboard like a child possessed – standing up from his bench and hammering the keys with small fingers that could scarcely reach the interval of a fifth. The playing came to an end as a cat entered the room. Wolfgang Amadeus, all of a sudden, leaped up to run after it. No more harpsichord for a while. As Barrington talked with his father, Wolfgang Amadeus found a stick, which he made into a hobbyhorse, galloping back and forth around the room.

The young Wolfgang Amadeus Mozart was more than impressive and Barrington wrote that the boy's musical talent was 'amazing and unbelievable, almost as it may seem'. Barrington's famous first lines of his observations started like this. 'Sir, If I was to send you a well attested account of a boy who measured seven feet in height, when he was not more than eight years of age, it might be considered as not undeserving the notice of the Royal Society.'[18]

Barrington also gave a touching insight in his observations into the Mozart boy's childlike nature, when he revealed that 'a favourite cat was often preferred to the harpsichord'.

Music, dance and language are three human expressive movements. All three arise from inner and outer movement. This combines music with dance, dance with language and language with music. But the musical creativity comes from composing, from creating musical compositions.

The practices of singing and playing begin to permeate society in the eighteenth century. Wolfgang Amadeus explored different possibilities by playing music and improvising, which then flowed into his compositions. First, however, he had to learn a traditional composition: this arose from the rules of the craft, a knowledge of instruments, the human voice and what the peculiarities of musical genres have to do with individuality.

His father taught him orally, but an interesting learning tool was apparently the music book that he – together with a person who has not yet been identified – made for his eight-year-old daughter Maria Anna.

Just as he stole the show from Maria Anna by playing the piano during concerts together with her, her younger brother evidently made his way into the music book from very early on – in the years 1760-1761. This was even noted by Leopold Mozart in the form of written notes in Maria Anna's little music book. Leopold already wrote down when Wolfgang Amadeus started to learn how to play each one of the pieces. From spring 1761, his first compositions were written down. Wolfgang Amadeus himself entered his music recordings three years later, in 1764. And over the time, Maria Anna's music book became Wolfgang Amadeus's music book, although his sister is said to have guarded this book like a shrine all her life.

The first aim of the lesson was the composition of minuets, which were called gallantry pieces. A minuet is a dance and has a very precise choreography that the composer must take into account. For a child as young as Wolfgang Amadeus Mozart was at that time, this meant to learn pictorial, melodic and tonal symmetries as well as correspondences and contrasts, bars and groups of bars.

Careful observers of music will discover that this learning objective is already reflected in the first compositions of the child Wolfgang Amadeus. It is for example reflected in the minuets 2, 4 and 5. Leopold Mozart had certainly corrected what his son actually played for him in his notations; it was his job, as a private music teacher, to give his son the form and the tonal progression. At that time, his son had already mastered metrical playing with components and playing with the typology of the simplest details – this can be observed in his first compositions, which were initially versatile and the pieces of music became longer and longer over the weeks.

Wolfgang Amadeus wrote his first symphonies scored for the strings, two oboes and two horns as early as 1764, when he was in London with his parents at the age of eight.

In the summer of 1767, the first piano concertos were written in Salzburg, known as the *Pasticco Concertos* KV 39-41. These were pieces set for him by his father as 'homework' as we would say now. Leopold Mozart's methodology was as follows. He took individual movements from sonatas by different composers including C.P.E. Bach, a German Classical period musician and composer, a son of Johann Sebastian Bach, or Johann Friedrich Schubert, violinist and composer – and wrote them into the score in such a way that Wolfgang Amadeus only had to make additions with orchestral passages and instrumentations. This is how the piano sonata became the piano concerto.

In order to learn vocal composition, Leopold Mozart brought his 5½-year-old son into contact with the theatre and managed to get him involved in a school performance at the Benedictine University where he performed as a 'salii', a member of the college of priests who performed weapon dances and sang ancient songs at the Feast of Mars. This was how Wolfgang Amadeus got his first contact with a theatre stage.

In the early opera, starting with *Euridice* (1600) by Jacopo Peri, which is now regarded as the first of its genre, there was a smooth transition between long narrative (recitative) and short melodic (song-like, dance-like) sections. The course and constant alternation of recitative and aria is preceded by an overture in the form slow-fast (usually a fugato)-slow, which, however, has no relation to the plot. Curiously enough, this form of the French overture in Italian opera prevailed over the actual Italian sinfonia (fast-slow-fast) at the beginning of the eighteenth century. The child dared to take its first musical steps by composing Italian recitatives and arias. Wolfgang

Amadeus already had the psychological disposition for this task. During the breaks between trips, he acquired the sphere of church music in Salzburg.

Wolfgang Amadeus's early role models include the German Classical period musician and composer, C.P.E. Bach and the Austrian composer Georg Christoph Wagenseil. In London it is said that Wolfgang Amadeus was raised at the knee of the German composer of the Classical era, Johann Christian Bach and played the piano with him. Bach began a fugue and then had Wolfgang Amadeus continue the piece. The boy certainly benefited from Bach's musical feeling and understanding during these visits.

Carl Friedrich Abel, a German composer of the Classical era and a renowned player of the viola da gamba, who produced significant compositions for that instrument, was visited in 1764 by 8-year-old Wolfgang Amadeus and his father in London to study his compositional movement. One of Abel's works became famous due to a misattribution. In the nineteenth century, a manuscript symphony in the hand of Wolfgang Amadeus Mozart was catalogued as his *Symphony No. 3 in E flat* (known as KV 18) and was published as such in the first complete edition of Mozart's works by Breitkopf & Haertel. Later, it was discovered that this E-flat major symphony (op. VII, 6) has been copied as sort of a role model and was found – evidently for study purposes – in Mozart's notebook, misleadingly as Mozart's *Symphony No. 3 in E-flat major*. That symphony was originally published as the concluding work in Abel's *Six Symphonies,* Op. 7.

In the eighteenth century, people composed with a view to a performance and the expectations of their audiences at the time. Difficult to grasp is Wolfgang Amadeus Mozart's peculiarity in these assimilation processes, so to speak, of all possible types of cognitive enhancement that are attributed to exposure to music by other composers who were his models, or to classical music in general.

When perceiving what is creative in the child, one should take the standpoint of the aesthetics of reception, what they ask about the intellectual and emotional perception of artistic works and to what extent it is already inherent in the object or only arises in the process of reception.

From 1769 – Wolfgang Amadeus was now 13 years old – Leopold started travelling with him alone as his father, teacher, impresario and servant – all in one person.

'The young Mozart is certainly a miracle for his age, and I love him infinitely',[19] wrote Johann Adolph Hasse, Empress Maria Theresa's favourite composer, to a friend in Venice in 1771. And he continues, 'The father idolizes his son a little too much and does what is possible to spoil him. But I have such a good opinion of the boy's natural sense that I hope he will, despite the adulations not let his father perish, but become a brave man.'[20]

Although the family life of the Mozarts was a very happy and harmonious one, it is hard to imagine that back home in Salzburg, mother and daughter would have welcomed every time the ambitious father Leopold and his spoiled little 'crown prince', as he called him, took off for months of triumphant journeys to *Welschland* – which was the name for 'Roman' countries like Italy or France and today French Switzerland.

While Italy was sort of a 'promised land' for many painters and architects in the Renaissance and Baroque periods, it became in the eighteenth century, due to the dominance of Italian music, the ambition of all composers to live and work there. Italian cities and courts welcomed streams of musicians in search of performing opportunities, official appointments or commissions, and steady jobs. The reason was that Italian works, conductors, singers and orchestras dominated the courtly musical life of the era throughout Europe and they were usually much better rewarded. And so, numerous Bohemian and German musicians even took on Italian names in order to make it easier for them to establish themselves in these countries.

Certainly, Wolfgang Amadeus Mozart's three journeys to Italy between 1769 and 1773 all shaped his musical development. In addition, he found that in Verona, Bologna, Rome and Naples, there would be successes in the magnificent palazzi and churches, on feudal country estates, in the Vatican, at the court of Archduke Leopold of Austria-Tuscany in Florence and at the Milan court with three opera compositions for the Archduke's brother Ferdinand as well. The Italian aristocracy admired his music for its 'melodic beauty, its formal elegance and its richness of harmony and texture', they spoiled and presented him with the weighty diploma of the Music Academy of Bologna.

At around this time, the family stayed together in Salzburg for just under a year. Mozart left for Italy together with his father when he was not even 14 years old; there was a desire to prepare for a bright, courtly music career that engaged both father and son alike. Wolfgang Amadeus became a pubescent youth who played his amusing games of independence and who sensed and recognized a great emancipation problem in relation to his equally talented father. Wolfgang Amadeus's early desire to assert himself professionally is entirely human. What was surprising, however, was the intensity and the increasing restlessness that filled him.

From the late sixteenth century, Italy was the country par excellence for opera and oratorio, the affective melodic style and thorough bass practice, and all subsequent musical innovations of the seventeenth and early eighteenth centuries arose in Italy. Composers such as Palestrina in Rome and Giovanni Gabrieli and Claudio Monteverdi in Venice made these cities extremely attractive addresses for young musicians from different parts of Europe at that time in order to learn and to continue their path in the art. It was a kind of must for them to get to know Italian composition and musical theatre practice on one side and, if possible, to make a name for themselves in the art industry in Italy.

George Frederick Handel, for example, who was a German-British Baroque composer well known for his operas, oratorios, anthems, *concerti grossi* and organ concertos, received his training in Germany, where he worked as a composer but also in Italy, before settling in London in 1712, where he became a naturalized British subject in 1727. He was strongly influenced by the German choral tradition and by Italian Baroque composers. In turn, his music formed one of the peaks of the high baroque style, bringing Italian opera to its highest, creating the genres of English oratorio and organ concerto, and introducing a new style into English church music. Handel was in fact called to London not as a German composer, but as a composer of Italian operas.

This was one of the reasons for Leopold Mozart to advance his son's career and he urged him to embark on this important journey. Of course, none of this was easy, because Wolfgang Amadeus was already going through puberty. It is also important to understand that at that time, a young man who was almost fourteen is not as fascinating as a seven-year-old child.

The suggestion was therefore made to Leopold Mozart that his son could acquire special musical Italian basics in Italy in order to then be able to prove himself in proper traditional movements in church compositions. Because, according to Leopold's friends who advised him, the 14-year-old was still 'far too immature' to write an opera and was not at all capable of asserting himself in a theatre at this young age.

And so, all of a sudden, the real goals of this new journey were beyond doubt. Wolfgang Amadeus's musical horizon should be broadened and chances for exploring other musical possibilities should be increased, in order to eventually gain recognition as an internationally recognized composer and musician. And Leopold Mozart thought that maybe a job in Italy was also possible.

There had been a lively cultural exchange between Austria and Italy for a long time, because Italian culture and art had been strongly represented since the Baroque at the Viennese court as well as in Salzburg. From the point of view of the Austrians, the centre of northern Italy was clearly Milan, and Leopold Mozart also saw it that way. It was logical to him that he had to build on old Salzburg contacts there. In addition, there were a few acquaintances, first of all the Austrian Governor General of Lombardy, Karl Joseph Gotthard, Count of Firmian, who was a nephew of Leopold Mozart's first employer in Salzburg. Another nephew of the Archbishop was the Salzburg High Steward Franz Lactanz Count of Firmian, who was an art lover and a science enthusiast.

In view of the clear objectives and the possible financing tasks involved in such trips, Leopold Mozart finally started his journey to Italy with only his son – without his wife or his daughter – on 13 December 1769. The father's plan to go to Italy and from there to prepare his son for a career that would span the whole of Europe was finally carried out. While on this trip, Wolfgang Amadeus added several letters to his father's reports in which he – like a typical boy of his age – practiced all kinds of languages and jokes, but in his statements about music he always showed attentive observation, a serious mind and an apt judgment.

The first important Italian stop was the city of Verona. As with the first musical journey, making the local fan base aware that they were back in the country was an extremely important marketing tool at the time. And all without cell phones, social media and computers, just by letters of recommendation and word of mouth. For this reason, father and son went to their local acquaintances to tell them at first hand that they had returned and paying their respects to important people in the city of Verona. And a first concert series with the adolescent Wolfgang Amadeus began; a series of private and public concerts given to the Veronese society.

The reputation of the child prodigy must have preceded him to Italy, because his schedule in Verona, shortly after his arrival, reads like that of a politician or manager plagued by appointments:

We were invited today by a certain honest man H: Ragazzoni general collector of Venice il Sgr: Luggiatti asked the

Cavaglieres to ask me to allow Wolfg: to be ground; it happened yesterday morning, and today after church he was supposed to sit for the second meal ... so we should be today come to H: Luggiatti in the morning after church to sit in front of the table one more time to watch the painter But ... the bishop of Verona from the house of Justiniani ... came, because he heard that one was in the process of making a portrait of Wolfg and we wanted to leave, he would let it happen ... They then continued to paint the portrait of Wolfg and we only went to eat at 3 o'clock.[21]

Wolfgang Amadeus also played organ concertos in Italy. Beside their music engagements, he and his father also took the opportunity to visit the theatre in Verona. They were both coveted guests and enjoyed this beautiful life. This was also the case when they both continued their travels to Mantua and to Cremona, both beautiful cities in Lombardy.

Mantua, 11th January 1770

We reached here yesterday and, one hour later, namely at 6 o'clock, went to the opera. We are well, praise God. Wolfgangerl looks as if he has been on a military campaign, namely slightly red-brown, especially around the nose and mouth, from the air and the open fire. As, for example, His Majesty the Emperor looks. My good looks have as yet not suffered much, otherwise I would be plunged into despair. I cannot yet tell you anything about this place. Today I called on His Eminent Highness the Prince of Taxis, but he was not at home, and his gracious lady under such obligation to write letters that she could not speak to us, her fellow countrymen. But downstairs in the house we saw a couple of soiled little kitchen goddesses who danced around quite joyfully on

seeing us, their fellow countrymen. It seems to me that they
do not particularly like being in Italy.[22]

Father and son finally arrived in Milan at the end of January 1770, and
they lived in the Augustinian monastery of San Marco. It was carnival
time and the Italians were happy and merry and this mood quickly
spread to the two Mozarts. Through the mediation of Count Firmian,
they soon got the chance to meet the Milanese composer Giovanni
Battista Sammartini. He was generous and presented Wolfgang
Amadeus with the libretti by Pietro Antonio Domenico Trapassi,
known under his pseudonym Pietro Metastasio.

As usual and well planned, everything was heading towards a
highlight of the stay in Milan. On 12 March 1770, Count Firmian
invited the nobility to a concert in his palazzo. That evening, Wolfgang
Amadeus played four soprano arias that he had composed using the
libretti written by Pietro Metastasio. The audience loved it, the guests
melted away and as a reward the next day he was commissioned to
compose an opera for the next carnival season in 1771. This was
a great opportunity for a young composer. The start of the Italian
journey was brilliant and it developed into an educational journey for
Mozart, who was now of an age when his critical consciousness was
awakening. In his letters from this period, he seems self-deprecating,
he plays with operatic affects and even borders on the obscene with
the feelings he describes. He sends out a look of affection that the
female addressees (his mother and his sister) certainly understood and
he wrote many letters to his beloved sister.

The next stops on the journey were marked by the numerous
contacts of Count Firmian and the names of the cities sound wonderful;
Bologna, Parma, Florence, Rome and Naples. It was obvious that the
two Mozarts did not travel as tourists, but that their main goal was
to experience image and prestige through this trip, as well as to make
new contacts to build up a real Mozart fan base during this time.

Leopold Mozart blossomed during these days into a career strategist, a top artist manager, who was constantly striving to make himself and his son known to the elite and to other prominent musicians. In order to keep their expenses low, both men were interested in being able to give a concert as soon as possible after their arrival in each city and then to leave again quickly, just like the popular artists on tour are doing today.

Bologna was an important city for the young Wolfgang Amadeus, there was the highly appreciated Academia Filarmonica, an important music library, that still exists today. Their letter from Count Firmian introduced them to Count Pallavicini-Centurioni, a leading patron of the arts, who immediately arranged a concert for the local nobility in his palace. Padre Giambattista Martini, the leading musical theorist of his day and Europe's most renowned expert in Baroque counterpoint and a special connoisseur of early music, lived in Bologna and attended this concert. The encounters between Padre Martini and Wolfgang Amadeus resulted in a special musical collaboration, namely on themes given by the Padre, for which Wolfgang Amadeus then composed suitable fugues. Regularly, and with an eye upon Wolfgang Amadeus's future prospects in the courts of Europe, Leopold was keen for an engagement with the great master. But because of their austerity policies, their time in Bologna was limited, and so Leopold promised to return in the summer for an extended tuition. The pair left on 29 March, carrying letters from Count Pallavicini-Centurioni that might make it possible for them to have an audience with Pope Clement XIV in Rome.

In Florence, Leopold Mozart expected a contact with a connection to Empress Maria Theresa, namely Leopold, the Grand Duke and future Emperor of Tuscany, who still remembered the performances of the two Mozart children at his parents' court and so he asked after Nannerl, expecting her to be there. After arriving in Florence, Wolfgang Amadeus and his father were received by him at the Pitti Palace and one day later there was a concert in the grand ducal summer residence Poggio Imperiale together with the violinist and composer Pietro Nardini. Purchased in 1550, the Pitti Palace was chosen by Cosimo I de Medici and his wife Eleanor of Toledo as the new Grand Ducal residence, and it soon became the new symbol of the Medici's power over Tuscany. It also housed the House of Habsburg-Lorraine (which succeeded the Medici from 1737) and the Kings of Italy from the House of Savoy, who inhabited it from 1865.

Nonetheless, after the long concert with Pietro Nardini, important contacts to the Austrian aristocrat fan base could be renewed in Florence and others were newly established. Many of these were to last until the young Mozart's time in Vienna. There was a particularly warm encounter in April 1770 between the violinist Thomas Linley (known as the Younger), who was the same age and the boys got on magnificently. Thomas often made music together with Wolfgang Amadeus. Thomas Linley was considered one of the most precocious composers and performers that had ever been known in England. Like Wolfgang Amadeus, he studied music with his father but started to play concerts at the age of seven. Linley is sometimes referred to as the 'English Mozart'. Leopold Mozart wrote a very long letter to his wife at the end of April in which he describes the musical creativity and harmony between the two boys:

> In Florence, we found a young English boy who is a student of the famous violinist Nardini. This youth, who plays beautifully, and who is Wolfgang's size and age, came to the house of the erudite poetess Sgra Corilla ... These two boys alternately produced the entire evening while constantly embracing each other... They played the entire afternoon alternately, not as boys, but as men! The little Tomaso accompanied us home and cried the most bitter tears because we were leaving the next day. But because he found out that we were not leaving until noon, he came the next morning at 9 a.m. and gave Wolfgang, accompanied by many embraces,

the following poetry, which Sgra Corilla had made him the evening before, and he then accompanied our coach to the city gates. I wish that you had witnessed this scene.[23]

Linley later would make a career as composer and violinist, but he unfortunately died way too soon in a boating accident at the age of only 22.

There were joint appearances in Florence with several other musicians, which was also the case in Rome, where the father and son regarded themselves as normal travellers. They arrived in Rome during Holy Week, after five days of travelling through wind and rain it was rumoured, then travelled uncomfortably 326 kilometres through beautiful Tuscany. But then they arrived in the Eternal city. They immediately went on sightseeing tours, which were common at the time and were undertaken together with other foreign guests, but also with diplomats and aristocrats, who mostly travelled incognito. They met with the Count's kinsman Lazaro Opizio Cardinal Pallavicino, Prince San Angelo of Naples, and Charles Edward Stuart, perhaps better known today as Bonnie Prince Charlie, Pretender to the throne of England. Wolfgang Amadeus played concerts in beautiful old aristocratic palazzi, while his father focused his interest on the papal court in the Vatican. In Rome, they quickly visited St. Peter's and then the Sistine Chapel. A particular fascination emanated there from the performance of *Miserere* by Gregorio Allegri, an Italian priest, composer and tenor singer, conductor at Fermo Cathedral, then from 1629 until his death singer in the papal choir of the Sistine Chapel in the service of Pope Urban VIII. Gregorio Allegri's *Miserere* is a famous a cappella setting of Psalm 51, '*Miserere mei, Deus, secundum magnam misericordiam tuam*' (God, be merciful to me according to your goodness). The work is surrounded by numerous myths. It is said that copying the score was forbidden under penalty of excommunication. According to the popular story (backed by a letter written by Leopold

Mozart to his wife on 14 April 1770), the ban was only lifted when Mozart first heard the piece during the Wednesday service. Later that day, he wrote it down entirely from memory, returning to the Chapel that Friday to make minor corrections:

Roma, 14th April, 1770.

We arrived safely here at midday on the 11th. It would have been easier to convince me that I was on the way to Salzburg than to Rome, as we had to travel from Florence to Rome for 5 days in the most abhorrent rain and cold wind. ....

.....You will often have heard perhaps of the famous *Miserere* in Rome, which is so highly regarded that the chapel musicians are forbidden, under pain of excommunication, to take any of the parts out of the chapel or to give it to anybody. But we already have it. Wolfgang has already written it down and we would have sent it to Salzburg with this letter but that our presence is necessary to perform it. Only the style of performance alone has to make a bigger contribution than the composition itself, so we will bring it home with us and, because it is one of the secrets of Rome, we do not want to entrust it to other hands but *non incurremus mediate vel immediate in Censurem Ecclesiæ.*[24]

It is clear that this story is one of the better ones to tell the fans of Wolfgang Amadeus Mozart. On Maundy Thursday, the two Mozarts went to the cardinal's table with a confident demeanour and in the best clothes they could wear and they had great success. Cardinal Secretary of State Lazzarro Oppizio Pallaviccini received the two; he was already informed about Wolfgang Amadeus and really enjoyed talking to this young special music talent. Apart from that, Wolfgang

Amadeus was busily composing. He wrote the *contradanse* KV 123/73g and the aria *Se ardire, e Speranza* (KV 82/73o), and finished the *G major symphony* that he had begun earlier.

After four weeks of meetings and concerts, the two men continued their travels to Naples, a city with the largest ancient historic centre in the whole of Europe and with a solid Catholic heritage and therefore more than 500 churches. They arrived on 14 May and with their letters of introduction in their hands, they immediately visited the Prime Minister, Marchese Bernardo Tanucci, and William Hamilton, the British Ambassador, whom they knew from a previous visit to London. They did performances in the palazzi of the imperial French and English ambassadors. Again, father and son toured the city and that took up a lot of time. They attended the premiere of Niccolò Jommelli's opera *Armida Abbandonata* at the Teatro di San Carlo. On the one hand, Wolfgang Amadeus was awestruck by both the music and the performance, but on the other hand he found them 'too old-fashioned and serious for the theatre'. And although he was offered the opportunity to write an opera for the next season in San Carlo, he unfortunately had to turn it down, because of a previous engagement in Milan.

When his son failed to receive an invitation for a concert at the royal court, Leopold decided to leave Naples but not until after they had both visited Mount Vesuvius, Herculaneum, Pompeii and the Roman baths at Baiae. The two departed for Rome on 25 June by stagecoach. For the first time, father and son Mozart made an extremely quick 27-hour return journey to the Eternal city. But Leopold suffered a leg injury that tormented him for several months.

Back in Rome, Wolfgang Amadeus received an audience with the Pope and was made a Knight of the Order of the Golden Spur. This was one of the most important awards in the eighteenth century. Cardinal Secretary of State Pallaviccini presented the insignia of the cross with red ribbon, the sword and the spurs on 5 July in the Palazzo Quirinale. He received the highest class of this order, which only Orlando di Lasso had received as a musician before him. A few days later he was received by Pope Clement XIV. In a typical way, Wolfgang Amadeus sometimes made fun of his award later on, but was also very proud of having received it.

From Rome, father and son made their way to the famous pilgrimage site of Santa Casa in Loreto and took the coastal road along the Adriatic Sea via Ancona and Pesaro back to the city of Rimini, protected by the military, because the road was under attack by pirates. From Rimini they moved inland and covered 120 kilometres before they arrived in Bologna on 20 July. The acquaintance with Padre Martini was deepened and led to the Padre wanting Wolfgang Amadeus to be admitted as a member of the music library Academia Filarmonica. Before that, however, the young Mozart had to prepare for an examination in October.

From August to early October, father and son lived on the estate of Field Marshal Giuseppe Maria Count Pallaviccini near Bologna. While Leopold's priority was to finally rest his injured leg, Wolfgang Amadeus was also working there on a composition for the Milan opera, *Mitridate, re di Ponto*. Since the summer, his interests had been focused on the Italian city of Milan and the opera.

On 9 October, he underwent examination for membership of Bologna's Accademia Filarmonica, offering as his test piece the antiphon *Quaerite primum regnum*, KV 86 (73v). What is interesting is that the results are still accessible today and one notices that the young boy was not yet firm in the strict contrapuntal Attico style. According to the American music scholar Robert W. Gutman, under ordinary circumstances Wolfgang Amadeus's 'floundering' attempt at this unfamiliar polyphonic form would not have received serious consideration, but Martini was at hand to offer corrections, and probably also paid the admission fee. Wolfgang Amadeus's membership was duly approved; and the Mozarts departed finally for Milan shortly afterwards.

Career aspirations apparently mutated into real opportunities in Milan and Mozart's biggest wish for his own life became more than clear – he wanted to pursue his musical career and show his father that he was a gifted musician and composer. The journey from Bologna to Milan was delayed by storms and floods, but Leopold and his son arrived on 18 October, ten weeks before the first performance of *Mitridate*.

One has to be familiar with the performance customs of the time in order to understand the repeated and long stays of father and son Mozart in Milan. No composer of the eighteenth century would have written his opera at home and then entrusted his music agent with the search for a performance venue and opportunity, which would be the case these days. Although the major opera houses sometimes commission specific composers, no opera director expects a composer to set to work on the spot and be in constant contact with him. Things were different in the eighteenth century – a finished opera first had to please the decision-makers; that is, the Prince who was paying for the operation of the Opera house or the Concert hall or the audience who paid for the tickets. The composer also had to take local circumstances into account and he also had to present the expensive singers who were involved in the best possible musical light. An opera mutated into a show, where each cog had its own function.

After the contract was signed and the texts had been received from the librettist, the composer began to work on that part of the opera that was, so to speak, standardized and did not require any special individualization.

This applied to the large amounts of text, the recitatives driving the action (i.e. singing in opera, cantata, mass or oratorio that is more like speaking), but also the chorus. The overture was usually written last. The arias of the singers were worked out when they were there and you could exchange ideas with them. In Wolfgang Amadeus' case, he was provided with an apartment in Milan for the duration of the composition and paid 100 guilders for the composition of the work. He had to send the recitatives to the theatre and be present in person from 1 November. Wolfgang Amadeus's mastery of Italian diction was revealed as the recitatives were practiced, and a run-through of the instrumental score displayed his professionalism.

The Mozarts arrived at the beginning of October and rehearsals began in December. The first performance took place on 26 December at the Teatro Regio Ducale, which was at the time the biggest opera house in Milan. Wolfgang Amadeus was very excited and did his best. He conducted the first three performances himself from the harpsichord. The play was an *opera seria* in three acts – the Italian technical term for an opera performance – with a story taken from antiquity.

The effort for the stage design was great, the opera lasted six hours with three ballets. The libretto was written by Vittorio Amedeo Cigna-Santi and with twenty performances *Mitridate* was a complete success for the young Mozart. The audience was mesmerized and applauded the talented young Austrian.

After this Italian opera success, father and son enjoyed the carnival season in Italy even more. The two finally departed in February 1771, driving from Verona not to the North, but to Venice and Padua. One thing was already becoming clear; wherever the two men went, they were showered with honours, receptions and further invitations to concert performances. It may seem odd, but the eighteenth-century stardom of a composer of the calibre of Wolfgang Amadeus Mozart was in some ways similar to that of a twenty-first century star. High-ranking aristocrats, bishops and even the Patriarch of Venice, musicians and merchants received the two in the friendliest manner.

At that time, it was more important for Leopold and Wolfgang Amadeus not only to receive commissions for concerts, but also to continue to receive commissions for compositions. So, March turned out to be a very lucky month. In Padua, Wolfgang Amadeus was commissioned to compose the oratorio *La betulia liberate*. And before that, he received 130 guilders for composing the carnival opera *Lucio Silla*. To the great astonishment of the Mozart family, Empress Maria Theresa from Vienna personally commissioned the composition of a festival opera *Ascanio in Alba* for the October 1771 planned wedding of the governor and general captain of Lombardy, Archduke Ferdinand, with Maria Riccarda Beatrice d'Este. Therefore, one can assume that father and son must have enjoyed their trip to Venice during the month of March very much. Aristocrats had offered them their gondolas and, together with Giambattista Abbrizio's guide, they toured the sights of the city. But in view of the three commissions for Wolfgang Amadeus, the two had to end their vacation and return to reality – that is, to the work table in Salzburg. At the end of March, the two men were back in Austria. But it was not to relax. They had many things to do and to prepare and above all – to compose the three commissions, because in five months, in August, the plan was to drive again to Milan to be present when the preparations for the festival opera would start.

On 15 October, the bridal couple came together and got married in the Cathedral of Milan. The wedding was a huge celebration spanning several days and was initially accompanied by several musical interludes – including a first concert that evening. The Duke of York (the Prince of Saxen Gotha) was already there. The Crown Prince, namely the father, and the mother of the Princess bride had also arrived. Count Sauerau was there. People were swarming everywhere, and 'one will have to suffer the greatest inconvenience to see everything', described Leopold later to his wife.

But the next day, the first opera, written by another composer, an old master Johann Adolph Hasse, was performed. Then, on the third day, Mozart's festival opera was to be performed after a float parade. In addition, Empress Maria Theresa had invited 220 bridal couples, married them immediately and prepared a huge buffet for them, so that they could eat. Horse and chariot races were organized to keep the crowds entertained, which was normal for such an occasion. This was followed by an artificial food fortress, which was a stunning epicurean extravaganza. At a special signal, the invitees waded through the mud, grabbing as much food as they could fit on their plates and drinking wine that came from a fountain, to the delight of the noble guests.

Such an event was traditional in Milan and other Italian cities, as nothing crowned a royal wedding or holiday more than watching hungry people wrestle for food. This very special buffet was set in the form of temples, pyramids or castles peppered with a wide variety of roasts, bread and cheese. This event was known under the name *Cuccagna*, which translates as 'abundance'.

But then the festival opera *Ascanio in Alba* followed. The wedding guests were gobsmacked and delighted at the same time. The opera and the art of the young composer were greeted with unanimous applause by the festival guests, and Wolfgang Amadeus was cheered to the rafters. The guests even shouted '*Bravissimo Maestrino.*' One thing became clear to everyone that day; Wolfgang Amadeus had once again surpassed himself. He was already able to inspire people with his phenomenal musical compositions. His festival opera completely overshadowed his predecessor, Hasse. This was of course communicated by Leopold to his wife in a letter. The festival opera by Wolfgang Amadeus was performed over several days, a total of three times, and each time the fifteen-year-old earned thunderous applause from the audience. Count Firmian took advantage of young composer's popularity and spontaneously decided to get Wolfgang Amadeus employed at the court in Milan. After an audience with Archduke Ferdinand, Leopold and Wolfgang Amadeus left Milan in the best of spirits on 5 December. But a week later, everything was completely different again and the family found themselves in the bitter reality.

Archduke Ferdinand himself had the idea of taking the young Mozart into his service and wrote to his mother to ask for her permission and her consent. But Empress Maria Theresa had advised her son in a letter not to hire the 'young Salzburger' after all. She replied on 12 December:

You ask me to take young Salzburger into your service. I don't know how, not believing that you need a composer or useless people. If that would give you pleasure, I don't want to prevent you. What I say is not to burden you with useless

people, and never to title these sorts of people as in your
service. It debases the service, when these people run around
like beggars; besides that he has a big family.[25]

It is unknown what could have led the Empress to reply so harshly
and indeed impolitely, and to disavow 15-year-old Wolfgang Amadeus
so much, even though he was a talented composer and musician and
already had an international fan base. His patron and mentor, Count
Firmian, will certainly have reproduced the empress' heavy words
in a more moderate tone. Musicologists suspect that she may have
foreseen that Wolfgang Amadeus, after getting a job in Italy, would
maybe repeatedly submitted requests for leave from Salzburg to the
Archduke and would probably have pestered him that he had to go
to his family. This was certainly understandable for a young man of
his age, but this did not fit with the strict regulations and rules of the
Empress.

Meanwhile, Leopold and Wolfgang Amadeus tried to distract
themselves with the other two commissions they had got from the
Italians. With the high reputation that the young composer now
enjoyed in Italy, at least that's what Leopold thought, the next step
would already be in the offing. They had plenty of time to forge a new
strategy in Salzburg before October 1772.

The Prince-Archbishop of Salzburg, Sigismund, Count of
Schrattenbach, was to celebrate his 50th anniversary as a priest on
10 January 1772. Wolfgang Amadeus had composed the dramatic
serenade *Il Sogno die Scipione* (KV 126) for this. But, one day after
the two men arrived in Salzburg, the Prince-Archbishop died. In
March 1772, however, the Bishop of Gurk, Hieronymus, Count of
Colloredo von Wallsee und Melz, whom Mozart had met in Rome,
was elected his successor. Behind the scenes, however, it turned out
to be an extremely unpopular vote in Salzburg, and the citizens of
Salzburg remained reserved and cold towards him to the end. Count
von Colloredo turned out to be an autocratic leader and his assertive,

almost domineering attitude towards various decisions repeatedly provoked the hostility of the cathedral chapter and city officials.

After the Count of Colloredo's election, Mozart decided to perform the composed piece of music for the arrival of the new prince archbishop. It was performed on 1 May 1772 in the archbishop's palace in Salzburg, only for a private audience and only one aria; the final chorus and the recitative were performed that day.

The third commissioned composition, the oratorio *La Betulia Liberata*, was composed in the same year, but unfortunately not performed in Padua.

In the autumn, Leopold and his son travelled to Milan to immediately start work on their first carnival opera *Lucio Silla*. Wolfgang Amadeus composed his arias at a breakneck speed and on 26 December the premiere was announced. The start was delayed by two hours due to the late arrival of Archduke Ferdinand and his wife and there were also some behind-the-scenes disagreements between the main actors. Ballet performances were also interspersed – which was normal at the time – so that the performance finally lasted until two o'clock in the morning. But the carnival opera once again proved to be a triumphant success.

The audience was beside themselves and cheered the young composer. It was such a huge victory that the opera was performed around twenty-six times – it was a milestone in Wolfgang Amadeus's career and his greatest operatic success. He and Leopold were passed around in Milanese society – everyone wanted to get to know them as well listen to their music. Several times Wolfgang Amadeus performed other compositions privately for invited guests at Count Firmian's palazzo. This atmosphere in Italy also made him compose on site, for example, church pieces like *Exultate, jubilate* (KV 165).

Father and son enjoyed the carnival in Italy to the fullest and Leopold even had to lie to his new employer in Salzburg, as he claimed to suffer from severe rheumatism which prevented his voyage, in order to extend his stay further. He gave the score of *Lucio Silla* to the Grand Duke Leopold I of Tuscany, and believed that he would let himself be persuaded and offer his son a job after all. This was closely supported by Count Firmian. They waited for two months for a response. But the Grand Duke of Tuscany remained firm and did not offer Wolfgang Amadeus any position in Florence. This refusal suddenly ended Leopold's hopes of an Italian job appointment for Wolfgang Amadeus and therefore father and son left Italy with a heavy heart in order to fulfil their obligations again in Salzburg. Their plans to make a career in Italy and possibly gain a foothold there were put on hold for the moment.

The truth was that Wolfgang Amadeus Mozart would no longer travel to Italy and there were no more orders from this country – which is surprising.

Leopold Mozart must have had taken this rejection badly. He worked on the next steps for his child's career and must have come to terms with the fact that Salzburg was not the hub of the world for talented musicians. Something had to happen, he must have thought, in order to get further commissions and to continue on the road to success.

After just four months in Salzburg, he and Wolfgang Amadeus embarked on their next journey. This time their destination was not Italy, but Vienna. In Vienna, the two men first met their old acquaintances to talk about Italy and new contacts with music lovers there were made. Mozart played many concerts in small circles. On 5 August, the two even had an audience with Empress Maria Theresa at Laxenburg Palace, which was situated outside of Vienna. Unfortunately, this audience did not bring the desired result, because Leopold in a letter to his wife hinted that the empress was 'very gracious' in receiving them, but that there was no result. He didn't want to write more in the letter, but rather tell her everything in person, as soon as he was back in Salzburg.

This career break happened at a bad time. While everything had looked so good at first, the success in Italy was ground-breaking, but apparently Vienna didn't want to play along. The best therapy in this case was to make music. Wolfgang Amadeus could have started a bigger career in Salzburg, but he didn't want to. He and his father also lacked the temperament to pursue such a career. What also made things more difficult was that Wolfgang Amadeus was getting older and not only developing internally, but also in all of his compositions. He became increasingly self-confident, imaginative and creative.

While he initially showed his child prodigy skills on his first trip to Italy by playing the piano like a fairy tale, improvising and implementing what the audience wanted from him and thus captivating his viewers and listeners with his melodies, on his second trip to Italy he suddenly became a real composer, who was also commissioned from Italy because people believed in him; his audience wanted these operas.

Mozart had picked up suggestions from everywhere, but he had noticed that the most realistic ones for him clearly came from Milan. The Milan symphony and chamber music offered him new musical horizons, which he wanted to continue in his compositions. Mozart also continued to deal extensively with the compositions of Pietro Metastasio. But beyond the richness of production and beyond his genius for assimilation, his creativity expressed itself in a very specific originality. Between 1772 and 1773 he performed strokes of genius in Milan and Salzburg and was apparently in a creative frenzy but was constantly exploring something new.

Chapter 3

Mozart's Style – Influencer and Freelancer

The Italian journeys were a great triumph overall for the whole family – especially for Wolfgang Amadeus. But from Leopold's point of view, they also included his own great failure. Indeed, one should not forget that the Mozarts were making good money in Italy due to the many concerts and orders that Wolfgang Amadeus got. He had emerged artistically as a respected composer and the Italians had responded with great enthusiasm. They became his fans in a matter of seconds and wanted to hear much more from this talented young man. They gave him gifts and invited him to do more concerts. But his father was somehow not able, despite his persistence, to secure a prestigious job appointment for either himself or for Wolfgang Amadeus. This often gave Leopold pause for thought and after a certain time he began to wonder what the real reason was for the lack of a permanent job in Italy – despite audiences and a papal award. He was probably unaware of the negative light in which he was sometimes seen, as a kind of 'pushy manager' of his talented young son. But he knew that their life had to continue and that the family needed regular money and reputation to live a decent life in Salzburg.

That is why Leopold decided to concentrate for the next months on Austria. He also believed that his family needed more space. For this reason, he decided to give up the apartment in Getreidegasse that had become too small for them, and he moved with his family to the Dance Master's House at Number 8 on the Makartplatz, where they had much more spacious living conditions.

Wolfgang Amadeus on the other hand, was absolutely not impressed by his father's musings and decided to continue his path and concentrated on working diligently to push his career in another direction. Compared to Leopold, he was not discouraged by the rejection of full-time jobs, but continued instead to focus on composing his next music pieces. By the end of 1773, he had composed the small *G minor symphony* and *Piano Concerto in D major* (KV 175).

As his father always had a tendency towards higher things, he kept himself and his family busy by accepting numerous invitations from the aristocratic and bourgeois high society of Salzburg.

Making music and organizing concerts was considered a status symbol at the time, and the three well-known aristocrats, the Counts Ernst Maria of Lodron, Carlo di Firmian and Karl Joseph Felix, Count of Arco, held leading positions in Austrian cultural life. Most of the baroque splendour of Salzburg architecture – still highly admired today – dates from the reign of Prince Archbishop Paris Lodron. At the time Wolfgang Amadeus was composing, the Prince Archbishop's family still owned two beautiful palaces in Salzburg, where aristocrats and the citizens of Salzburg regularly met on Sundays for academies, which were occasionally even supervised by Leopold Mozart. In the house of Count Georg Anton Felix von Arco's family, there were even what he used to call retreat-academies on Fridays. Actually, the Count was very attached to the Mozart family and this led many respected and rich bourgeois families to emulate this aristocratic role model.

During his years in Salzburg after his trip to Italy, Wolfgang Amadeus increasingly devoted himself to the genre of divertimenti, serenades and night music – one could even say he was committed to them. Many of the pieces in this style composed at that time were written for certain music-making circles in the aristocratic houses. These include the *Haffner Serenade* (KV 250) or the *Lodronsche Nachtmusiken* (KV 247, 287 and probably also KV 289). The latter, which Wolfgang Amadeus called *Two Cassations for the Countess*, he composed as a 'name-day serenade' for Countess Antonia Lodron of Salzburg. Luckily, she celebrated it on 13 June, so that there was usually nothing standing in the way of an open-air performance, since the self-designated title *Cassation* was derived from the expression '*go gassatim*' in the sense of making music on the street and therefore referred to the mentioned custom of serenading in the open air. These were truly princely serenades, which followed the tradition of the Austrian divertimento in their instrumentation (strings and horns) and in their six-movement structure. Wolfgang Amadeus also composed the *Concerto for Three Pianos* (KV 242) for the countess.

Official duties at court were not really as unpleasant for Wolfgang Amadeus as he seemed to find them, because the new Prince-Archbishop of Salzburg was an enlightened prince and very art-loving just like Empress Maria Theresa, though unfortunately just as frugal as she was. He started to restrict the courtly representations and preferred to concentrate on the celebration of the liturgy in the church and on communicating with the population. The Wolfgang Amadeus he met was no longer a cherubic prodigy but a cocky and urbane teenager. As a composer, Wolfgang Amadeus also had to adjust to this and he composed a lot of church music, though this was mainly simpler in style. But he was not a fan of his patron and employer Prince Archbishop of Salzburg; even if he was the youngest among the employed court composers, he was given, for the first time, officially and in an employment relationship, the opportunity to present himself musically on important occasions in front of large and appreciative audiences.

Some of the private concerts the Mozart family presented at their own home, in the larger lodgings on the Tanzmeistersaal. At their disposal was a large hall, which was formerly used by the local dancing master and was then suited for the regular musical and social gatherings, which involved music-making, playing cards or shooting sessions. Many of Wolfgang Amadeus's instrumental concertos and divertimentos were composed for performances in such semi-public environments.

In 1775 he received the commission to compose a new piece of music for the visit of Archduke Maximilian Francis of Austria in Salzburg, the youngest son of Empress Maria Theresa, who was passing through Vienna. It was to be a two-act serenata entitled *Il re pastore* (KV 208), with a libretto by Pietro Metastasio. Two musicians from Munich were hired, a castrato and a flautist. The principal psychological theme of the opera was the demands of love against the demands of kingship.

Wolfgang Amadeus worked diligently on the opera for six weeks, but he was uneasy that it was only a special event and that it would not be performed more than once, if it was successful – which he was so used to in Italy. This situation annoyed him beyond measure. The petty conditions in Salzburg provoked resentment and uneasiness in him. In Wolfgang Amadeus's philosophy, artistic advancement experienced by such banal concerts for just one single performance could not be compensated for with the harmony and comfort of life in Salzburg.

However, as he had absolutely no intention of risking his first job in Salzburg lightly, he did it diplomatically by casting an eye across the border towards the Bavarian residence in Munich. An interesting opportunity arose there with the help of an envoy at the papal court, who had seen the opera *La finta giardiniera* in Italy and hatched the idea of also commissioning a *Finta Giardiniera* opera for the next carnival season in Munich.

The Prince Bishop of Chiemsee, Ferdinand Christoph Reichserbtruchsess, Count of Waldburg Zeil, who was a big fan and patron of Wolfgang Amadeus, as well as the Electoral Court Theatre Director Graf Seeau, commissioned the work. He received the contract in the late summer of 1774 and began to compose that autumn. In December, he travelled to Munich with his father and was received by the Elector Maximilian III Joseph, who was – like his sister Maria Antonia Walpurgis of Bavaria – very skilled in music, but due to a need for strict frugality, no post could be offered to Wolfgang Amadeus. The premiere of *La Finta Giardiniera* took place on 13 January 1775 in the presence of the Elector Maximilian III Joseph at the Salvator Theatre in Munich. The public was amazed by the young

Austrian. The Mozarts stayed for a while in Munich and spent the carnival with parties and musical invitations to various private houses. Unfortunately, Wolfgang Amadeus's new opera was only performed twice and was not a great success. Nevertheless, at the beginning of March, the two men returned home to Salzburg.

In the next two years, Wolfgang Amadeus's musical life was put to the test; the comfort of Salzburg unfolded more and more, as did his compositional activities. At the same time, his patience had also been put to the test. On the one hand, he was quietly mourning his triumph as freelancer-composer in Italy, on the other hand he was employed at the Salzburg court and received constant commissions to compose. He couldn't always withstand the pressure his parents – especially his father – put on him during those years. He never showed the typical pubescent rebellion. He was totally focused on his music and the perfection of his art. He was a young, employed musician, but still a free spirit and through his art an influencer of his time. You don't need a mobile phone or a laptop to become a real influencer.

His burgeoning love life was quenched with a little flirtation from his sister's best friends. Nothing special. He was much too young for a permanent relationship. However, the energy he had accumulated over the years was suddenly released in the middle of 1777, neither against his parents, nor against his sister. Wolfgang Amadeus was fed up with constantly composing for his strict employer, who was very unpopular in Salzburg and who kept pestering him.

He wanted to leave again in order to give concerts, but when an application for leave of absence was not approved by his employer, Wolfgang Amadeus decided that day that it was time to say goodbye to the permanent job. It was like lightning swept through the palace when he finally delivered his letter of resignation to his employer, the Prince-Archbishop of Salzburg, on 1 August 1777. 'Your Highness will not take this most humble request ungraciously, since three years ago, when I asked permission to travel to Vienna, you very graciously declared to me that I had nothing to hope for and would do better, to seek my happiness elsewhere.'[26]

You weren't recalled from Salzburg unless you were constantly working somewhere else. Wolfgang Amadeus had worked hard for the Austrians. And his father Leopold had repeatedly sent vacation requests to Prince-Archbishop of Salzburg – over time, however, the number increased because the stays abroad had become overwhelming. At first, the archbishop took it calmly and allowed vacations, but over time he became more and more reticent, which of course slowed down their son's career – in the eyes of the Mozart family – quite a bit.

And now Wolfgang Amadeus decided to go on a new musical journey. This time he was accompanied by his mother. The reason for this was that his father had serious doubts about his son's pragmatism and sense of reality. Therefore, in order to calm the situation and to watch over the now 21-year-old, his mother Anna Maria was sent along.

On 23 September 1777 at 6:00 am, mother and son left Austria and headed for Munich. They wanted to reconnect with the contacts that were cultivated during the performance of *La Finta Giardiniera* two years ago. At first, it all went according to plan. The people he met were again the Elector, the theatre director, the episcopal sponsor and the owner of the hotel Zum Schwarzen Adler. But this time, the Mozarts wanted a job at court and that was more difficult than getting a commission for a music-piece or, even better, an opera.

Unfortunately, efforts to get a job at the court were unsuccessful. Count Josef Anton of Seeau remained 'much more serious and not as natural as the first time' during the conversation with Wolfgang Amadeus and his mother. And so, the Bishop of Chiemsee, Count Sigmund Christoph of Waldburg-Zeil-Trauchburg, decided to support the young man from Austria and spoke to the Electress Maria Anna Sophie of Saxony to improve his mentee's chances. Unfortunately, the Electress's feedback was a disaster; she 'just shrugged her shoulders' and that was it.

But Wolfgang Amadeus didn't give up that quickly. It turned out that a court musician who was also a cellist, Franz-Xaver Woschitka, wanted to arrange an audience with the Elector. There was also a short conversation with Elector Maximilian III Joseph, who unfortunately had to cancel because there was no vacancy at court. Then Wolfgang Amadeus met together with a diplomat, with Count Seeau and other aristocrats. But nothing happened except that he enjoyed a few nice days in Bavaria and distracted himself with music games.

During a two-week stay in Augsburg, a town in Swabia not far from Munich, he often met an uncle's daughter, named Maria Anna Thekla Mozart. He affectionately called her Bäsle, which is a diminutive form in German, meaning 'little cousin'. Together with her, he confidently threw himself into social life, was interested in other musicians, made contacts with them, and kept an eye on everything that revolved around music. He also gave music academies. At one of these academies, he met an old friend from Paris – Melchior Grimm. During these weeks Mozart was extremely happy, mainly because he had escaped from his father's strict, demanding gaze and felt free and inspired in this new life. He needed to conspire with other artists and exchange ideas with them. He missed it so much in Salzburg.

Nevertheless, his latent restlessness persisted, because he wanted to give his career a new impetus. But his father, who had stayed behind in Salzburg with his daughter, remained concerned about the career of his son, who was losing his touch with reality and wallowing in illusions. Meanwhile, Wolfgang Amadeus enjoyed his time (told through the exchange of letters), when he didn't have to look him in the eye, but only wrote about specialist musical and unessential things and thus played the loving, very good son, which in truth was not true.

After he had left Augsburg and arrived in Mannheim at the end of October 1777 to stay there for a longer period, a written relationship between him and Bäsle continued to develop, a relationship where he was used to calling them both by colourful nicknames – that was his style, that was his volatile personality. Like in the following letter, where he calls himself her nephew instead of her cousin 'If you love what I love myself, you too then must love yourself, Your Very affectionate nephew, Wolfgang Amadée Augsburg, 25th Oct., 1777 Mozart.'[27]

His late-pubescent effusions in this very special openness could – as Mozart researchers interpret – also be a fictional game from a distance. But his, until then, childish letters were over time transformed and they suddenly began to contain not only a very special humour, but also pretended that he was in a completely inverted world that no longer had anything to do with reality. Ten letters from their later correspondence survive today: they were all written by Wolfgang Amadeus to Maria Anna. These are called the Bäsle letters. They impress us with their wealth of scatological and sexual humour:

> Now write her a sensible letter for once; you can still have fun writing, but write that you have received all her letters safely, then she will not need to worry and fret about them.

> Ma très chère Nièce! Cousine! fille! Mère, Sœur, et Epouse!

> Heavens above thousand sacristy, Croatians, dire straits, devils, witches, fays, heavenly hosts without end, by the elements, air, water, earth and fire, Europe, Asia, Africa, Jesuits, Augustinians, Benedictines, Capuchins, Minorites, Franciscans, Dominicans, Carthusians, Maltesers, Canons Regular and Irregular, and all lazybones, rogues, cowards, sluggards and pricks in a heap, donkeys, buffalos, oxen, clowns, simpletons and fools! What manner of action is this one hears, 4 soldiers and 3 bandoliers? – A packet like this and no portrait? – I have been full of longing – I firmly believed – for you did of course write to me yourself, not long ago, that I would have it very soon, very soon indeed. Do you perhaps doubt if I, on my part, will keep my word? – I certainly hope

that you will have no doubts about that! Now, I beg you, send it to me, the sooner the better. It will hopefully be as I requested, namely dressed in the French style.[28]

His letters become more and more difficult to translate as they contain a lot of puns and silliness, for example onomatopoeic repetitions, word distortions or sexual allusions.

Mademoiselle [Mannheim, 28th February, 1778]

ma très chère Cousine!

You will perhaps believe or even opine that I am dead! – have kicked the bucket? – or am in the knacker's yard? – But no! Do not believe it, I beg you; for believing and shitting are two different things! – How, then, could I write so beautifully if were dead? – How could that be possible at all? – For such a long silence on my part I do not wish to excuse myself at all, for in this case you would give me no credence; yet what is true remains true! – I have had so much to do that, although I may have had time to think about my little cousin, it was too short to write, so I have had to let it be.[29]

Mannheim was an attractive and respectable place, but the Mozarts could only rave about a possible career there. Unfortunately, the reality was different. Indeed, at the Kurpfälzische Residenz there was an opulently equipped art and cultural life – because the orchestra was considered the best in Europe of that time. And, of course, there was excellent music there, otherwise nothing would be as it actually was. And then it happened – all the musicians who worked there contacted Wolfgang Amadeus, on one side out of curiosity about the famous young man and on the other side, out of politeness. Among them was Christian Cannabich, a violinist, composer and conductor of the classical period, and also the oboist Friedrich Ramm, who worked in the orchestra of Charles Theodore, Elector of Bavaria in Munich and in Mannheim. Wolfgang Amadeus developed a good friendship with them both, sustained by their families.

The Kapellmeister Ignaz Jakob Holzbauer introduced him to court music director Count Louis Aurel Savioli, and then the Count did the same to the Electress Elisabeth Auguste of Sulzbach. And what Wolfgang Amadeus had hoped for many months, suddenly happened – just a week after his arrival in Mannheim, he was able to hold an academy in the palace and in the presence of the electors, have an exchange of views on philosophical, spiritual or cultural issues coupled with music.

A few days later he was allowed to play the organ at the service in the court chapel. He was cheered and even received a gift afterwards, namely a watch. In the days that followed, Wolfgang Amadeus Mozart felt like any internationally successful artist would feel today. He was courted by the rich and invited nearly everywhere in Mannheim. He was passed around, applauded, spoiled, women clung to every word from his lips and every note from his keys. It seemed that his music united the German souls. He played again private concerts in several noble houses in Mannheim. His achievements were celebrated. In between he continued to try to contact the Electoral Family and he finally succeeded with the help of their children, who also made music and to whom he donated some scores.

Count Savioli seemed to become Wolfgang Amadeus's mentor. Meanwhile, Leopold, in Salzburg with his daughter, began to hope that his son this time might get a temporary contract. On the other hand, it would now be good for Wolfgang Amadeus to finally travel to other German cities, such as Mainz, Frankfurt and Bonn. However, Leopold Mozart was initially sceptical about his son's plans to travel on to Paris. He knew that Paris would incur costs and that his son would not get any appointment without a letter of recommendation.

At the same time, Wolfgang Amadeus urged his mentor to finally intercede for him before the Electoral Family. But Savioli remained adamant, silent and preferred to wait.

In December 1777, Wolfgang Amadeus received a negative written decision from Savioli and he and his mother had to travel on. It was a sad step and he did not like it, but he decided to tell his father the truth. Then he started more planning and continued to aim high.

The next step of his strategy was to speak to Joseph Mesmer. He had been the master mind and the school director of the first 'Normal school' in Vienna since 1770 (which was an elementary school, a junior high school and a teacher training college at the same time, as the 'source and centre of the Maria-Theresan school reforms'). Mesmer would arrange – with the help of the Viennese court – for a letter of recommendation to be sent to Marie Antoinette, daughter of the Austrian Empress Maria Theresa and Queen of France.

Wolfgang Amadeus let himself fall into a completely different fantasy world, but only in the music, in his diverse musical activities and in his compositional productivity did this strategy work. Nevertheless, he managed to cover his living costs and that of his mother, who accompanied him. On the one hand he received a loan from his family, on the other hand he gave many concerts and received gifts that could later also be turned into money. In addition, he taught regularly in Mannheim. This helped him to get a calculable income but did not change much in the current – rather hopeless – job situation in Mannheim. This manoeuvring was viewed with great suspicion by Leopold in Salzburg, and there was increasing tension in the communication between father and son.

Before his dismissal in Salzburg, Wolfgang Amadeus had made extremely derogatory remarks about the musicians at the court there, but in Mannheim everything was suddenly different. In Mannheim, the young man formally cheered his German colleagues and was already making plans with three of them – namely the oboist Friedrich Ramm, the flautist and composer Johann Baptist Wendling and the ballet master Etienne Lauchéry – to go to Paris together and pursue a career there. To Leopold, all this seemed very ill-considered. He wrote this in a very long letter on 11 December 1777 to his son where he analysed the situation for him:

> But they tried to entertain you so well in different places right at the beginning that you had to forget everything and allowed your thoughts to rest, full of hopes, only on what people dictated to you, without thinking further ahead and without finding out means with which to be more certain of achieving it.
>
> One can never think up too many paths when one wants to reach a goal, because one can never foresee all unfavourable hindrances. What you write about a journey to Paris with Herr Wendling etc. etc. is not to be dismissed: there is still time to give an answer on that – it depends where you are this coming Lent. At young Sigerl Robini's I saw Duets for 2 Violins del Sgr. Lauchery, Danseur de S:A:SS: l'Electeur Palatin etc.
>
> What can be earned in Paris I know myself, and I have written to you about it in previous letters. If Msr. Grimm is there, your luck is made; if not, we shall no doubt find and make acquaintanceships. In short! When it comes down to it, you will receive all due guidance from me.
>
> Simply read through my previous letters several times, and make some notes from it all for yourself, otherwise something will be forgotten at once, and who wants to read the whole letter through every time? – If you do not stay – or if you are no longer in Manheimm, there is no other choice than to go to Paris, and I will then at once send a letter flying to

Msr: Grim and let you have the list of all our acquaintances and do some thinking ahead in every possible way.[30]

In the previous weeks, Wolfgang Amadeus had been quite sarcastic towards his father in his letters for the first time, almost verbally hurting him. In reality, he had made every effort to explain to his father his reasons for the importance of a trip to Paris, but Leopold saw it differently. Wolfgang Amadeus kept trying to make peace with his father at the end of his letters:

I wrote that your last letter caused me great joy: that is true! Only one thing vexed me a little – the question of whether I might have forgotten about Confession? – But I have nothing to say against that. Only please allow me one request, and that is: Do not think so very badly of me! I like to have fun, but rest assured that despite all of these things, I can be serious. Since I have been away from Salzburg – and in Salzburg itself, too – I have met such people that I would have been ashamed to speak and act like that, although they were 10, 20 and 30 years older than me! – So I ask you once again, and most submissively, to have a better opinion of me. To Herr Bullinger, the best of all my friends, I ask you to convey my compliments and the most friendly wishes for New Year. My compliments to all good friends, both gentlemen and ladies. N.B. to Father Dominicus.[31]

So, it went back-and-forth for weeks with miserably long letters between the worried father and the son who had fled Salzburg. But at the same time, a good reason suddenly developed for Wolfgang Amadeus to stay in Mannheim. It was the love for a young woman. However, when Leopold found out who the girl was and what family she came from, it did not suit him at all. He felt his son slowly but surely free himself from his grasp, which unfortunately led to lifelong conflicts between father and son.

At the age of 21, Wolfgang Amadeus only wanted to present himself to his father as a man full of plans and reasonable musical activities. For this reason, he decided to travel to Kirchheimbolanden in the Rhineland-Palatinate in the coming days, on the advice of a Dutch officer he knew, in order to get to know Princess Caroline von Nassau-Weilburg. The princess was a woman with an affinity for music and had already proved to be the ideal patron of the Mozart family in 1765 in The Hague.

He also told his father about this plan and explained to him that he had sent her some of his compositions. In the course of his correspondence he suddenly mentioned a 16-year-old singer, whom he had been teaching for some time. He raved to Leopold about her father Fridolin Weber, saying that he was born in 1733 as the son of a bailiff in the Schönau family. His path through life was quite adventurous. He is said to have studied law in Freiburg and acquired a theological doctorate. In 1754, he was named as his father's successor in office. He was also a good singer, and in this capacity Charles Theodore, the Elector of Bavaria, drew him to Mannheim, where he appeared as a bassist from 1765-1778 with a salary of 200 fl, then later 400 fl. Apparently, the low income had prompted him to get a second job as a copyist and one as a prompter. Nevertheless, his circumstances remained less than modest, especially since he had a large family to support. He had been married to Marie Cäcilie Stamm from Mannheim since 1756 and had five girls and one boy with her. In 1777, the four daughters Josepha, Aloysia, Constanze and Sophie were still alive. Unfortunately, Fridolin Weber earned far too little money for the large family.

Wolfgang Amadeus Mozart himself was a trained boy soprano[32] who was tutored during his childhood – between 1764 and 1765 – by the famous Italian castrati Giovanni Manzuoli. Manzuoli first sang as a soprano and later became an alto. Incidentally, up to the age of 13 Mozart repeatedly appeared in public, not only as a musician but also as a singer – after that his puberty was probably an obstacle to further performances.

At the time of the lesson in 1777, Aloysia was by now a very advanced student. Wolfgang Amadeus even had the feeling that she already had an excellent vocal cantabile style. However, he felt that she could use some work on highly virtuosic passages of fast notes.

Wolfgang Amadeus Mozart's project was to travel without his mother, but with the young soprano and her father for a week to the Princess of Nassau-Weilburg. Together they played several concerts with the usual success for Wolfgang Amadeus.

Immediately afterwards, Wolfgang Amadeus gave up his plan to travel to Paris with his three friends and fellow musicians, Wendling and Ramm, as well as with ballet master Etienne Lauchéry. His mother, who had stayed at home, received numerous letters and nonsense poetry from him, which spilled over slightly into the erotic and he was – as he later clarified to his father - sort of 'unconsciously provocative' while he was deeply in love with a woman. Then, Wolfgang Amadeus suddenly told Leopold Mozart that he was planning to go to Switzerland with Mr Weber, his singing daughter Aloysia and her sister Josepha. He even suggested that there was the possibility of driving to the Netherlands as well. It sounded as if he had fallen in love with the young singer Aloysia and in his admiration for her, he did not consider that his father would not approve.

In fact, it was even worse, because nonsensical plans of this kind enraged Leopold. He knew that without an order and without a letter of recommendation, nothing was possible in the world of music. No money would flow and no concert would ever take place. But his creative son had no idea about management and the work behind an order. This time, Leopold was so outraged that he told his son in clear words that he was becoming too distracted.

The mood between father and son became noticeably hotter and was taken to the extreme when Wolfgang Amadeus began writing that he intended to take Aloysia to Italy and make her famous there. Then came an answer from Leopold in which he replied honestly, but full of anger to his son:

My dear son!   Salzburg, 12th Feb., 1778

I have read through your letter of the 4th with amazement and horror, and I am beginning to answer it today, the 11th, when I have not been able to sleep the whole night, and am so feeble that I have to write slowly, word by word, and must gradually bring it to an end by tomorrow. I have been well, praise God, the whole time up till now, but this letter, in which I no longer recognize my son except by the mistake that he always believes the first word that people say, revealing his too kind heart to everyone at the prompting of flattery and good, fine words, allowing himself to be led to and fro, as they choose, into every idea that is presented to him, and allowing himself to be brought, by sudden ideas and unfounded prospects lacking adequate consideration of their realisability, to the point of sacrificing, to the advantage of third parties, his own name and advantage and even the advantage and help owed to his old, honest parents; I was all the more oppressed by this letter because I had been storing reasonable hopes in myself that some of the circumstances you had already encountered, and the reminders I had given you verbally here and in writing, should have persuaded you of this: in order to seek one's fortune as well as what is even merely common advancement in the world and, finally, to achieve the sought after aim among such various kinds of good, bad, happy and unhappy people, one must guard one's kind heart with the greatest reserve, undertake nothing without the deepest reflection, and never allow oneself to be carried away by enthusiastic fancies and chance, blind whims.

I beg you, my dear son, read this letter thoughtfully – take the time to read and reflect.[33]

In the course of this 6-page letter, the father also reminded his son of the basic concerns of his family:

Off to Paris with you! and soon; place yourself close to great persons – *aut Caesar aut nihil*; the mere thought of seeing Paris would have kept you safe from all flighty ideas. From Paris, the reputation and name of a man of great talent goes out throughout the whole world, since the nobility handle persons of genius with the greatest condescension, esteem and courtesy. There one sees a fine way of life which is in astonishing contrast to the coarseness of our German gentlemen and ladies at court and there you acquire a solid mastery of the French language. As far as keeping company with Wendling etc. is concerned, you do not need them at all. You have known them long enough, and didn't your Mama notice it, were you both blind? No, I know how it will be, you were taken in by it, and she was not allowed to dare to contradict you. I am angry that you both lack the trust and forthrightness to tell me everything in detail and with honesty; You did the same thing with me concerning the Elector, and in the end all the truth had to come out after all. You both wanted to save me vexation, and in the end you suddenly poured over my head a bowl of lye filled with vexations which are almost robbing me of my life. You know, and have 1000 examples of it, that our gracious God gave me sound powers of reason, that my head is still turned the right way, and that I have often found an escape from the most entangled matters, and have foreseen and guessed a multitude of things: what, then, kept you from asking me for advice and always acting according to my will? My son, you must see me more as your most sincere friend than as a sharp father. Reflect on whether I have not always dealt with you in friendship and served you as a servant does his master, and have also procured for you every possible support and helped you, often at my own great inconvenience, to obtain every honest and respectable pleasure?

This letter might have provoked something. The weeks passed. And on 14 March Wolfgang Amadeus decided to drive to Paris with his dear mother – without Aloysia Weber and her family.

A lot had changed in Paris in the twelve years since Mozart was last there. There was a new king, Louis XVI, whose Austrian wife, Marie Antoinette, was the daughter of Maria Theresa. That was a good omen for Wolfgang Amadeus. But the intellectual and artistic scene had also changed during the years of his absence. However, some of Mozart's contacts were still living in Paris; for example, the patron of the child prodigies, Friedrich Melchior, Baron von Grimm. And the Mozart family was still in contact with him.

But it was the Parisian music scene which had changed a lot for Mozart, who was now again in France on the stage. Of course, no one could have expected the enthusiasm for him to be the same as it was twelve years before. In art, too, the stars were progressing and, above all, new stars were emerging who also want to have a stunning career.

During Wolfgang Amadeus's stay in Paris, the Piccininist Controversy, a politically instrumentalized use of Piccini in the minds of those interested in music, was raging. The protagonists of the controversies were two outstanding composers, Nicolas Piccini representing Italian opera and Christoph Willibald Gluck representing French *tragédie lyrique*.

But the great and admired artist among the composers was the Belgian André Ernest Modeste Grétry, who, however, was not able to assert himself very much against Gluck.

The start for Wolfgang Amadeus in Paris was not particularly rosy and for Leopold it seemed quite predictable. But in view of the cultural circumstances in Paris, he was still very successful, because he obediently stuck to his father's patterns of action.

It all started when, equipped with a few letters of recommendation, he sought contact with German diplomats and merchants. Friedrich Melchior, Baron von Grimm and his mistress, Louise D'Épinay, helped him a lot – among other things with the search for an apartment for him and his mother. They very quickly brought Wolfgang Amadeus into the action. He was first paired with the singer, composer and director of the Concert Spirituel, active since 1777, Joseph Legros, followed by the French dancer, ballet master and creator of Ballet d'action, Jean Georges Noverre.

It seemed as if Wolfgang Amadeus had found his new path with these great contacts. At least his mother was enthusiastic and expressed this in a letter to her husband, writing that her son was famous and popular again. It was all well and good for Leopold, but he knew that one could not live from composing commissions alone. You needed an official mainstay – for example as a busy composer at the court. For this reason, he constantly urged his son to finally give it a try. He even mentioned the palace of Versailles. And if this should not work out, Leopold even focused on the chapel of a prince.

At the beginning of May 1778, Wolfgang Amadeus wrote in a letter to his father that the hornplayer, violinist, music teacher and composer Jean-Joseph Rodolphe offered to get him a well-paid position as organist in Versailles. Leopold seemed positive and advised him to accept this position to be in constant touch with the nobility. But his son declined.

Six weeks later, Wolfgang Amadeus was complaining about the lack of success of his situation. Though he was constantly running around in Paris, auditioning and getting access to imperial court and nobility, he could not get one job offer, though he did get huge compliments. But one cannot survive financially only with compliments and the situation had to change. In his opinion, Paris had changed a lot since the last time he had enjoyed the vibrant city.

The French people were ruder and their cultural taste had changed for the worse. Although he gave music lessons to the daughters of well situated French people and earned some money, it was not enough for him and his mother.

Of course, there was always a balancing act between hope, perseverance, self-esteem and a correct assessment of the situation in France. Leopold and his son repeatedly settled their disputes in long letters on these topics. One could almost speak of a generational conflict between the two men. The young Wolfgang Amadeus wanted to get good jobs that suited him, but his father stuck to the letters of recommendation, which had always been fruitful up to that point. Still he didn't understand, because he observed in person how the city of Paris and the French really behaved in those days. He couldn't believe, and therefore accept, his father's advice. On the other hand, one thing was totally clear between both men; Wolfgang Amadeus should avoid contact with the Italian symphony and chamber music composer Nikolo Piccinni and the Belgian *opéras comiques* composer André Modeste Grétry as much as possible. They could represent dangerous competition for him. However, this resolution led to a certain loneliness in Wolfgang Amadeus's time in Paris.

Meanwhile, his mother spread good cheer to her husband in her letters by sugar-coating the situation and repeatedly defending her beloved son. But in June 1778, she suddenly fell ill. It is reported that she went out for the last time on 10 June. She did not feel well afterwards and started to constantly complain of headaches, so she bled herself on 11 June. That doesn't seem to have helped because by 19 June she was bedridden, developing a severe fever and losing her hearing. Wolfgang Amadeus was again invited by Count Sickingen to play him the new *Paris Symphony* (KV 297), which had been premiered on 18 June with great success. Meanwhile, Wolfgang Amadeus, as he reported to his father, had prayed a rosary for this success, and then celebrated alone in a Parisian café with a good ice cream.

Unfortunately, by this time, his mother's condition was worsening from day to day. Even the doctor, who had been summoned, could not save her. As a precaution, she received the last rites on 30 June, dying three days later at the age of 57 of an undiagnosed illness in the presence of her son, a nurse and Franz Joseph Hainas, who had taken great care of her in Paris. She was buried at the cemetery Saint Eustache.

Her son was broken. On her deathbed, he first wrote to Abbé Joseph Bullinger in Salzburg, asking the friend of his family to carefully prepare his father and sister Nannerl for the news of his beloved mother's major illness and death.

Paris, ce 3 julliet 1778

Best of friends!

Entirely for you alone. Mourn with me, my friend! – This was the saddest day of my life – I am writing this at 2 o'clock at night – I must tell you, sir, my mother, my dear mother is no more! – God has called her to himself – he wanted to have her, I saw that clearly – accordingly I have surrendered myself to the will of God – he had given her to me, he could also take her from me.[34]

He then wrote that same evening his most famous letter of four pages to his father, where he strictly avoided giving written testimony of his mother's death, wrapping it instead in a meditation on the need to 'submit oneself to the will of God':

Paris, ce 3 de julliet 1778

Monsieur mon très cher Père!

I have to give you some very unpleasant and sad news, this is also the reason that I have not been able to reply sooner to your last letter dated the 11th. – My dear mother is very ill – as is her wont, she had her blood let, and this was also very necessary; and subsequently she was doing well – yet for some days afterwards she complained of shivering, and at the same time was feverish – developed diarrhoea, headaches – at the beginning we used only our household remedies, antispasmodic powder, we would also have liked to use the black powder, but we had none left, and we could not get it here, nor is it known under the name pulvis epilepticus. – But because it got constantly worse – she could hardly speak, lost her hearing to the extent that one had to shout – Baron Grim sent his doctor here – she is very weak, still has hot flushes, and is delirious – they are speaking of hope, but I do not have much – I have been between fear and hope day and night for a long time now – but I have surrendered myself entirely to God's will – and hope that you and my dear sister will do the same; what other means do we have, then, of being calm? .....– ...... Let us hope, but not too much; let us have our trust with God, and comfort ourselves with the thought that all goes well if it goes according to the will of the Almighty, since he knows best what is profitable and useful for both our temporal and eternal happiness and well-being.[35]

In this long letter to his father, Wolfgang Amadeus first reported his Parisian successes and the compositional effects of his Parisian symphony, but suddenly he starts to alternate from his successes to the approaching death and praying the rosary, when being a good Christian. He then wrote a third letter, which is unfortunately lost today, to Fridolin Weber and his daughters in Mannheim, to inform them about the death of his mother. It seemed obvious that he was in shock and in pain. Still wondering how this could have happened, because he didn't see her death coming. As we know today, she might have died of typhus. The hardships of travel to France, the cold and damp accommodations, her loneliness and her homesickness probably shattered Maria Anna Mozart's delicate health. Perhaps the fateful development of her son's career in France also played a role. She grieved because he had completely escaped his father's influence and was completely fixated on the Weber family – above all fixated on this 18-year-old singer Aloysia – whose slynessness he didn't want to recognize.

However, the Webers took their time with an answer. Franz Fridolin Weber finally replied to his '*Très cher et plus cher amy*' with a veritable begging letter for money, which upset the grieving Wolfgang Amadeus so much that he immediately forwarded the request for 1,000 guilders 'for the remaining years' to his father in a four-page letter to him with the encoded announcement of his mother's passing. He hadn't mentioned Aloysia to his father for over four months. But now that his mother had died, he received the begging letter from her father. Leopold Mozart began to realize that Aloysia and her family had taken control of his son's feelings during his whole time in Paris and that they hadn't stopped begging him for money over the months.

With the death of Wolfgang Amadeus's mother, all hope of a dazzling new career in Paris died for him. But neither Wolfgang Amadeus nor Leopold knew it. However, one of the close friends of the Mozart family, Friedrich Melchior Grimm, who had hosted Wolfgang Amadeus and his mother, understood the situation and reacted quickly. He informed the father in a letter, telling him the truth as well as all his observations in a very open manner. In his letter from 13 August he mentioned that Wolfgang Amadeus was too 'guileless' and simply not energetic enough, but that he was also easily deceived and was unfamiliar with the means that could lead to great success.

To make it in Paris you had to be shrewd, enterprising and daring. Leopold understood this as easily as the next man and he reacted by searching for a job for his son at the Salzburg court. And he was successful. Towards the end of August, he was informed by the court that 'everything was agreed', that his son was hired as concertmaster and that he would earn 500 guilders.

Wolfgang Amadé – as the young man called himself during his time in Paris – nevertheless first resisted this job announcement. He felt that he still had good chances in Paris. But, as luck would have it, when he received the Weber's begging letter, he began a streak of financial bad luck which seemed to have been interrupted since his departure from Mannheim. One of his debtors, the extremely rich Adrien-Louis de Bonnières, Duke of Guînes, headed the ranks of defaulters; he owed Wolfgang Amadeus big sum for his harpist daughter Marie Louise Charlotte's lessons as well as for a piece of music – the *Concerto for Flute and Harp* (KV 299) – that he and King Frederick of Prussia had commissioned from him. But when Wolfgang Amadeus requested payment, the duke's head butler settled at half the agreed amount.

For this reason, Leopold Mozart turned on Friedrich Melchior Grimm, who had once mediated this connection with the rich duke, leading to tensions between them. Because of this, Wolfgang Amadeus then decided to belittle Grimm when he wrote new letters to his father claiming that Grimm talked 'harshly, simple-mindedly and stupidly' to him, that he was 'wrong' – and that he constantly tried to 'suppress' him. On the other hand, he understood his father's concerns and seemed ready to return home to Salzburg. In a letter dated 11 September 1778, he explained his feelings to Leopold:

> I would have moved out next month and got into a house where things are not as simple-minded and stupid as with him – and where you always have it set right before your nose if someone does you a favour – presented this way, I really could forget a favour – but I wish to be more generous than he – I am only sorry that I am not staying here just to show him that I do not need him – and that I am capable of just as much as his Piccini – although I am only a German; the

greatest good deed that he showed me consists of 15 louis d'or which he lent me little by little during my blessed mother's struggle between life and death – can it be that he is anxious about this?[36]

Wolfgang Amadeus not only played the indignant and self-confident son for his father, he was already in a bad mood and in a bad situation. Aloysia was the magnet with which the Weber family shook Wolfgang Amadeus and asked him to pay. Again and again they pretended that she became the 'victim of an intrigue', but, incomprehensibly, her father did not explain who the *infami cujoni* were. In such situations, Wolfgang Amadeus tended to belittle other people.

He did this when he met Johann Christian Bach again at the end of August, the man who had taken care of him so kindly when he was in London with his parents and his sister Nannerl. Bach, who arrived with the castrato Tenducci, introduced Wolfgang Amadeus to Marshal Louis de Noailles, 4th Duke of Noailles, who he met at his castle in St. Germain–en–Laye, where he maintained a court orchestra made up of German musicians. Now, he introduced the young Mozart to the Duke de Noailles, who belonged to one of the most prestigious noble families in French history and who also basked in the grace of the court of Versailles. Wolfgang Amadeus happily wrote to his father about the new encounter from the palace in Versailles, but pointed out, that he 'will not gain anything here'.

He spent almost three weeks in the castle of St. Germain–en–Laye and probably had the happiest time of his Parisian life, inspired by the beauty, the spirit and the grace of French polite society. Here came what he had always been looking for, namely aristocracy, artists, a good orchestra, entertainment, friends and a wonderful ambience. There were also triumphs when making music in front of the duke and his famous guests. It can be assumed that some copies of Wolfgang Amadeus's scores were also sold at court. He even composed a scene for Tenducci (KV Appendix 3). In a letter to his father, he compares

France with Germany and that the people 'were fobbed off with praise'. Leopold never got to know this endless chain of verbal insults and bad taste during his travels. In France of all places, he assumed, extravagance was always the essence of noblesse and artistic delights had always been highly rewarded.

Although Bach and Tenducci were extremely supportive of Wolfgang Amadeus with Marshal de Noailles, he unfortunately did not hire him for his court music. On 8 September, the world premiere of Wolfgang Amadeus's *2nd Paris Symphony* (KV Appendix 8) took place in the Concert Spirituel. What was shocking afterwards was that he was supposed to get 275 guilders for this piece of music, but the money never came. Several hundred guilders should also have been paid from the publisher for three piano concertos and six sonatas for piano and violin. But nothing happened there either. He spoke to his father about it.

Whenever Wolfgang Amadeus was in a hopeless situation, as he currently was in Paris, he tended to flee into fantasies of other places and had many new goals. One of his biggest and most important goals was to be together with his first and new girlfriend, the young singer Aloysia Weber.

Aloysia was originally supposed to come to Paris with her father and to join Wolfgang Amadeus. But then they had no more money and when it became public that she was to receive a contract for the Munich court theatre and would move to Bavaria, Wolfgang Amadeus was convinced that he should present his girlfriend to the Archbishop of Salzburg as a fashionable, young singer. Leopold Mozart supported his son and also intervened on behalf of Aloysia with the Archbishop of Salzburg. In addition to this, Wolfgang Amadeus wanted to flee to Italy with her, which is why he wrote a few letters in Italian to her, beginning with the greeting and opening '*Carissima Amica*'. For his father Leopold, this Italian-project was absolutely out of the question.

On his journey home, Wolfgang Amadeus repeatedly ignored his father's requests to return faster, because a job was waiting for him. This can be interpreted as the long-overdue release from the childhood bond between the now 22-year-old musician and his father. He had already outgrown his childhood prodigy years and he became meanwhile a renowned composer. So, instead of hurrying back to Salzburg, he stopped in Nancy and in Strasbourg to earn money, before staying a little bit longer in the German city of Mannheim.

During these five weeks, he lived in Mannheim with Maria Elisabeth de la Motte, lady of the bedchamber to the Duchess of Zweibrücken, who was married to the composer and conductor Christian Cannabich. After Charles Theodore was appointed Elector of Bavaria in 1778, he had to move his residence to Munich and asked Cannabich to take over the management of instrumental music in Munich. While her husband started his job and had already moved to the Electorate of Bavaria, Wolfgang Amadeus lived at the apartment of Maria Elisabeth who, a year ago, had been enjoying the young composer's emerging eroticism. She was 'almost beside herself with joy, when she saw me again', he later wrote. Wolfgang Amadeus also communicated this to Maria Elisabeth during his time in Paris. The few surviving lines about being with her reveal a deep, astonished happiness and friendship with this warm-hearted, lively woman, as well as an intoxication and a certain blissfulness. Wolfgang Amadeus gave daily keyboard lessons to her daughter, Rosa, for whom he composed the *Sonata in C*, (KV 309). He liked and admired Maria Elisabeth's husband immensely, observing in one of his letters, that

> Then furthermore, and perhaps for this reason, the musicians are not very popular in Salzburg, and receive no respect at all – yes, if the musicians were organised as in Mannheim! – the subordination that prevails in this orchestra! – the authority that Cannabich has – everything is done seriously; Cannabich, who is the best director I have ever seen, has the love and fear of his subjects. – He is also respected throughout the town, and so are his soldiers – but they also

behave differently – display manners, are well-dressed, do not go into the inns and carouse – but this cannot be the case where you are, unless the Prince puts his trust in you or me and gives us complete authority for whatever is necessary for the court music – otherwise it is pointless …[37]

But the extraordinary journey home from Paris to Salzburg, which lasted from the end of September to mid-January 1779, brought a final disappointment. Aloysia, the woman with whom Wolfgang Amadeus was in love, got a permanent engagement in Munich. She therefore met him only for a short time, but rejected his request to go with him on a trip to Italy. Her coolness and distance towards him plunged the acclaimed young artist and composer into despair. He understood that it was the end of their love, before he became angry with her and called her 'false' and a 'coquette'. He then decided to contact his cousin, Maria Anna Thekla Mozart from Augsburg and ask her to join him in Munich and to travel together with him to Salzburg. Bäsle agreed and stayed with him and the Mozart family for a few months. It was a distraction for both of them and in a certain way, she became a substitute for his deceased mother and the – so called – 'Carissima Amica' Aloysia. His love for Aloysia would remain only through music; he continued to compose arias for Aloysia and he also sometimes performed together with her.

Back in Salzburg, Wolfgang Amadeus was appointed as court organist and earned not more than 450 guilders and 50 guilders for piano lessons for noble boys. In addition to that, he was supposed to take over his former position as concertmaster, playing in the orchestra again as the first violinist, which he thoroughly hated.

In reality, the archbishop had no intention of making any concessions to Wolfgang Amadeus. Not only was his offer pathetic, it was a mockery. The Count of Colloredo knew that the Salzburg court no longer wanted Wolfgang Amadeus, who had become known as a difficult person and artist. And he only took him on as long as his father could manage to rein in the extremely exhausting muddle-headed son.

The whole thing seemed like a humiliation for Wolfgang Amadeus. Two full-time jobs, both well below his abilities. But where was the time for creativity and compositions? A shameful offer, compared to the nearly 4,000 guilders he had received in Paris for his first composition. Nonetheless, he accepted the job. This was only a small consolation for all the professional and the private disappointments he had suffered during his stay in France and he struggled with very sad career disillusionment.

The lively musical world of the France of the eighteenth-century appeared to have a long-lasting influence on him as his *opera seria Idomeneo* and some of his instrumental works would later indicate. Especially Paris was – and will always be – a city that attracts artists from around the globe. Artists detected new trends and were inspired by them, and the French themselves were always on the alert for new styles, new creative – but most of all – younger talents. Once they were discovered, some of them quickly disappeared.

In 1778 it may have been such issues that diverted the attention of French people from Mozart. Although he wanted to succeed in France, now it was too late. His chance was gone. The inner unrest he had been struggling with since his stay in Paris had to find a way out and eventually end in some sort of massive outbreak.

For Wolfgang Amadeus, as for many other musicians and composers in the eighteenth century, performing and composing represented two sides of the same coin. And he described good sight-reading as playing a piece in such a way that you might suppose that the performer had composed it himself. Players and singers were supposed to continue the creative work of the composer. Improvisation at the keyboard, his stock in trade during his whole career, represented his most complex merging of performing and composing into a single creative act. This was his constant act, and he was good at it. In improvising for his audience, he had these activities reinforce each other, as critics recognized when referencing both his playing and features of the music produced; ideas, themes and harmony. He was capable of playing valiantly, to improvise for hours off the top of his head, producing the best music ideas according to the current taste. Like the words he wrote, Wolfgang Amadeus's career was shaped by involvement as a performance composer. His intimate relationship with renditions of his own music also affected what he wrote primarily or exclusively for others to perform. He learned his compositional craft as a performer on his trips: compositional weaknesses, including harmonic and gestural unevenness in the accompanied sonatas, attributable to a desire to exploit concomitant performing opportunities. Exuberant ornamentations and embellishments in the early accompanied sonatas also gave a flavour in notated form of the enthusiastic performances that the audiences of his renditions would have enjoyed throughout Europe. After his trips to Germany and France without his father his intention was to exploit his skills as a performer-composer to procure a post away from Salzburg. At least in his principal career aspiration, Mozart focused his mind on the future and where he wanted to direct his energies.

Fulfilling an order from a third party and exploring one's individuality as an artist are two demands that are difficult to reconcile – and yet a composer will try to square the circle. If he refuses to do so, he challenges himself immensely, which may be to the benefit of the work that is being created. But he will not go unpunished by those with the power to perform works and audiences that cultivate certain listener expectations.

At that time, this was particularly true for large-scale works such as operas, oratorios, symphonies or a piano concerto. One could rather be solipsistic in the composition of small pieces with little effort, or even in works to play oneself. Of course, there is also a group-solipsism – artistic communication in circles of initiated connoisseurs, which can be just as stimulating and fruitful, as it can lead to a rigid assimilation of two cultures, in which one culture is assimilated into another. Culture A matches Culture B's traits to their own and the members of Culture B assimilate to the applicable standards by entering Culture A.

Avant-garde circles combined in a group of pioneers of intellectual developments and the associated progress, but isolated eccentric geniuses have existed in western musical history from the very beginning. It was decisive for a composer's reputation to convince with works in the major genres, especially operas, festive masses and oratorios, which were particularly suitable for performances on representative, official occasions.

Because he was constantly thinking about his own career – which, of course, also simply meant securing his own economic existence – Wolfgang Amadeus had to regularly work on getting commissions for operas. He was not very pleased that the archbishop of Salzburg, Count Colloredo, who was oriented towards enlightenment, restricted the scope of and expenditure on church music, especially the one for festive masses.

The correspondence with his father over several years showed Wolfgang Amadeus's wishes and strategic considerations to get commissions for opera compositions in Italy. But, as already described, no more orders came from Italy. Father and son continued to play the game, but without further success. They even asked Padre Martini from Bologna to mediate with potential clients. But how could this famous music theorist and church musician have obtained an attractive opera commission for the Mozart's?

Another problem at that time was that opera houses kept placing orders, but usually it was just a premiere and then possibly a first series of performances. But very rarely were the opera pieces taken over again and adapted or even performed by other opera houses. Today it is the case that a work is performed on countless opera stages. But at that time, one was happy if it at least found a positive expression and was played on an opera stage.

It is also known at this time that certain pieces were picked up again and again and played with modifications – also on other stages.

Certain arias could reappear as favourites in entirely different operas. It was also an honour for composers to be asked to write a single aria for another composer's opera and Wolfgang Amadeus did this sometimes. However, Mozart's pieces did not find their way into this repertoire. His three Milan operas were never played anywhere, let alone adapted.

Mozart never skipped over the abilities of the musicians and the comprehension of the audience as confidently as the later Beethoven. It was a matter of course for him to compose for certain performers and for a certain audience. This is particularly evident in large-scale works such as the opera and piano concertos. However, his communicative compositional behaviour cannot always be understood from this.

Nonetheless, the reaction to his mature music, which ranged from spontaneous approval to persistent reserve, must be attributed to its character and to the composer's mischievous desire to explore his expressive imagination, both seriously and cheerfully, despite all human commitment.

Even a talented person like Wolfgang Amadeus Mozart first had to learn manual skills and experience what other composers created in order to articulate his own music in such a way that we can trace an inner essence to his work. By the time of his stay in Italy he had acquired this sovereignty.

In concrete terms, Wolfgang Amadeus's pleasure in skill can be understood, and it may amaze each of us here and there, if we can't find an explanation for such a phenomenon. But in truth, one has to say that the pleasure in skill begins with the desire to fail. This was evident in the summer of 1764 in London, when Leopold Mozart lay ill and his son began to compose without his father's supervision. What he wrote down in his London Sketchbook during this period is now known as *Piano Pieces* (KV 15).

Some things in his earliest compositions seemed skilful, others helpless or hair-raising, contradicting all compositional rules and creative conventions.

But what might be more important for the evolution of the artist was that he broke out of his father's domestication. He was determined to break certain conventions and this process was very important for him personally. Even failure can be a positive stimulus. Ten years later he was, of course, much more talented and could compose professionally, and he was also aware of it. He was able to use his skills in a targeted manner like a businessman does with his capital. And this is where his second desire and joy came into play, namely the willingness to experiment.

On the basis of manual and technical skills, a creative individual suddenly moved, playing with his basic skills and at the same time exploring his entire ability to express himself. And this under the eyes of observers – namely an international audience. All of this reflected his lust for skill and for expression.

Had Wolfgang Amadeus followed the eccentric leaps of his mind that appear in some of the pieces in his beloved London Sketchbook as a guide, he might not have been as successful in music. His pleasure in being able – for example in the symphony – expressed itself differently. He maintains a conservative framework and fills it with varied interiors. In addition, there is a completion of him as an individual. This process includes the development of one's own abilities, aptitudes and opportunities to express beliefs, attitudes, opinions and perspectives. The aim of the process is a step-by-step awareness in order to recognize and realize oneself as something unique.

In his compositions he deals with the expectations of his environment. His lively Italian symphonies have something to do with what the listener expects. His G-minor Symphonies, on the other hand, speak – as the Austrian musicologist Gernot Gruber later described it – of his urge to express himself and his striving for unification of compositional technique.

The *Piano Concerto in E flat major* (KV 271), the *Jeunehomme Concerto*, could reveal when Wolfgang Amadeus confronts us as the master we are looking for in his works. From a concert one expects a dialogue between a soloist and the audience, which proceeds in certain forms. First it begins with an orchestral tutti (this happens when all the players in the orchestra play together), where the character of the piece is established and important melodic themes are introduced. Then the soloist appears and presents himself with an introduction, which is designed in a similar way to the intro. Then there is an interplay between orchestra and soloists. But in KV 271, Wolfgang Amadeus lets the piano soloist intervene as early as the second bar. To the astonishment of his audience, he then constantly switches the roles of the soloist and the orchestra, never conforming to convention.

He used this drama to captivate the viewers and listeners. He amazed his fans, who were not used to such stylistic elements from the other composers – and that was his special musical secret. He didn't follow the usual rules in order to be heard and applauded, and consequently built up a very special fan base during this time. The psychological portrayal of the main actors was an important element in operas, a new form of dramatization was found in the opera or *opera seria* in order to disentangle the conventional emotional images into flexible processes and to achieve this portrayal of the characters.

Furthermore, Wolfgang Amadeus used the *accompagnato* recitative more frequently than any other composer of his time. Specifically, what matters here is that the singer is accompanied by an orchestra, which is involved in the compositional interpretation of the sung content, which results in a stricter rhythmic connection. Using the *accompagnato* recitative as a grid of landmarks, he constantly raised the ambivalence of the opera's protagonists' feelings by inverting and changing what has already been heard beyond the text.

In the operas *La Finta Giardiniera*, or *Lucio Silla* (1772) and in the *Jeunehomme Concerto* one can see the demands Wolfgang Amadeus made in these works and to what extent his audience made them in the context of an everyday social situation of an opera performance, in reality overwhelmed by its individualizing musical design.

In *Lucio Silla* the story is about the Roman dictator Lucius Sulla, who covets Giunia, the daughter of his enemy Gaius Marius. Giunia, on the other hand, loves the exiled Senator Cecilio. The story in *La Finta Giardiniera* follows Count Belfiore and the Marquise Violante Onesti who play a pair of lovers, before Belfiore stabs Violante to death in a fit of rage. In fact, the story begins with the revived Violante and her servant Roberto, disguised as Sandrina and Nardo, working silently in the mansion of the town's Podestà (mayor). Violante discovers that Belfiore has become engaged to Arminda, the Podestà's niece, and when Belfiore confesses his enduring love to Violante, Arminda jealously conspires to kidnap the other woman. When Violante is found, she and Belfiore lose their minds, believing themselves to be Greek gods. When they regain their senses, Violante forgives the Count and they hug. Arminda returns to Cavalier Ramiro, her rejected suitor, and Roberto falls in love with Serpetta, another of the Podestà's servants.

Leopold Mozart believed from the beginning that his son should first make his name as a pianist when in other countries, like for example in Paris, and then as a composer. Wolfgang Amadeus should simply exploit the reputation he had earned. His son, on the other hand, made it crystal clear that when he came back to Austria, especially to Salzburg, he wanted to get a much better job offer than his father would even imagine. In reality, Wolfgang Amadeus was tired of being underestimated. In line with standard eighteenth-century practice, he tailored opera and concert arias to the needs of individual singers. Not only did he respond actively to the vocalists' strengths and weaknesses, but he also combined this with his knowledge of timbre and use of the most modern instruments, as this period marks the beginning of a huge technological and timbral revolution, for example the French horn, with its valves and huge textural palette, and the clarinet, which, along with the flute became completely separate from their medieval and earlier counterparts. He is known as to have composed with astonishing ease and speed and under circumstances that were not always favourable. He was, without a doubt, a remarkable improviser, gifted with creative exuberance and possessed an exceptional memory, which served him well when taking the smallest of ideas and turning them into the powerful and by turns delicate music he composed. His creative urge was so strong and fast that sometimes the mere waiting for ink to dry before turning a page could be too long a wait and the muse had left him before he could continue. Also, his life was so hectic that events often interrupted the polishing or even the completion of works, so what we have may not be exactly what he intended.

After all, Wolfgang Amadeus knew that he didn't want to get a simple job offer as a straightforward violinist of earlier years in Austria, but indeed as an enhanced role of quasi-Kapellmeister of the wonderful city of Salzburg – and maybe more in another prestigious city.

Chapter 4

Mozart and his Father as his Mentor

After his return from Paris, Wolfgang Amadeus stayed in Salzburg for about twenty-two months. He had to learn to overcome his private disappointments in the recent years when he was on tour with his mother, including her sudden death, which had caused him great distress, and then the rejection by the singer Aloysia Weber, whom he had not only coached and supported, but also loved very much. That is why he focused – more than ever – on the next steps of his career.

Of course, he'd taken a setback job-wise, and he found time and time again that there was obviously a need to settle for second best sometimes in order to be successful in the music business. Unfortunately, he also had to pay off debts to the total of 1,000 guilders.

For this reason, his father and sister decided to give him a particularly pleasant family atmosphere in Salzburg. When Wolfgang Amadeus was at home, he should simply feel good and forget the daily stress as a court organist.

This striving for harmony can be seen clearly in a famous family painting from this period made by the Austrian painter Johann Nepomuk della Croce, who was a student of Pietro Antonio Lorenzoni, and who painted at the time of Wolfgang Amadeus's departure from Salzburg. It conjured up a close relationship that, strictly speaking, was already a thing of the past at that point in time. The portrait of his dead mother hangs on the wall as a picture within a picture. Incidentally, when the painting was completed in the winter of 1780/81, Wolfgang Amadeus was already in Munich to perform his new opera *Idomeneo* there. The similarity between mother and son in the painting claimed by contemporaries seems to be confirmed here by the forehead, eyes and parts of the nose of both of them.

During his stay in Salzburg, Wolfgang Amadeus did not fall into a resigned lethargy, but on the contrary – the tension between being and wanting increased, the compositional productivity remained unbroken, and interesting perspectives arose. It seemed as if, in his offended pride, Wolfgang Amadeus felt challenged to offer high quality, especially in disputed areas. Despite all the tensions in the relationship with his employer, the Prince-Archbishop Colloredo, he covered a wide spectrum of compositions in church music, ranging from small German hymns to festive masses, and with the so-called *Coronation Mass* (KV 317) and the *Cathedral Mass in G major* (KV 337) created particularly successful works that are still popular today.

The main obligation on the court musicians was the provision of music at the cathedral on feast days. At other times, each group of this orchestra fulfilled independent duties, from small-scale chamber music to elaborate theatrical productions at court and from day-on-day services at the cathedral to fanfares at court. Aside from the cathedral, several other religious institutions in Salzburg also provided opportunities for large scale church music. But these performances of church-music outside of the cathedral were radically curtailed from the beginning of Archbishop Colloredo's reign onwards, as a central agenda of his reforms was to limit the excessive splendour of the church. Staged operas and other dramatic pieces with music were a common part of festivities under Schrattenbach, but they were reduced to a minimum under Colloredo. While the tradition of school dramas, called Final Comedies (*Finalkomödien*), at the end of each school year, in three or five acts, with prologue, choruses and epilogue, were a future within the calendar and were even given on religious feast days or in honour of visiting guests, they were written by a member of the court music and instrumentalists from the court took part in the events. But it seems that these opulent baroque stage dramas must have been a particular nuisance to the Prince-Archbishop Colloredo of Salzburg. And so, immediately after his accession to the archbishop's see, he firstly set out to reform them and then abolished the school plays permanently in 1778.

This certainly played a part in the growing discontent of the whole Mozart family with the musical environment in their hometown. Both Wolfgang Amadeus and his father often complained about it. And from then on, they decided to call the litanies at court with great sarcasm 'beer litanies', since their brevity made it possible for the deacons to quickly return to the nearby inn, in order to continue quietly to drink.

But on the other side, there were even – more than ever before – new opportunities in Salzburg to write music for the theatre in the years 1779 to 1780. Johann Heinrich Böhm, an actor, singer, theatre manager and theatre director from Moravia, made guest appearances with his troupe in the spring and again in the winter of 1779 in Salzburg. Leopold Mozart was enthusiastic about him and gave him high praise for his performance practice. This is how Wolfgang Amadeus came into contact with him and started to work for Böhm's Theatre on various occasions. As Emperor Joseph II, in 1776, was in the process of setting up an opera company at the *Burgtheatre*, that he called German National Theatre, for the purpose of performing German opera. One condition required of the composer to join this company was that he should write a comic opera. For this reason, the two men began to work together on a Singspiel in 1779, for which Andreas Schachtner, who was a good friend of Leopold Mozart, wrote the libretto, which was set in Turkey. Presumably he used impresario Franz Joseph Sebastiani's book *The Seraglio – a German Operetta* as a model.

It was popular at the time for operas to depict the rescue of enslaved Westerners from Muslim courts, as pirates found slaves off Mediterranean ships. In this story, Zaïde tries to save her lover Gomatz. The play is now known as *Zaïde*, although it was then entitled *The Seraglio, or The Unexpected Meeting in Slavery between Father, Daughter and Son*. Two acts with arias and ensembles were composed by Wolfgang Amadeus, a third – unfortunately lost – act remained unperformed. What is amazing about this music project is the experimental aspect of the use of melodrama. The enthusiasm that he developed in Mannheim for the works of the Bohemian conductor and composer Georg Anton Benda is also expressed here. The strategy depends on the genre and the subject. But the contact with the Bavarian impresario, dramatist, actor, singer, and composer Emmanuel Schikaneder, who also made guest appearances in Salzburg with his theatre troupe in 1780, where thirty-four actors performed ballets, operas and spoken plays, is said to be even more momentous.

Schikaneder showed plays by Shakespeare, such as *Hamlet*, but also by German authors such as Lessing, Goethe, Schiller and German Singspiel by Benda, Hiller and Umlauf.

The Mozart family watched the Bavarian impresario and rarely missed one of his shows. And over time they became good friends with Schikaneder; they spent their free time together, went dart shooting and bowling together. As a composer, Wolfgang Amadeus was able to learn a lot from the experienced theatre man. And he also started thinking about what a move from Salzburg to Vienna would mean for him. But it was still a little too early for a change.

Wolfgang Amadeus received a new assignment from Munich – he should write a carnival opera. Great joy and a positive surprise after his unsuccessful performance of *Finta Giardiniera*. The reason for the commission was that when the Mannheim court orchestra moved to Munich in 1778, some of his friends also came along; Christian Cannabich as concert master and director of the orchestra; the tenor Anton Raff; the flautist Wendling and his wife Dorothea; the oboist Friedrich Ramm and many others with them. A sponsorship from his friends, who worked for the theatre manager Count Joseph Anton von Seeau was decisive this time. High-ranking women also supported him, including the Bavarian Electress Maria Anna von Gatterburg, as well as the elector's mistress, Maria Josepha Barbara Johanna Nepomucena Gabriele von Lerchenfeld, Countess of Paumgarten, who was Lady-in-Waiting (*Hofdame*) at the Bavarian court. Count

Joseph Anton von Seeau allowed himself to be persuaded from several sides to hire Wolfgang Amadeus for this music project. He began to do the preliminary work for the piece of music in Salzburg before he set off for Munich on 5 November 1781. But there a whirlwind of work, pleasant social obligations and challenging, exciting contacts with musicians awaited him. He was in high spirits and wrote so to his father in several letters. When he had to leave Munich in January 1779, he even badmouthed Salzburg and there was a certain bitterness in his words. 'I swear to you upon my honour that I cannot tolerate Salzburg and its inhabitants: I am speaking of the Salzburg natives – for me their language – their manner of living is entirely unbearable – you would not believe how I suffered during Madam Robinig's visit here.'[38]

But then, he wrote again from Munich and was enthusiastic to his father:

> Next Monday it will be six weeks that I have been away from Salzburg; you know, my dear father, but I am only in out of consideration for you – for – by God, if it was up to me – I would have wiped my bottom with the last decree of appointment before setting off this time, for by my honour it is not Salzburg – but the Prince – the proud noblesse that become more unbearable to me by the day – so I would look forward with pleasure to his having a letter sent to me saying he no longer needs me.[39]

And after that Wolfgang Amadeus threw himself into the kind of over-the-top planning, that was typical for him:

> I would also be sufficiently secure, in view of the great patronage that I currently have here, against present and future circumstances – with the exception of deaths – for which no -one can give surety – but which can do nothing to harm a person of talent who is single, – yet – for your sake

anything in the world – and it would be still easier for me if one could only get away occasionally for a short time to snatch breath – you know how hard they made it to get away this time. Without a major reason there is no point thinking about it – one could weep when one thinks about it – so away with it – Adieu! – I kiss your hands 1,000 times and embrace my sister with my whole heart and forever yours.

Come to me soon in Munich – and hear my opera – and then tell me – if I am wrong to be sad when I think about salt . . ! – Your most obedient son Wolfgang Amadé Mozart.[40]

These movements seemed a bit confused, but here too, Wolfgang Amadeus was still busy with the completion of his opera and the approaching performance and once again concentrated on the finalization.

In fact, *Idomeneo* is Mozart's great choral opera and is considered as his boldest contribution to the history of *opera seria*. On one hand, the opera is still in the baroque tradition of an *opera seria* with its extended recitatives and great emotions, but on the other hand, Wolfgang Amadeus and his librettist from Trentino, Giambattista Varesco, have already broken with this traditional form in many ways. This opera is a pure *tragédie lyrique* in Italian, influenced by Mozart's trip to Paris and the Mannheim Orchestra in Munich. The fact that action and reflection, which in conventional *opera seria* were divided into simple recitatives and arias, was often brought into a closed, consistently motivating line in *Idomeneo*, which continues with its own lawful consistency (this can be studied in the opening scene), is characteristic of the *tragédie lyrique*, as well as the high proportion of choral and ballet scenes.

One can see only too well that Wolfgang Amadeus's great joy in music-dramatic experimentation, received a great uplift here from the hopeful special situation of a new composition task abroad. Indeed, *Idomeneo* is about a truly tragic rift; the opera's protagonist finds himself in an all but impossible situation as he will have to sacrifice a relative to save his people. The ancient story specifically tells of the Cretan king Idomeneus, who, after returning home from the Trojan War, feels compelled to sacrifice his own son Idamante in order to appease the sea god Neptune and to restore peace in the country. In fact, this opera deals with the relationship between humans and gods. The fact that Wolfgang Amadeus particularly relies on a strong choir and the opera ends with an interesting ballet scene is based on conventions. He oriented himself in this composition on Christoph Willibald Gluck's *Iphigenia in Tauris*.

Nevertheless, Wolfgang Amadeus made demands that were difficult for this ensemble to cope with. This was evident in the arduous rehearsals with the singers. Even an excellent orchestra must have had its difficulties with his scores, otherwise his father's well-intentioned advice would be incomprehensible:

> In the whole town there is general talk of the quality of your opera. The first stir was created by Baron Lerbach; the Court Chancellor's wife said to me that he had told her that the opera had been exceptionally praised in every detail. The second was Herr Becke's letter to Fiala, which he caused to be read everywhere. My wish is that the third act should have the same outworking, and am all the certain in this hope in that the great affects make their appearance here and the subterranean voice will necessarily be very surprising and spine-chilling. Enough, I hope that they will say: *Finis coronat opus.*

> Just try to keep the whole orchestra in a good mood, flatter them and retain their favour with laudations for every one of them, for I know your way of writing, in which the uninterrupted and most astonishing attention is called for in all instruments, and it is indeed no light matter when the

orchestra has to go through at least three hours of nervous strain with such effort and attention. Everyone, even the worst viola player, is most deeply touched when one praises him tête à tête, and as a result becomes more zealous and more attentive, and courtesy of this kind costs you nothing more than a few words.[41]

An extremely intensive professional correspondence developed between Wolfgang Amadeus and his father, which became part of the preparation for the opera. During this time, Leopold Mozart also became a mediator between his son and the librettist of the Opera, Giambattista Varesco. There was evidently also an interest from the court, and even from the elector himself, in the planning, elaboration and rehearsals.

With this opera, Wolfgang Amadeus was concerned for the first time with the correct conveyance of the weights and accents in the overall plan of the drama, but also with the plastic modelling of the dramatic connections. And this time, an opera became a special masterpiece with new means. Because the decisive turning point in *Idomeneo* does not occur this time in a typically logical way or even psychologically, but through the intervention of a special, supernatural power, following a baroque tradition through a deity, who gave the events in the libretto the final turning point. The oracle of a subterranean voice of the god Neptune finally turned the tragedy to a happy ending, the miraculous became questionable in the Age of Enlightenment stage. Wolfgang Amadeus never commented on the dramaturgical disputes, but he knew the discussion and the facts very well. Specifically, the preferred subject of discussion was Shakespeare's *Hamlet*:

The aria is not at all to either my or his liking; regarding the era, I will not say anything at all, for that is always wrong in such an aria. Metastasio has it from time to time, but extremely seldom, and these arias are not his best either; and what necessity is there for it there? – Moreover, it is also not at all as we wished it, namely it should show nothing except peace and contentment, and it shows this here only in the second line; then we have seen and felt enough of the disaster and all that he had to withstand throughout the whole opera, but he can surely speak about his present state. Nor do we need a second part at all – all the better. – In the opera *Achille in Sciro* by Metastasio there is such an aria in this manner, and in which manner Raff wishes to have it.[42]

A letter discussion then ensued between the two men, during which Leopold Mozart repeatedly brought suggestions for compositions and Wolfgang Amadeus did not respond to them, but instead continued on his own musical path. Apparently, he had a precise idea of his opera and wanted to carry it through in exactly the same way. The strategy he finally puts to his father through his letters to him is well thought out and filled with a pinch of humour:

Mon très cher Père!

My head and hands are so full of the third act that it would be no wonder if I became the third act myself. – It alone costs more effort than a whole opera – for there is hardly a scene in it, which is not extremely interesting. – The accompaniment for the subterranean voice consists of nothing more than 5 parts; namely of 3 trombones and 2 hunting horns, which are positioned in the same place as the voice comes from. – At this point the whole orchestra is silent – the main stage rehearsal is quite certainly on the 20th – and the first performance on the 22nd – neither of you need to take anything with you except black clothing – and other clothing – for every day – if you do not go anywhere except to good friends where one does not pay any compliments so that the black clothes can be saved a little – and, if you want, a more attractive one for going to the ball and the concert masquée.[43]

Leopold Mozart had fundamental doubts as to whether the material and the lengthy libretto could have any chance of success 'because of the so-called populars', but Wolfgang Amadeus was confident that his music would inspire the audience, it was 'for all kinds of people, except for long ears'. While Leopold felt inclined towards the characteristic musical theatrical effects, his son insisted more on reducing the means to the essentials. An interesting, modern approach for a composer of less than 25 of this time. But, in fact, Wolfgang Amadeus had everything in his mind and also knew how he wanted to use it.

> Tell me, do you not find that the speech by the subterranean voice is too long? Consider it thoroughly. – Imagine the stage, the voice must be terrifying – it must penetrate – one must believe that it really is so – how can it achieve this if the speech is too long, a length which will increasingly convince the listeners of its emptiness? – If the speech of the ghost in Hamlet were not so long, it would have an even better effect. – The speech here can furthermore be shortened easily, it gains more from that than it loses.[44]

It was Wolfgang Amadeus's wish to touch the audience – above all, through the memorability of the expression, as well as to the rule of God and nature to the ongoing psychologization of the people and their actions. Nevertheless, he struck a good balance between what is characteristic and without going beyond the generic name of the opera. The finale also served this purpose in the form of a ballet, musically a large orchestral suite, which is, of course, more than just a transition to other carnival pleasures.

On 25 January, shortly after Wolfgang Amadeus's 25th birthday, *Idomeneo* premiered. Two reprises took place in February. But the response to it was critical. Unfortunately, his father was right. There were those who saw it as a great success, such as the Elector, as well as those who knew Wolfgang Amadeus's work and some of the nobles, but the general public was not enthusiastic.

The performance achieved only a partial success; instead, the equipment and the stage effects received special mention. Another performance did not take place and the work did not bring Wolfgang Amadeus the job he had hoped for, although the music is among the best that he wrote. For him, *Idomeneo* remained his favourite stage work alongside *Don Giovanni*.

The usual career fictions, which he usually had with a touch of high spirits, had already set in at the beginning of his stay in Munich. This time, however, his fantasies revolved more around the free artistic life that he wanted to live than a permanent position at court, which his father also wanted for him.

Then February came, the carnival arrived in Munich and it was celebrated extensively – also by the Mozart family. Leopold and Maria Anna came all the way from Salzburg and celebrated this time with Wolfgang Amadeus in high spirits. But with the end of the carnival season, they left again.

Wolfgang Amadeus also left, but not for Salzburg. This time he travelled to the federal capital Vienna on 12 March. The truth behind this decision was that with the death of Empress Maria Theresa at the end of November 1780, Emperor Joseph II was at the beginning of a sole reign and the balance of power threatened to change. That is why Archbishop Colloredo had travelled to Vienna and acted as prince in the Habsburg residence city. It was precisely on these occasions that a prince appears with his court and orchestra. And Wolfgang Amadeus was at the centre of this court as the attractive young musical gem. For this reason, the archbishop ordered the composer to join him in Vienna. The dream of an artist's life in Munich was buried, but that in Vienna came closer and closer.

Chapter 5

Mozart and his Escape from Salzburg

Wolfgang Amadeus Mozart fled Munich as well as the provincial confines of Salzburg with its clerical constraints to Vienna, a multicultural metropolis characterized by a liberal spirit of optimism, in the golden decade of the sole government of Joseph II. Vienna was one of the world metropolises at this time. The city had 200,000 inhabitants, was culturally one of the most important cities in the world and Emperor Joseph II, who had ruled since 1763, was a stroke of luck for the city. Fourteen years before, he had made the former court park – the Prater – accessible to the general public, was considered a liberal prince who was very interested in culture and also had music lessons in his youth. By 1790, Joseph II had already introduced one reform after another, thereby sparing his country a bloody revolution like that in France.

Wolfgang Amadeus arrived on 16 March 1781 and stayed in the house of the Teutonic Knights order, where the Prince-Archbishop Colloredo also lived, not knowing that now a great turning point in his life would begin. He had hardly arrived in Vienna when he dashed off to visit the Weber family. They seemed to be his fixed point of contact in the federal capital. There was no denying the fact that there was a bit of curiosity about how his secret flame Aloysia Weber was doing. Fridolin Weber had already died of a stroke in 1779 and Wolfgang Amadeus's great love Aloysia was now married to the widowed court actor Joseph Lange and pregnant by him. Cäcilia Cordula Weber, Fridolin's widow, lived with her three daughters Josepha, Constanze and Sophie on the second floor of the house with the name God's Eye (*Zum Auge Gottes*). Nothing is known about her son Johann Nepomuk Weber.

For Cäcila Cordula Weber, however, Wolfgang Amadeus again became suddenly interesting. The attractive 25-year-old musician, composer and court organist from Salzburg, who was sent away from Munich after two years and had now travelled from Salzburg to Vienna with Prince-Archbishop Colloredo, had blossomed into a rising star in Viennese musical life. He could make a great son-in-law, Cäcilia Cordula Weber thought.

Wolfgang Amadeus immediately realised that Prince-archbishop Colloredo was keeping him on a much shorter leash in Vienna than in Salzburg. He had to report to him every day, eat in the kitchen with the other servants, was only allowed to give concerts with the court orchestra, and if he wanted to give concerts himself (at his own expense), Prince-Archbishop Colloredo usually refused. Only when Wolfgang Amadeus's aristocratic friends and patrons interceded with Colloredo was he was finally allowed to give a concert in the Vienna Artists' Society, which was a tremendous success for him. Now it became clear to him, that he could gain a foothold in Vienna and be successful.

On the first evening, Wolfgang Amadeus was presented as a pianist alongside the Campanian violinist Antonio Brunetti and the Umbrian castrato soprano known for his grace and excellent singing technique, Francesco Ceccarelli, to many guests, specifically 120 people of the highest Viennese noblesse. Right at the beginning of his stay in Vienna, the court organist from Salzburg, who the Viennese knew from his earlier years as the incredibly talented child prodigy, had given concerts for the Russian Ambassador and philanthropist Prince Dmitry Mikhailovich Gallitzin, for the Vice Chancellor Count Philipp of Cobenzl, who was not only Habsburg ambassador in Paris, but also a patron of the arts. He then gave a concert for Maria Caroline Countess Thiennes de Rumbeke, who immediately became his first piano pupil in Vienna and also for the German Hofrat Carl Adolph von Braun and for the prince Colloredo, as well as some concerts at the Schönborn Palace.

The first encounter with Antonio Salieri must have taken place there. The scene in the film *Amadeus* in which Salieri meets Mozart describes this very vividly. Salieri has prepared a *March of Welcome* for Wolfgang Amadeus and presents it to the emperor, who sits immediately down and plays it on the piano – the whole piece of music not yet perfect and in a very unprofessional way. As Wolfgang Amadeus is guided through the rooms of the Imperial palace, he can hear the music. As soon as he arrives, the emperor questions him about his latest music project, which was *The Abduction of the Seraglio*. Then, the emperor asks him to play the *March*. Wolfgang Amadeus smiles, sits down at the piano and begins to play and then to embellish the piece of music in a certain way, that is so typical of him. This childish approach to the music leaves Salieri gobsmacked.

Also, in the first week Wolfgang Amadeus met one of the most important women in Viennese musical and social life, who would remain his patron until the end of his life, Countess Maria Wilhelmine von Thun und Hohenstein. This woman was famous for her intellect, her warmth and her personal magic, but also for her open house in which she received many talented people. She played host to a musically and intellectually outstanding salon in the metropole Vienna and she was highly appreciated for her patronage of music.

Prince-Archbishop Colloredo had received Wolfgang Amadeus on the day of his arrival in Vienna extremely coldly, because his last 'holiday trip' of six weeks had unfortunately turned into four months and this was not acceptable for the Prince-Archbishop. That is why there was a palpable tension between the two men from the outset. What happened in detail can only be analysed on the basis of the correspondence between Wolfgang Amadeus with his father, who he called – for the first time ever – 'my dear friend' instead of 'my dear father' in his first letter from Vienna:

Mon très cher ami,

Yesterday, the 16th, I arrived here, praise and thanks be to God, utterly alone in a postchaise; – I almost forgot the time:

– 9 o'clock in the morning; – I drove as far as Lower Haag with the post-coach – but this burnt my arse and what it hangs from so badly that I could not possibly hold it out – so I wanted to continue my journey with the ordinaire.[45]

At the end of this letter he even dares to criticize the Prince-Archbishop Colloredo. 'In the evening we have no meal, instead everyone is given 3 ducats – with that one can leap a long way. – The esteemed Archbishop is so kind as to glory in his retinue – robs them of their earning opportunities – and does not pay them for it.'

Wolfgang Amadeus was certainly very well looked after with his accommodation, the food and drinks which were served, his wonderful colleagues, the violinist Antonio Brunetti and the soloist Francesco Ceccarelli, who were allowed to live in the same building, and the company he had. While Leopold was in favour of him earning additional money, the Prince-Archbishop Colloredo only allowed it in the context of court service, but not for the own benefit. For Wolfgang Amadeus this was absolutely not acceptable in the long term. Of course, he wanted to earn more money and who would blame him for that? Therefore, he started to repeatedly criticize the archbishop in his letters to his father. The situation was not bearable for him. When once Prince-Archbishop Colloredo made an exception and Wolfgang Amadeus was allowed to perform as a pianist and play his own symphony at a charity event concert in the Kärntnertor-Theatre, Wolfgang Amadeus criticized him again in a letter to his father:

I have already written to you recently saying that the Archbishop is a great hindrance to me here, for he has caused me losses of at least 100 ducats which I could quite certainly have made from a concert in the theatre – for the ladies had already spontaneously offered to distribute tickets. – I can certainly say that I was extremely satisfied with the Viennese public yesterday. – I played in the widows' concert in the

Kärntnertor-Theatre. – I had to start from the beginning again because there was no end to the applause. – What do you think I might earn if I give a concert for myself now that the public knows me? – only our arch-boor does not allow it – does not want his people to make a profit, but a loss – but he cannot achieve this goal with me, for if I have 2 pupils here, I am in a better position than in Salzburg – I do not need his board and lodging…[46]

When Wolfgang Amadeus uses the word 'our arch-boor' for the Prince-Archbishop Colloredo in this excerpt of a letter to his father, one gets the impression that he is venturing quite far forward in his criticism for the first time in this letter. At the same time, the withdrawing from his family begins. In Vienna, Wolfgang Amadeus made the firm decision to stay almost as soon as he arrived. He felt so good in this city and was accepted and acclaimed – not only by the Austrian nobility, but also by the numerous guests of the hosts of his concerts. This certainly was another life, a life that he had always wished to live. What happened in Vienna, was an inspiration and a challenge at the same time for Wolfgang Amadeus. And that is why he pursued in his letters to his father his wish to be allowed to stay there, in that wonderful city, with all the intellectuals and art lovers.

Nevertheless, it didn't work. His father refused. As a result, Wolfgang Amadeus started to neglect his duties in the Archbishop's Viennese residence, became unpunctual and cheeky to boot. He was reprimanded, but fortunately not released from his post. The talented 25-year-old was allowed to continue making music, because he had a lot of fans in the city. In further letters, Wolfgang Amadeus described to his father how he had many admirers in Vienna, in the most well-known houses, and that he could not understand that pressure was being exerted on him and that he was not allowed to stay in Vienna, where he could continue to pursue his art and could compose much more.

All that would convince his father, however, was a permanent job. Unfortunately, Wolfgang Amadeus couldn't come up with that in Vienna. The question was, did he want to expose himself to the shame of living as a musician without a job in this thriving cultural metropolis?

Viennese society was more spoiled and demanding in the field of music than any other society in the world, because most of the greatest musicians of that time – like Joseph Haydn, Gluck, Salieri, Bonno or Righini – also gave their concerts or even worked there permanently. Constantly travelling composers and virtuosos were also always present. Everything was of high rank; it started with theatre, continued with opera and ended with concerts. When Wolfgang Amadeus appeared before the nobility in Vienna, he was usually greeted by a personal valet, together with his colleagues – the violinist Antonio Brunetti and the soloist Francesco Ceccarelli – and was led into the company at the right time by another servant. But Wolfgang Amadeus had his own way of proceeding inside the building; he walked straight ahead, leaving the other two artists behind him. Then, he quickly walked through the different corridors, until he came to the music room he already knew. After that, he walked straight up to the host and appeared like a sovereign. As a musician, confidently confronting a nobleman with the right respect came from a deep conviction.

When Wolfgang Amadeus described such scenes from his life in his letters to Leopold, he also wanted to show the true face of Prince-Archbishop Colloredo and thus, his relationship with him. The archbishop was described as a person who constantly used the work of an artist, singer or musician – like Brunetti, Ceccarelli and Wolfgang Amadeus – for his own benefit. He used artists only as a decoration in his everyday life. The artist was not recognized or even respected by Colloredo and therefore he kept hindering him. However, Wolfgang Amadeus was highly respected and valued in the highest circles of Viennese nobility. The letters he wrote to his father on this subject contained page-long descriptions of various examples of incidents involving Prince-Archbishop Colloredo. In one of these letters, however, Wolfgang requested that his father – instead of Prince-Archbishop Colloredo – would allow him to travel to Vienna every year at carnival time, because 'if he doesn't want to allow it, I'll go anyway, it's my misfortune not, certainly not', he wrote.

But Leopold Mozart, on his side, continued to try to keep his son in a good mood and gently dissuaded him from leaving the Salzburg service. However, Wolfgang Amadeus would disguise the true course of events a little in his letters.

The Prince-Archbishop Colloredo had fixed the return trip to Salzburg for the artists for 8 April 1781. For those of the artists who still wanted to stay longer in Vienna, he stipulated that from then on they had to pay for themselves, although they were allowed to stay in their accommodation – they didn't have to pay anything for that. From then on, they were allowed to do whatever they wanted.

The potential for an argument between Prince-Archbishop Colloredo and Wolfgang Amadeus had increased in recent weeks. Although the violinist Brunetti had already left Vienna, Prince-Archbishop Colloredo and Wolfgang Amadeus were both still there. And one thing was clear now – Wolfgang Amadeus didn't want to leave Vienna at all.

On 27 April, the Prince-Archbishop organized a musical academy for his father. Wolfgang Amadeus enjoyed this evening particularly. After his concert, his enthusiastic Viennese fans – in this case, women from Vienna's high society – asked him to continue to play an encore on the piano. Wolfgang Amadeus sat down again and played variations on a theme according to a specification given to him by the Archbishop. After the encore, Prince-Archbishop Colloredo departed.

But only a few days later, on 1 May, the order came for Wolfgang Amadeus's return to Salzburg with Prince-Archbishop Colloredo's entourage and he was told that he had to move out of his room immediately. Although the caravan of Salzburg court carriages travelled in several stages, Wolfgang Amadeus was clever and had already been staying with the Weber family since the end of April. He had also missed several official departure dates and he resisted and used a lot of excuses as to why he couldn't go on this or on that day. A few days later, he was summoned to the Prince-Archbishop. There, a heated argument suddenly broke out between Prince-Archbishop Colloredo and Wolfgang Amadeus. After this, Wolfgang Amadeus wrote immediately to his father that he was extremely angry. The Prince-Archbishop had scolded him and he pretended that Wolfgang Amadeus was slovenly, depraved, childish, crazy and arrogant – 'the most slovenly man he knew, a scoundrel, a rascal'. However, this meant, that Wolfgang Amadeus took this as an opportunity, because he felt offended and resigned right away from his work in Salzburg.

Before the Mannheim-Paris trip, Leopold Mozart was always a mentor who agreed with his protégé. He suffered with him, when something didn't work well, and he got upset with him about the impertinent world out there, which didn't approve of everything for the brilliant child prodigy Wolfgang Amadeus. But now, suddenly, Leopold couldn't do that anymore. He had the feeling that somebody had intervened in the background and that the result of this intervention was that his son wanted to stay in Vienna. That is why quite unexpectedly, an intense and bitter fight started between Leopold Mozart and Cäcilia Cordula Weber over the influence she exerted on his son. Leopold Mozart was beside himself. But step by step, Cäcilia Cordula Weber conquered the territory. Leopold Mozart emerged from this quarrel more and more exhausted; one can only imagine how many anger-filled letters to Vienna and sleepless nights this fight for his beloved son cost him in the state of his nerves.

Leopold Mozart also contacted Count Georg Anton Felix von Arco, with whom he was always on good terms and who was supposed to get in touch with the Weber family and to intervene for him and for Wolfgang Amadeus. He was sceptical, but on the other hand wanted to help the Mozart family. However, he did not succeed in convincing Wolfgang Amadeus to return back home to Salzburg. Even more strangely, Wolfgang Amadeus said later in a letter that von Arco had called him a 'stumblebum' and forcibly prevented him from running to the Prince-Archbishop Colloredo to deliver his resignation letter. Wolfgang Amadeus even alleged that he got kicked by the count and that he had to tear himself away. In any case, he begged his father not to believe anything other people would tell him about the incident. But interestingly, Prince-Archbishop Colloredo refused to accept Wolfgang Amadeus's resignation.

Mon trés cher Pére!

I am still completely galled! – and you, as my own dearest, best of all fathers, are surely with me in this. – My patience was tested for such a long time – but finally it did fail after all. I am no longer so unfortunate as to be in the service of Salzburg – today was the day of good fortune for me; just listen: – Twice already the – I do not know at all what I should call him – uttered to my face the greatest insults and impertinences, which, in order to spare you, I have chosen not to write down, and only – because I always had you, my best of all fathers, before my eyes did I refrain from taking vengeance on the spot. – He called me a boy, a wretched lout – told me I should be on my way – and I – suffered everything – felt that not only my honour, but also yours, was impugned in the process – but – you wanted it this way – I remained silent.[47]

Leopold Mozart was still trying to use persuasion and authority. He wanted to use all means to dissuade his son from leaving Salzburg for Vienna. He also wanted to get him out of the Weber family's spell. He took this opportunity to remind his son of their machinations in Mannheim and the sad end in Munich. But all this seemed to be in vain. Wolfgang Amadeus seemed to be bewitched. The fascination for the Weber family was back and more than ever. Leopold warned him in his letters tirelessly, but after a while he admitted that he had lost his son to the Weber family.

In Holy Trinity Church, Leopold and Nannerl Mozart were on their knees again and asking for the support of the Almighty. As always, Nannerl was condemned to passivity, although this time it was not just about the dark mood at home and her care, but now it was about her favourite emotion; happiness. She was already 30 years old and Franz Armand d'Ippold, an Imperial and royal captain and director of a college in Salzburg, who had been courting her for years, wanted to finally be allowed to marry her. Leopold Mozart agreed at first, but Nannerl had no dowry, since the debts from her brother's Mannheim-Paris trip still had to be repaid and her brother, who was living in Vienna, didn't want to help her financially. Despite the fact that he repeatedly regrets it in his letters to her, there is nothing to be done about it. For this reason, Leopold Mozart withdrew his consent.

Nannerl and Leopold could clearly see why Cäcilia Weber would not want to let her rescuer go, as long as he earned enough money and brought some of the splendour of the aristocratic world into her apartment. With the loss of the position in Salzburg, a new spectacle began, which in the father's eyes threatened to lead to the next catastrophe in his son's life. 'If one writes a play, one must exaggerate somewhat, if one wishes to receive applause and not remain so precisely faithful to the truth of the matter – and you must also give these gentlemen some credit for their readiness to serve.'[48]

Wolfgang Amadeus was not saying that about himself, but rather he is referring to Count Georg Anton Felix of Arco, who, he assumed, told Leopold Mozart details about the events in Vienna. Those were weeks of inner turmoil for Leopold Mozart. He also had received complaints about his son from the Prince-Archbishop, which must not have been very pleasant for him.

Wolfgang Amadeus had violated the feudal patriarchal thinking of his time and that was not welcome. Interestingly, Count Georg Anton

Felix of Arco's made a remark to the effect that Leopold Mozart's son would not quit his job without his father's consent. The fact that Wolfgang Amadeus wrote to his father about it is one of his clever tactics and indicates that he probably wanted to show his father that he was willing to talk and that he had trust. This threatened to lead to a profound estrangement between father and son. In the course of the next letters between father and son, we learn that Mozart intended to marry, but his father wanted to prevent this and, seeing his influence on his son waning, would not allow it. At that time, getting married without parental consent was considered the ultimate taboo. To emancipate oneself from one's father was even more difficult than to emancipate oneself from a prince.

The Webers evidently had a genuine sense of family, which led Leopold Mozart to criticism and to use the derogatory term 'Weberian'. When Aloysia Weber began her engagement in Munich in 1778, she had also negotiated a position for her father at the theatre.

As a singer, Aloysia earned three times what Wolfgang Amadeus earned in Salzburg. A year later she had an engagement as the best-paid singer at the National Theatre in Vienna, again under the same conditions for her family. When Mozart came to Vienna, Aloysia had already been married to the painter Joseph Lange for a while. Her late father had left his family with many debts. Therefore, the situation of the family was less favourable than Aloysia's considerable fee of 1,700 guilders. Above all, her mother was determined and energetic. In her apartment on St. Peter's Square, she tried to earn money by renting out individual guest rooms. Her two daughters Constanze and Sophie were still unmarried. Therefore, Wolfgang Amadeus was a welcome and well-trusted lodger for Cecilia. Wolfgang Amadeus already knew many prominent Viennese from the nobility, so it would have been easy for him to get a beautiful apartment for himself. But probably, after all the excitement with Prince-Archbishop Colloredo, he wanted – above all – to find someone to talk to on a daily basis, as well as a family connection, in the form that he had previously only experienced with his own family in Salzburg.

Leopold Mozart feared that his son might get caught up in a whirlwind of completely unrealistic plans again, with the help of the Weber family. He expected to get some pressure from Salzburg because of this. But instead, during this time Wolfgang Amadeus was married off to 19-year-old Constanze Weber by her family. Even when he left the Weber family after four months at his father's incessant urging and no longer lived on Petersplatz, around the Church of St. Peter, but rather on the Graben, which is today a promenade and shopping street in the city centre – he in reality didn't move at all, as it was a corner house with two different addresses. Leopold was maliciously deceived – and Wolfgang Amadeus was already pairing up with Aloysia Weber's older sister. And – to tell the truth – he was more intimately and firmly pairing up with this woman than he ever had been before. The rumour that he was going to get married was put out by Constanze's mother with great single-mindedness. And this rumour reached eventually Salzburg in July – much to the chagrin of Leopold Mozart, for whom, as a father, the alarm bells started now to ring and Wolfgang Amadeus meet them with displeasure and condescension. Although there was apparently a new woman in his life, Aloysia was still not indifferent to him. He even composed three concert arias for soprano for her.

The truth was that Wolfgang Amadeus felt very comfortable with the three Weber women and thought that cheerfulness and teasing had never yet forced a man into marriage. He did that often enough in Salzburg under the watchful eye of his father, but also in Mannheim. Back then, in Germany, he squabbled far more intensely with Aloysia Weber and courted her stormily, so that everybody in Mannheim spoke about their love and passion. At the time, Cäcilia Cordula Weber was not worried about her daughter and her reputation. Also, the violent affair with his cousin, Bäsle, which got as far as Salzburg, caused no worries about a marriage obligation between the two of them. And

The only surviving apartment of the composer Wolfgang Amadeus Mozart in Vienna at Schulerstraße 8/Domgasse No. 5 is also the most elegant, largest and most expensive. It is the only one in Vienna that has been preserved. Important works such as *Le Nozze di Figaro*, as well as the *F major, D minor, C major, E flat major, A major* and *C minor* piano concertos were all created here. © *Judith Grohmann*

The staircase inside the house, which dates from the fifteenth century. Changes made around 1716 led to the house that Wolfgang Amadeus would recognize, when he moved in with his wife Constanze in 1784. The rent (including stable rent) was 480 guilders. © *Judith Grohmann*

When entering the third floor, dedicated to the topic of Vienna in the Era of Mozart, visitors are welcomed by a paper cutting of the composer and various lighting displays. © *Judith Grohmann*

Wolfgang Amadeus was an avid fan of the Freemasons and was himself a member of various Viennese fraternities. These items symbolize his connection with the ideas of the organization.
© *Judith Grohmann*

Items belonging to Wolfgang Amadeus including a musical card game, a painting of a bridge in an adjoining district, a punch ladle, the inheritance treatise after his death and books written by contemporary authors, Johann Pezzl and Joseph von Sonnenfels, who were also brother Freesmasons of the composer. © *Judith Grohmann*

A frock coat in the style of the one Wolfgang Amadeus received from Baroness Martha Elisabeth von Waldstätten, who was his music student and sponsor. In a letter to her he said, 'Because of the beautiful red frock [coat], which tickles my heart so cruelly, I asked someone to tell me where to get it and how much it costs - because I have to have a frock [coat] like that so that it's worth the trouble. Putting buttons on it, which I have been thinking about for a long time: These are mother-of-pearl, with some white stones around on the side and a beautiful yellow stone in the middle.' Also shown here is an eighteenth-century Harlekin-costume.
© *Judith Grohmann*

Various paper cuttings of the cast for *Le Nozze de Figaro.* © *Judith Grohmann*

Interactive Mozart: videos showing key scenes from the opera *Le Nozze di Figaro* from the Salzburg Festival in 2006. © *Judith Grohmann*

Wolfgang Amadeus Mozart´s father, Leopold, switched from studying the Law to a more 'profane life' of music. In 1743 he played fourth violin with the Salzburg Court Orchestra and published a textbook: *A Treatise on the Fundamental Principles of Violin Playing.* © *Judith Grohmann*

Furniture and other objects from Wolfgang Amadeus' time act as clues to the probable functions of a room. An example of this here is a table for board games such as chess or trick track. © *Judith Grohmann*

A scene from Wolfgang Amadeus' last opera, *The Magic Flute*. The Queen of the Night's phenomenal aria, 'Hell's Vengeance Boils in My Heart', is renowned as an extremely demanding piece to perform, because the vocal range covers two octaves, from F4 to F6, and requires a very high tessitura, A4 to C6. © *Judith Grohmann*

Several pictures of the residents of the Viennese city centre apartment: Wolfgang Amadeus and his wife Constanze; their 9-day-old son Carl Thomas; and two years later a second son by the name of Johann Thomas Leopold. There were also several servants and numerous guests, as well as pets. © *Judith Grohmann*

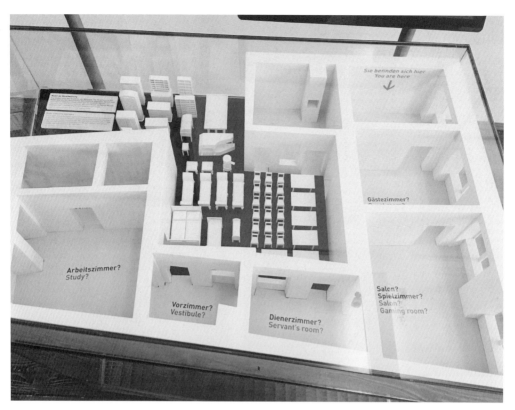

Wolfgang Amadeus lived in this apartment from the end of September 1784 to the end of April 1787. This 3D floor plan shows the various rooms and their functions. Remember that during his lifetime, no indoor toilets meant that chamber pots were used for human waste. The contents were often poured out of the window onto the street, or emptied into cesspools, which were emptied once or twice a year. © *Judith Grohmann*

An original chair from Wolfgang Amadeus' flat.
© *Judith Grohmann*

Wolfgang Amadeus was passionate about playing games, not just with words and musical notes, but also by playing cards and billiards. His friend, the singer Michael O'Kelly, wrote, 'He was an avid carom player and had a pool table in his house'. © *Judith Grohmann*

The view from the Mozart House down Blutgasse. The houses in this small street all date from the eighteenth century. © *Judith Grohmann*

This magnificent golden flute clock (c.1796) is an absolute highlight of Wolfgang Amadeus' apartment and plays a variation of the *Andante for a roll in a small organ* (KV 616). The piece was probably composed just for this clock. © *Judith Grohmann*

A cradle used by Constanze and Wolfgang Amadeus' children. © *Judith Grohmann*

The famous Camesina Room. Albert Camesina, a plasterer, lived in the apartment before Mozart and his family and had decorated this particular room with stucco. It later became Wolfgang Amadeus and Constanze´s bedroom. © *Judith Grohmann*

Artists were given dramatic license to paint Wolfgang Amadeus as they wished, giving rise to many different interpretations. © *Judith Grohmann*

Countess Maria Wilhelmine Thun-Hohenstein's salon was of particular importance to Wolfgang Amadeus during his years in Vienna. The two had a very close relationship and the Countess was also his critical interlocutor during the composing of *The Abduction from the Seraglio*. He gave music lessons to her three daughters, nicknamed affectionately by the Viennese as the 'beautiful graces'. © *Judith Grohmann*

A glance through the rooms of the Mozart House shows that they were large and had double doors. © *Judith Grohmann*

Wolfgang Amadeus Mozart came into the world on 27 January 1756 in the yellow Hagenauer Haus at Getreidegasse No. 9, in the city of Salzburg. © *Heather Williams*

The Mozart statue, sculpted by Ludwig Schwanthaler, can be found in the centre of Salzburg's *Mozartplatz*. It was ceremoniously unveiled in the presence of his sons on 4 September 1842. The Bavarian king, Ludwig I, was an important sponsor and donated the marble base. © *Heather Williams*

The Mozart family lived at the Dance Master's House on the Makartplatz in Salzburg from 1773 to 1787. The spacious eight-room apartment on the first floor is now home to one of the many Mozart museums in Austria. © *Heather Williams*

The Mozart statue in Vienna has been in the Burggarten in the inner city's 1st district since 1953. The 7.5-metre high structure was created by architect Karl König and sculptor Viktor Tilgner and originally unveiled on 21 April 1896 on Albrechtsplatz (now Albertinaplatz). The sculpture is made of Lasa marble (from Vinschgau, South Tyrol), while the steps of the base are made of dark diorite. © *Judith Grohmann*

St Marx Cemetery is situated in Vienna's 3rd district. It was laid out in the eighteenth century before closing in 1874. It is now a listed area, having preserved the appearance of the Biedermeier age and conveys a rather romantic mood. © *Judith Grohmann*

A sign directs visitors to the composer's grave, with people from all over the world coming to pay homage.
© *Judith Grohmann*

Wolfgang Amadeus Mozart was buried in 1791 in an unmarked grave in the Masonic style of the era. The tombstone dates from a later period. © *Judith Grohmann*

The entrance to Wolfgang Amadeus Mozart's funerary monument at the Vienna Central Cemetery. © *Judith Grohmann*

The statue commemorating Wolfgang Amadeus at the Vienna Central Cemetery is one of fifty-five such monuments honouring well-known musicians. © *Judith Grohmann*

Salzburg confectioner Paul Fürst created the world-famous Salzburger Mozartkugel in 1890. Consisting of a marzipan and pistachio core, wrapped in nougat and dipped in dark chocolate, it quickly became the most popular sweet for all Austrians, not to mention the friends of Wolfgang Amadeus Mozart. © *Judith Grohmann*

Bavarians also created their own version of the Mozartkugel. These Reber Mozart chocolates are an ingenious composition of the finest pistachio marzipan, with fresh almonds and hazelnut nougat, doubly coated with alpine milk and fine dark chocolate.
© *Heather Williams*

now he was supposed to be wary of Constanze Weber, because he was joking around with her and teasing her – and all this in the Weber family's apartment?

From then on, Wolfgang Amadeus no longer tried to be as assertive towards his father as he had been weeks before in the conflict with the Prince-Archbishop Colloredo, but he rather tried to calm down and trivialize the situation. Stories about his musical successes, his fame in society and his career opportunities should have had this calming effect, as well as the reassurance that marriage was not even on the horizon at the moment – and if he married, then he actually wanted to be happy with an extremely rich woman. But what he allowed himself to pretend here, was a very special comedy that he staged. In order to avoid the gossip of the Viennese, Wolfgang Amadeus left St. Peter's Square and switched to a completely different accommodation.

Cäcilia Cordula Weber was not indifferent to this behaviour of Wolfgang Amadeus. She wanted to realize her plan and bring her daughter together with this dazzling composer and musician, whatever the cost. For this reason, she sent Johann von Thorwart, Constanze's guardian, to see him. Thorwart was the commercial director of the National Theatre and in a way rather uncomfortable for him. This man managed to get Wolfgang Amadeus to agree to marry Constanze Weber within three years, otherwise he would have to pay her an annuity of 300 guilders a year from then on. In mid-December, after six months of playing hide and seek in his letters to his father, Wolfgang Amadeus unfortunately told Leopold Mozart about it at length. This was so disastrous and shocking for the family in Salzburg, that Leopold Mozart became extremely furious. As a result, he neither wished his son a Merry Christmas nor a Happy New Year.

Not only was Leopold angry, but also Maria Anna also resented this step. They hated the Weber family so much and they knew that the Webers were playing a dirty game with their beloved son and brother. But the reality was that they didn't want to allow that, but couldn't prevent it either.

Many letters went back-and-forth between father and son, often with Wolfgang Amadeus praising the talents of his love and Leopold standing his ground and refusing to let his mind be changed. Indeed, Wolfgang Amadeus found Constanze very attractive, although he played down this point to his father in one of his letters one year before the wedding:

But who, then, is the object of my love? – Do not let yourself be startled here either, I beg you; surely not one of the Webers? Yes, a Weber – but not Josepha – not Sophie – but Costanza; the one in the middle. In no family have I encountered such unevenness of disposition as in this. – the eldest is a lazy, coarse, false person with hidden cunning. The Lange woman is a false person of bad thoughts, and a coquette. – the youngest – is still too young to be anything. – is nothing but a good but too lightheaded creature! May God protect her from seduction. – But the one in the middle, namely my good, dear Constanze, is – the Martyr among them, and for just this reason perhaps the best-hearted, most adept and, in a word, the best of them. takes on all the tasks in the house – and still never does it properly. Oh, my own, best of fathers, I could fill up whole sheets if I were to describe all the scenes which took place with the two of us in this house. If you request it, however, I will do that in my next letter. Before I let you escape from all my chatter, I certainly must make you more closely acquainted with the character of my dearest Constanze. She is not ugly, but also nothing less than beautiful. Her entire beauty consists of two small, black eyes and a beautifully shaped body. She has no wit, but a healthy understanding of people so as to be able to fulfil her duties as a wife and mother. She is not inclined to extravagance, that is fundamentally false. – On the contrary, she is accustomed to dressing simply. – For the little that the mother could do for her children she did for the two others but never for her. – It is true that she likes to be dressed tidily and cleanly, but not propre. And she can make most of what a woman needs herself. And also she dresses her own hair every day – She understands how to run a household, has the best heart in the world – I love her, and she loves me with her whole heart. – Tell me whether I could wish for a better wife?[49]

Wolfgang Amadeus then decided to describe Cäcilia Cordula Weber and Thorwart in his letters as 'the bad guys' and Constanze, as a young woman who had to be saved by him. That is why he writes that he wants to quickly free his Constanze from the hands of her family, because 'the poor girl is being tortured to death along with mine', he writes to his father, who has meanwhile travelled to Munich, to talk about his son's unfortunate involvement in Weber's plans with his friends from Mannheim, to get some advice and to find a way out of this dilemma. It appears that Leopold Mozart was given some terrible details about the Weber family and probably also about their daughter Constanze – because the letters in reply from his son from this period (30 January to 23 March 1782) have disappeared.

One has to imagine, that this described martyrdom, that now changed into how a suddenly malicious, nagging, always drunk mother had caused her daughter, encouraged Leopold Mozart to be against this connection even more.

Cäcilia Cordula Weber saw her power over the possible future son-in-law dwindling and began to intensify her strategy, so that Constanze could be married off quickly. It was interesting to note that on 30 August 1782, a new law came in Austria into effect that Joseph II had enacted, about the 'engagement godparents', in which marriage vows were 'completely annulled'.

Unfortunately, Cäcilia Cordula Weber had to recognize one thing, because at the beginning, it looked to her as if little Mozart was putty in her hands. He let her incite him against all sorts of people and take his money out of his pockets. He let himself be blackmailed and even got engaged to one of her daughters. But when it came to marriage, he would do nothing without his father's blessing. When she found out about this she was horrified and showed her future son-in-law how offended she was. That situation was unbearable in the long run. Wolfgang Amadeus was tormented by the constant accusations from both sides – his own family, as well as Constanze's. In addition, his future mother-in-law used all sorts of tricks to get him to keep his vow to marry her daughter within three years. She even threatened him with a police vice squad.

In the course of the summer of 1782, the scenes in the Weber household escalated into a scandal. When neither tears, harassment nor illness led to the goal, Cäcilia Cordula Weber went to extremes. Her young daughter Constanze was lovingly driven into Wolfgang Amadeus's bed.

When he was no longer allowed to enter the Weber's apartment, Constanze fled straight to his new apartment from her mother's outburst of anger. And the case was closed. One thing was sure; Wolfgang Amadeus and his future bride needed spiritual and material help at this time. And this came from a libertine woman from Viennese society, Baroness Martha Elisabeth von Waldstätten. The baroness was a rich lady who took piano lessons from Wolfgang Amadeus. She generously supported him in many matters. He also thanked her for the beautiful red frock coat with mother-of-pearl buttons and gold embroidery, which – on her advice – became Wolfgang Amadeus's trademark in the future for his various concerts.

The baroness was enthusiastic about Wolfgang Amadeus as an artist and, in her patrician, friendly manner, resolved that everything had to turn out well for both families. Since Constanze also had problems with her mother because of the marriage plans, the baroness took the young woman into her house, introduced her to society and gave her a certain social polish. In addition, Mozart was able to meet Constanze discreetly in her apartment.

The baroness corresponded amicably with Leopold Mozart, who was understandably upset about the marriage, but she was the only one who managed to appease him. After the marriage consensus – this signed act of will, where a man and a woman accept each other in an irrevocable bond – had arrived in Salzburg, Wolfgang Amadeus was finally able to marry his Constanze on 4 August 1782 in St. Stephen's Cathedral. The witnesses were Franz Anton von Gilowsky, a young body valet and court surgeon, who was also the publisher of the *High Prince Salzburg church and court calendar*, who made his living playing loose pranks in Vienna – Wolfgang Amadeus used to call him the windmaker – and the district administrator Carl Cetto von Kronstorff, presumably an acquaintance of the guardian. Wolfgang Amadeus described the solemnities in his letter to his father like this:

> At the wedding there was not a person present except her mother and her youngest sister; Herr von Thorwart as guardian and aide to both of them; Herr von Zetto: chief regional administrator accompanying the bride and Gilowsky at my side. As we were joined together, both my wife and I began to weep; everyone, even the priest, was moved by that, – and they all wept, since they were witnesses of how moved our hearts were.[50]

After the ceremony, Baroness Martha Elisabeth von Waldstätten had arranged the wedding dinner for Constanze and Wolfgang Amadeus at her apartment.

Wolfgang Amadeus's great love Aloysia and her husband Joseph Lange were not present at the wedding. And Wolfgang Amadeus had forced his father's blessing, which now followed immediately, with the news that the night had passed in his apartment, but due to the hasty wedding, it arrived one day too late.

One thing was sure; Leopold and Nannerl would always love their Wolfgang Amadeus, admire him and let no harm come to him. They would continue to do everything they could for him in the future, encouraging and applauding him, sending him many parcels, looking for the musical scores he needed and those Salzburg delicacies he longed for so much. Leopold Mozart continued to maintain important contacts for Wolfgang Amadeus; with publishers, clients and theatre directors.

But one thing Leopold made clear to him after his lightning marriage to Constanze Weber; he would no longer pay for his financial escapades and debts in the future. That was what the 'Weberians' should do in the future.

The young couple decided to move into a new apartment in Vienna. They were finally established in the federal capital. And believe it or not, but Constanze was – in many ways – indeed the perfect partner for Wolfgang Amadeus. She was probably more than a match for his sometimes flighty, left-field humour; she was down to earth and she could run a house well. She was also well-educated and, in addition to being musically gifted, she spoke excellent French and Italian, as well as her native German. In many ways, she therefore was the ideal wife for a composer, something which Wolfgang Amadeus heartily believed.

Chapter 6

Mozart Settling Down in Vienna

The striking change that took place in Wolfgang Amadeus's new life in the years 1781 to 1782 consisted mainly in the fact that he finally settled down in one place that he loved so much, which was the prestigious city of Vienna. For more than 200 years, what Wolfgang Amadeus Mozart really meant for the music world has been connected with that part of his oeuvre that was created in Vienna and which was composed from the year 1781 to the year 1791. The dominance of the masterpieces from the Vienna period has remained. His rise to stardom and to become the real King of Pop all started – in reality – here. Additionally, he started a family and throughout his life never made any attempt to settle anywhere else. He remained loyal to the city of Vienna, so to speak, even though there were several chances to change the city, and thus also his workplace. Like his father, he may have maintained an inner distance from Salzburg. But now, for the first time in his life, the talented composer and musician Wolfgang Amadeus Mozart simply got involved with a place and its people. In a certain way, Vienna must have been a highlight for him.

During his first year in Vienna, full of personal tensions and quarrels with his new family, the Webers, Wolfgang Amadeus's ascent to fame, honour and money took place. As almost everywhere he had landed before – be it Paris, Munich or London – the most extraordinary opportunities suddenly opened up for him in the glamourous city of Vienna. Although, in terms of compositions, the first year in Vienna was poor by his standards – apart from the first two acts of the opera *The Abduction from the Seraglio* – he wrote nothing more, except a few sonatas, arias and one serenade.

Critics have pointed to parallels between Wolfgang Amadeus's life in the years 1781-1782 and characters and situations in *The Abduction from the Seraglio*; his descriptions of Colloredo and Osmin (one of the main characters in this opera, who was Bassa Selim's servant and an overseer of Bassa's Country House [Bass/Buffo-Bass]), the rescuing of another main character in the opera with the name of Konstanze, who was the mistress of the nobleman Belmonte, from the harem and his future wife Constanze from her dominating mother, as well as Konstanze's defiance in tortures of all kinds as she says and Mozart's defiance towards his father and the authorities from Salzburg. These connections between his future wife and the main character in *The Abduction from the Seraglio*, which were in fact suggestive parallels, probably caused Wolfgang Amadeus to smile wryly to himself.

On the other hand, he caused a sensation, as the young and charming piano virtuoso that he was, so that he decided to take advantage of every opportunity to which he was called, because of the dazzling income he got at the end from these jobs. Already in the first five months he performed in about twenty different aristocratic palaces, embassies and bourgeois salons of the wealthy Viennese. Word of Wolfgang Amadeus's 'delicacy in the Fortepiano beating' got around quickly in the city and he was therefore enthusiastically celebrated almost everywhere.

Emperor Joseph II, who returned in September from many months of travelling abroad, was downright infatuated with Wolfgang Amadeus's piano playing and he therefore always gave him monetary gifts – usually between 112 and 450 guilders. Mozart, the young virtuoso, who was very spoiled by his tours abroad, found it somehow lacklustre at the beginning of his journey and he thought about moving to Paris after only six months, because of the better pay in France. But the Emperor – when he was in Vienna – rarely failed to attend one of Wolfgang Amadeus's concerts. He had attended all the salons in which Wolfgang Amadeus made music and also his public academies.

Sometimes he even ordered him to come to the Hofburg Palace and to perform a concert there, so that his protegee earned a stunning 1,500 guilders a year, solely thanks to the imperial casket.

However, it should not be forgotten that his private life also played an important role and therefore Wolfgang Amadeus's new relationship required some stability in his life.

For the young composer, Vienna was in a way a burdened place in which he had already experienced quite a bit. First, at a very young age the wonderful performances made as a child prodigy in front of Empress Maria Theresa and her family. Emperor Joseph II probably had a certain memory of this time, when Wolfgang Amadeus reappeared in Vienna and the emperor remembered the child prodigy days of that time.

However, the past changed Wolfgang Amadeus and, for more than a year, there was a new impetus for him in the federal capital. The very special atmosphere of this time, the Josephine decade from 1780 to 1790, must have triggered something in him too. From a historical perspective, the Josephinism undertook many Enlightenment reforms in the Austrian political system, including the introduction of a relatively extensive freedom of the press through the censorship patent in 1781. As a reaction to this, numerous brochures that called for further reforms were written, but at the same time praising Joseph II as the realization of the idea of an enlightened ruler. Wolfgang Amadeus's sparkling and agile personality fitted in very well with the spirit of optimism, at least of the early 1780s. The emperor probably also noticed that about the young composer.

While Joseph II continued the reforms of his mother Maria Theresa, his greatest goal was to expand the Habsburg power positions and establish a modern, tight domestic order. Joseph II has been therefore called a 'revolutionary by the grace of God'. When he became King of Austria and Hungary, Prince of Brabant, he finally had a free hand and radically modernized the empire in the spirit of the Enlightenment, even against the old power structures.

In 1781, Joseph II began a revolution from above in the Habsburg Empire and pushed through a series of reforms. He restricted the clergy and nobility with the edict of tolerance, then he abolished hereditary serfdom and established the bishoprics of Linz and Sankt Pölten, which replaced the Passau diocese. He started to build a general hospital and at the same time introduced German as the official language. He then repealed the county constitution in Hungary and introduced a general civil code. Although a Catholic himself, on 29 November he decreed the abolition of 'useless monasteries'. By this, he meant contemplative monasteries, whose primary task was prayer and which did not engage in charitable (such as nursing), educational, or pastoral work. In doing so, he abolished more than 700 monasteries in the Austro-Hungarian region. There are over fifty closures in the Duchy of Brabant. The goods of the monasteries were incorporated into a religious fund, which was intended to serve ecclesiastical, charitable and educational purposes.

Joseph II also stipulated that none of his subjects may walk more than an hour to the nearest parish. As a result of that, many branch churches were converted into parishes. Long before that, the Council of Trent had decided that every baptism, wedding and burial had to be noted in a church register, but this was implemented hesitantly and only a century later.

Emperor Joseph II also authorized the sale of wine in his own house and thus he laid the foundations for the famous *Heurigen*-restaurants, which make Austria still so famous worldwide today. The reason for this new regulation was, that in what was then called the Crown lands (Cisleithania), the applicable rights were often interpreted against the farmers. That is why Emperor Joseph II decreed that every producer was free to sell his own wines at all times of the year – including to seated guests – without a formal licence to serve to need to give away. As a result, he won the hearts of the Austrians, who immediately set about turning the whole country into a long-term wine tavern.

Although Emperor Joseph II succeeded – over time – in breaking the old rules, fierce battles broke out against his radical reform steps in Hungary and in the Austrian Netherlands. But many of his other reforms – such as the abolition of serfdom and the death penalty, the patent of tolerance, the legal improvement of the Jews or the relaxation of censorship – brought a necessary progress to the country. His cultural policy was about weakening the supporting institutions of art and music; the court and the church. One can observe that for this reason, well known composers – such as Joseph Haydn or Wolfgang Amadeus Mozart – hardly composed any church music in the 1780s. The reason for this was that there was, apparently, no need for larger church-sized works in these years. The ban on instrumental music in the church in 1783 interrupted a special tradition in Austria of all places. And so, all of a sudden, musical interests shifted to other areas. The elimination of classical court music on a larger scale promoted musical life in the city palaces and castles in the countryside of the aristocrats, among the bourgeoisie and in the remaining monasteries. For Wolfgang Amadeus this time must have been very similar to the time in Salzburg; just like Prince-Archbishop Colloredo of Salzburg, Joseph II had a very strong sense of economy and focused primarily on simplicity. However, Joseph II had much more power than Colloredo and he also had a suitable environment and implemented radically up-to-date Enlightenment ideals, but also tried to develop Austria into a modern state.

This was also reflected in his personal attitude and appearance. He appeared most of the time as Count von Falkenstein (since he was originally from the House of Habsburg-Lothringen), avoided representative appearances and large church ceremonies, reduced courtly culture and liked to move around in aristocratic salons. His attempts to make public events such as theatrical performances or balls accessible to members of all classes served the tendency to combine simplicity and unity among the people of the state. Alongside numerous other composers, Wolfgang Amadeus wrote dance music for these balls, which then took place in the Redoutensaal of the Hofburg Palace, in the late 1780s.

For the emperor, music as well as musical theatre meant a special area of entertainment and relaxation, not part of an imperial representation, but instruments used for new political purposes. This led to a combination of centralism and enlightenment, using the consistent subordination of social affairs to the state administration of Austria according to the principles of Josephinism. The merging of these endeavours had its target in the metropolises and residential cities of the time; Vienna benefited here from the fact that it was a city that was in transition and on the move. The cultural plurality of the entire Habsburg Empire was concentrated here. And Vienna was the most polyglot city in the world at the time.

Among the officials at Emperor Joseph II's centre of power, there were representatives of all strata together with representatives of a new bourgeoisie. Emperor Joseph II's motto was *Virtute et exemplo* (With virtue and example). And with this comprehensive mixture of representatives from all classes, social utopias were developed. The site of a social avant-garde was formed by the Masonic lodges, which were already spreading at that time. There it happened – what seemed otherwise never to have been possible – namely that a prince could offer a non-nobleman the *tutoiement*, which meant that they called each other with their first names. Members of different social classes suddenly made music together to a greater extent. Making music and socializing with one's people as a singer or musician had a long tradition, especially among the Habsburgs. For example, all baroque emperors were composers – such as Leopold I, a music lover who played several instruments and who conducted his own chamber orchestra. With 230 works, Leopold I left lasting cultural traces. This had a role model effect on both the population and the nobility. The then much-admired Viennese musicians in string quartets, piano trios and solos, had a courtly chamber music tradition behind them.

Another interesting change of the time seems to be the rapid development of a journalistic public. The Josephine flood of pamphlets began as early as the 1770s. This is a derogatory term for the large amount of small-scale printed matter (2,000 to 3,000 titles) published in Vienna as part of the relaxation of censorship under Joseph II in 1781, giving extended freedom of the press on the basis of the 'basic rules for the determination of a regular future book censorship' of February 1781 and the Censorship Decree of 11 June, up to their tightening in the years 1792-1795. Cultural and theatrical life was hotly debated precisely in these media.

The social and political atmosphere of this decade can be summarized with the single word 'explosiveness'. The political situation was always endangered, as it oscillated between the reforms of Emperor Joseph II, his attempts to create new freedoms and the resulting setbacks and disappointments. Interestingly enough, this also applied to the behaviour of the emperor himself. Although Joseph II promoted the mentioned cultural awakening, he tried to steer it in his interest and to adapt it to the centralist aspirations for power. However, under the pressure of real events, resistance and wars, he had to withdraw from most of his plans and reforms that had already been initiated. You would like to believe that his reign followed a unique curve, the ups-and-downs of which also had an unmistakable impact on the cultural life in the beautiful city of Vienna. And in this very hopeful, positive beginning of Emperor Joseph II's solo reign, Wolfgang Amadeus had suddenly showed up in Vienna.

It is true that he started out with no secure income and without anyone to bankroll him. His livelihood depended unambiguously on artistic and financial success as a performer and composer achieved through activities in both areas and including publishing as well as a limited amount of teaching piano and music.

Within fifteen months of arriving in Vienna, Wolfgang Amadeus had already experienced a wide range of activities related to instrumental music-making in the city. It started with private concerts, went on to public concerts and to outdoor concerts, then to teaching, to publishing his music, to weekly soirees and even to a keyboard duel.

Despite all the confusion in the process of breaking away from Emperor Joseph II and his father in Salzburg and despite his understandable glorification of the situation in Vienna, Wolfgang Amadeus had not forgotten everything he had previously experienced in similar situations of having to gain a foothold. He knew how important it was to be able to get an appointment with his Emperor as quickly as possible, to win his favour and to attain his very respectable position at court. He also knew how much this was connected with the other, attracting the interest of high society and causing a sensation as an artist among them. Wolfgang Amadeus also promised that he would do everything possible to get to the Emperor Joseph II as quickly as possible. As long as he was in the service of the Prince-Archbishop Colloredo of Salzburg, that had never been possible.

Despite all the bitterness and all the strife, there was an advantage to his service, namely that he was constantly presented to the Viennese nobility by Prince-Archbishop Colloredo – and it was precisely at these moments that Wolfgang Amadeus was always ready to show himself from his best side. An artist's great opportunity lay in making new contacts. Having resigned from his princely service in Salzburg had not seemed to do him any harm in Vienna, quite the contrary, in fact. Apparently, he was even encouraged in the federal capital to further advance his career there. What could be better? Above all, women and men from the aristocracy emerged as major supporters. And in a short time, he had set up an exciting network of helpful personalities in Vienna – which, by the way, was never the case in Salzburg.

Wolfgang Amadeus was a euphoric artist and composer who knew how to act in this artistic environment in order to be successful. He was skilful, eloquent and very fond of writing letters – that was the best way to communicate in those days, even though time passed and not everything could be done immediately. One should remember that this was a completely different time; without mobile phones, without computers and you only scored with your own personality, your own commitment and immense respect for the supporters.

His means of earning money were music lessons for wealthy clients and inquisitive students, appearances at piano concerts, work as a composer and thus the creation and development of new pieces of music as well as the arrangement of the associated printing of the scores. The high point, however, was the composing of a new opera and its successful performance – at best over several weeks. For example, Wolfgang Amadeus's first pupil came from the circles of the high aristocracy, with which his entire family had already found contact during his first trips to Vienna.

In the first few weeks in Vienna in 1781 he was a guest of the famous Countess Maria Wilhelmine Thun-Hohenstein, whom he described to his family in Salzburg as 'the most charming, dearest lady I have seen in my life'. Countess Thun-Hohenstein was considered the supporter of a musically and intellectually outstanding salon and the patron saint of music, especially of that of Wolfgang Amadeus (see Chapter 5) and she became in fact a huge supporter. She was extremely taken by him and his musical genius. And through her huge support and encouragement of the young composer, other people from the Viennese society also became aware of him. For example, Johann Philipp Graf von Cobenzl, Vice Court and State Chancellor of the Habsburg Monarchy in the Austrian Empire, one of the most powerful men in the monarchy. He brought Wolfgang Amadeus together with his cousin, Countess Maria Caroline Thiennes de Rumbeke. The Countess became Wolfgang Amadeus's first piano student in Vienna. But in the summer of 1781, his income suddenly faltered. Showing off as a pianist and composing for the piano was one of the two main focuses of Wolfgang Amadeus's musical talent. He constantly wrote to his father about his enthusiasm for the piano in Vienna and told him, that he was so happy to be in 'Clavierland'.

It was – of course – clear to the young Wolfgang Amadeus that his talent existed, but that his audience's enthusiasm was waning.

Because, as soon as the attraction of variety was no longer just the personality of the artist, then you had to satisfy your fans with a new, extraordinary form of performance from him. Organizing academies together with other artists had a certain tradition – especially in Vienna. And because of the proliferation of such events, a new breed of entrepreneurs was making a name for itself in Vienna as they seized the moment by experimenting with new forms of performance. One of them was Philipp Jakob Martin, who served as impresario for Mozart's concerts by organizing first so-called 'dilettante concerts' in Vienna from 1781-1782. Dilettantes were originally those people whose training produced a wide range of skills and this was geared towards the active participation of a free citizen in the community. The ability to make and judge music was highly valued, but a professional (instrumental) musician was considered a philistine.

Philip Jakob Martin was the first professional concert promoter and impresario in Vienna. From 1781 he organized concerts with amateur orchestras at the Mehlgrube (Vienna's first district, Neuer Markt 5), in the Prater (Vienna's second district) and Am Hof (Vienna's first district). The Augarten Concerts was founded by him in the summer of 1782 and became particularly well known. He led it until the year 1791 and Wolfgang Amadeus also played an active role there from the spring of 1782.

The Augarten was an imperial park and an old baroque garden that was redesigned and restored in 1705 by Emperor Joseph I according to the taste of the Viennese. In 1712, the new monarch, Emperor Charles VI, commissioned landscape architect Jean Trehet – who was also responsible for the design of the gardens at Schönbrunn and the Belvedere Palace – to carry out new plans to develop the whole park, in French style. Emperor Joseph II took over in 1755 and opened it; he laid out additional shady avenues, set up benches to rest and even introduced nightingales for acoustic accompaniment. The centre of the complex was a hall building, the remains of the former Old Favorita, dedicated to Emperor Ferdinand III, an imperial pleasure palace. In addition to the music, food and drinks, a wide variety of games, billiards and a casino were also offered here.

The guests were enchanted with performances that took place at the most unlikely times. For example, the morning concerts that have gone down in music history and became a meeting place for the elegant world. These concerts were deliberately held in the morning, because at this time of the day the high society was undisturbed by the mob – the common people were still at work.

Wolfgang Amadeus was present and was employed at these concerts as a composer, pianist and also as a programmer. The special attraction of these events lay in the diversity of the offer and the Viennese society felt very comfortable here and enjoyed the time with the young musician. With the astonishingly large number of experts in the aristocracy and in the new civil service, it was no wonder that such elite musicians' circles were formed in Vienna at this time. Wolfgang Amadeus very quickly found access to the socially most important circles of artists. It was that of Gottfried Freiherr van Swieten, who was a Dutch born Austrian diplomat in the service of the Habsburg monarchy, a librarian and governmental official, but also a patron of several great composers of classical music. He was in the time of Joseph II, succeeding his father, the famous Gerhard van Swieten, Prefect of the Main Library and President of the Study Commission, and with this career, a man of extreme influence.

Working as an Austrian ambassador in Berlin in the 1770s, the composing aristocrat came into contact with personalities from the former circle of Johann Sebastian Bach, such as his son Philipp Emanuel Bach and the composer and music theorist Johann Philipp Kirnberger. Van Swieten was particularly enthusiastic about older music, such as that of George Frederick Handel and Johann Sebastian Bach. He cultivated this preference intensively in Vienna in the 1780s. But it wasn't quite as exotic here as one might think. Among the professional musicians there was knowledge and appreciation for the instrumental music of Bach. Handel became a very prominent figure in Europe, because of his Oratorios, large musical compositions for orchestra, choir, and soloists. On Sundays, Van Swieten invited the Viennese and well-known musicians to matinees in his official residence as court librarian in the Imperial Library.

Among the musicians he invited was Josef Starzer, composer and violinist at the Burgtheatre in Vienna and also at the Imperial Russian court in Saint Petersburg, and the Austrian organist, Kapellmeister and composer, Anton Teyber, who had just returned from Bologna in Italy where he had studied with Padre Martini.

During these special musical circles, dealing with the strictly contrapuntal genre of the fugue had become an elitist fashion. Fugue, based on the counterpoint between two or more voices, centres around the repetition of a theme in different registers and with differing textures and dynamics, these themes are often repeated throughout a piece, and were seen as a highlight. The contact with Van Swieten and the familiarity with him became more than a social advantage for Wolfgang Amadeus.

The risks of freelance work were well known to Wolfgang Amadeus, and he learned to live with them as long as he was artistically active, because artists could not count on a regular income either from teaching or from giving concerts. But as a pianist, at the beginning of his time in Vienna, he trusted in the chances of success, despite the fact that the nobility shaped their lives in flexible summer and winter cycles and in alternating attractions.

Wolfgang Amadeus did not really fear that his fan base in the aristocracy might turn to another artist. But his father was extremely worried about his son during this time in Vienna and communicated this to him. Then Wolfgang Amadeus tried to calm him down and he did so on 2 June 1781:

Mon très chère Père,

From my last letter you will have gathered that I have spoken with Count Arco himself; praise and thanks be to God that everything went off so well. – Do not be worried, you do not have the least reason to be afraid of the Archbishop – for Count Arco did not say with a single word that I should not forget that it could be to your detriment – and when he said to me that you had written to him and complained strongly about me, I interrupted him at once and said: And not to me, are you sure? – what he wrote to me was such that I often thought I would go crazy over it – but, regardless of how I reflected on the matter – I simply cannot etc.... – There is no doubt that the Viennese enjoy bringing people down - but only in the theatre. – and my specialty is too popular here for me not to be able to keep myself.[51]

Great successes at the theatre were far more lucrative and therefore more important than successes in the so-called 'Clavierland'. In the field of operas, Wolfgang Amadeus had not yet had any outstanding and long-lasting successes. So far, he hadn't said a word about it, but he registered it and it bothered him immensely. He did not receive a new piece to edit through his contact Gottlieb Stephanie – about whom he wrote in a letter in 1781 as a 'man with a bad reputation – but in the end he called him a 'good friend'. Wolfgang Amadeus probably chose him because Stephanie was known for his particularly effective plays; in fact, he did 32 plays in 393 performances at the Vienna Burgtheatre, where he started in 1769 at the age of 28 and worked there as actor, stage manager and dramaturge until his death.

Stephanie gave Wolfgang Amadeus the arrangement of a very special piece by a Leipzig merchant, Christoph Friedrich Bretzner, who was famous for writing librettos to which a musician, composer and music publisher of the Classical period from Offenbach am Main in Germany, Johann André, had already composed *Belmonte and Konstanze, The Abduction from the Seraglio*. Stephanie gave the story a different, happy, ending. While Bretzner's Bassa von Belmont recognized his son – Nestroy liked to use this kind of happy ending – Stephanie has put the idea of humanity in the foreground.

Voluntarily, out of nobility, the Bassa pardons the two lovers Belmont and Constanze.

One thing was clear from the beginning; the collaboration between the two creative men was intense. Wolfgang Amadeus accepted Gottlieb Stephanie as an arranger of someone else's play. Cooperation and agreements with him also had an official order as a requirement.

Wolfgang Amadeus had always been smart because he had urged his father already when he was in Mannheim in January 1778 to ask Viennese friends 'with good contacts at court' to politely ask the Emperor as the German National Theatre was founded, to try out the talented Wolfgang Amadeus for an opera project.

A family friend, Franz Edler von Heufeld, an Austrian comedy writer, literary critic and theatre manager, gave the advice to compose a good opera and that a presence in Vienna was urgently needed. But now the time had finally come and Wolfgang Amadeus was in Vienna. The background for this spectacular project is probably Count Franz Xaver Wolfgang von Orsini-Rosenberg, who knew Wolfgang Amadeus from his time in Italy and who commissioned him to write a good opera. This is how he also came into contact with Gottlieb Stephanie. Although von Orsini-Rosenberg was one of the courtiers of Joseph II at his palace in Vienna, he was at first opposed to Wolfgang Amadeus's idea of writing an opera in German instead of Italian, but switched finally to German – thanks to the emperor, who chose to allow Mozart to write the opera in German. This shocked many people.

The work began in early August 1781. Wolfgang Amadeus went all out. He knew he could count on great interest in the material to be worked on by the music-loving Viennese – so a success seemed to be inevitable. Gottlieb Stephanie offered him the best ensemble at the time in Vienna.

The work on the piece lasted exactly ten months until the end of May 1782 and coincided with the private quarrels with his mother-in-law and his own father. It is as clear as day that Wolfgang Amadeus was actually thinking of his own great love Constanze when he portrayed

Konstanze in *Belmonte and Konstanze, The Abduction from the Seraglio*. When creating the role of Konstanze, however, he thought of the soprano opera singer Caterina Magdalena Giuseppa Cavalieri, who was trained by Antonio Salieri, and not of his wife, who was also a trained singer. As the composer of the opera, Wolfgang Amadeus went into the texts very thoroughly, down to the last detail, not only with the characters Konstanze and the Spanish nobleman Belmonte, but also with Osmin, who is the overseer for the Pasha. There were countless letters between him and his father, who stood by him in an advisory capacity. Wolfgang Amadeus wanted to show his father that they had a common ground on a professional level.

Wolfgang Amadeus had the great will to bring a special work into the world in a precarious, decisive situation on his path in the field of opera-dramatic compositions. It may be understandable to produce outstanding composer performances in a rather irritable state, but it is astonishing that he managed to muster the concentration for another creative arc that an opera composition required, namely in addition to being overburdened with his important work in the 'Clavierland' and the time-consuming effort to be constantly present in Viennese society – without television, radio, computers, and social media such as Instagram, Facebook, Twitter, TikTok etc – and despite all private problems with family and in-laws.

Only three weeks before his marriage to Constanze, on 16 July 1782, the opera *Belmonte and Konstanze, The Abduction from the Seraglio* was premiered. And it was really successful. The Singspiel was performed thirty-four times in the same theatre up until 1788. This also became Wolfgang Amadeus's only operatic success in the German-speaking arena, which, however, came rather slowly at first.

The premiere was, so to speak, not a great spontaneous success. Wolfgang Amadeus spoke of the second time the Singspiel was played and of an even stronger 'cabal', because of the first act, which was hissed by the public. But nevertheless, the public 'could not hinder the loud shouts of "Bravo!" during the arias'. There was probably some behind-the-scenes intrigue – the usual, opera pundits say. But what was much more interesting, was how the new depth in the musical design of this Singspiel was received by the audience for the different kind of expectations. First of all, the Singspiel took some getting used to.

The smug and terse remarks of a Saxon-Austrian civil servant Count Karl von Zinzendorf – who served the government of Austria in a variety of capacities, including as governor of Trieste and who then rose to high rank at the Habsburg court – which he noted in his well-known diary, sums up an impression that most members of Viennese society might have shared with him. 'This evening at the show *The Abduction from the Serail*, opera, whose music is plundered from various others.' But this otherness of the Singspiel he peddled, could in fact not stop the reception of this new opera from developing. It even encouraged it.

The new Singspiel was noticed by the public far beyond the borders of Vienna and discussed in various media-forums of this time. The 'kidnapping' had become more than 'just' a Singspiel. This is basically what the German poet, playwright and critic Johann Wolfgang von Goethe thought, 'All our efforts to shut ourselves off [in the Singspiel] from the simple and limited were lost when Mozart appeared. The abduction from the Seraglio crushed everything.' The *Abduction from the Seraglio* became the greatest stage success during Wolfgang Amadeus's lifetime. Posterity has long counted it – between *Idomeneo* and *The Marriage of Figaro* – as one of his seven great master operas. As a result of this success, the image of Wolfgang Amadeus as a Singspiel composer emerged in Germany, which greatly overshadowed many other things.

A question that can be asked is, how much did this particular success of this Singspiel depend on the support of a royal, which in this case was Emperor Joseph II, for Wolfgang Amadeus as a composer? Did he make more money? Did he get more attention?

The Emperor had his idea of a national theatre – the Burgtheatre in Vienna – as a sort of the nation's school of morals, where primarily

German language drama had to be promoted. Over the years, the theatre even achieved a leading position among the German-speaking theatres. The financial security provided by the court made it possible to keep theatre stars in Vienna together in an ensemble. The actors were given the same status as court officials and received a state pension.

But this did not correspond at all to Wolfgang Amadeus's demolition of the Singspiel genre by incorporating elements from other music theatre forms. The purity of genres was required for the theatre by the imperial adviser Joseph von Sonnenfels – who was an Austrian and German jurist and novelist – and who stood in the way of Wolfgang Amadeus. It is rumoured that after the premiere of the singspiel, Emperor Joseph II commented, 'Too beautiful for our ears and a tremendous amount of notes, dear Mozart!' Wolfgang Amadeus is said to have countered with the following, extremely self-confident as he was, 'Just as much, Your Majesty, as is necessary.' One might even think that Wolfgang Amadeus has miscalculated with his latest composition, and then only when he intended to influence the Emperor's taste. But in reality, Wolfgang Amadeus was once again only concerned with one thing; to realize his full potential and to act as a music–dramatic experimenter. That was his strength; influencing people through the music he created. And with this in his mind he succeeded admirably in this Singspiel.

In order to diversify the program in the National Theatre, then Burgtheatre, Emperor Joseph II introduced the German National Singspiel in 1778, which clearly reached its climax with *Abduction from the Seraglio*. The Emperor slipped into the role of the director of the Burgtheatre; he saw the theatre as a tool for enlightenment and its social reforms. As a moral authority it was intended to be a means of educating and disciplining the audience.

Emperor Joseph II was not uninterested in music or uneducated, he had only received the usual Habsburg musical training in his youth and his understanding of music in his mature years also showed recognizable characteristics. He conducted very frequent discourses on music and particularly valued his treatise *Gradus ad Parnassum* from 1725 by the late baroque Viennese court conductor, composer and music theorist Johann Joseph Fux; the mastery of counterpoint influenced countless composers, through.

But the Emperor was also a particular lover of opera. And he took the theatre seriously as the nation's school of morals. However, it did not really fit into this picture that he left the design of spoken theatre to a relevant court commission, but intervened in the selection of the operas himself. If one looks through the reports in the media at the time, one will notice that he obviously played through much-discussed opera scores himself or even had them played for him. He did this over and over again. He also took care of administrative details and even found time to attend rehearsals, select plays and appoint actors. Even on trips abroad, he looked for talent for the Viennese stage and sent 'talent scouts' across Germany. He was torn between politics, which he was trying to shape through his decrees, and culture, especially music and opera, to which he was also attached. He wanted to see bourgeois virtues on the stage, but he seems to have appreciated a subtle criticism of the aristocracy. As emperor, he promoted the German-language national theatre and also loved Italian operas. Over time, while living in Vienna, Wolfgang Amadeus realized how this influenced the emperor's feelings and wishes towards his musicians and artists. 'Now, my main aim here is to gain access to the Emperor in a fine manner, for I *absolument* wish that he should get to know me. – I would like to whip zestfully through my opera for him and then nicely play fugues, for that is his thing.[52]

But Wolfgang Amadeus's achievement of his goal was of course entirely dependent on the emperor and his wishes; he could only move as far forward as the emperor would allow. When he left Salzburg, the emperor was abroad and when he returned to Vienna, a series of diplomatic visits followed, which he had to do for political reasons. Joseph II sought a change of alliance from Prussia to Austria with Tsarina Catherine II – the Great. Catherine II was the country's longest-ruling female leader. She came to power following the overthrow of her husband and second cousin, Peter III. Under her reign, inspired by the ideas of the Enlightenment, Russia experienced a renaissance of culture and sciences, many new cities, universities and theatres were founded, a large number of European immigrants moved to Russia, and Russia was recognized as one of the great powers of Europe.

Needless to say, the two monarchs got along very well. They had already met in the summer of 1780 for the first time and a year later, they concluded a defence alliance with important consequences. This should then be stabilized in Vienna, so Emperor Joseph II invited the Russian heir to the throne and later Emperor Paul I of Russia – he was the only son of Catherine the Great – and Duke Friedrich II August von Würtemberg moved to Vienna with their families. With the arrival of the nobles in November 1781, the Emperor began showing his guests the culture of Vienna's glittering city. Wolfgang Amadeus was able to present himself a little.

The emperor was impressed by a competition organized at court between Wolfgang Amadeus and his pianist rival Muzio Filippo Vincenzo Francesco Saverio Clementi, who was a composer, pedagogue, conductor, music publisher, editor, and piano manufacturer, mostly active in England. The emperor proved to be jovial towards Wolfgang Amadeus and he often praised his compositions and, as a sort of 'thank you' repeatedly invited him to his home to show his craft to his guests. When the Grand Duke Paul I of Russia came again for a visit to Austria in October 1782, Wolfgang Amadeus was allowed to show him his new opera *The Abduction from the Seraglio* and conducted it at the Burgtheatre. Wolfgang Amadeus was also given access to the Russian embassy and the envoy Prince Nikolai Dmitriyevich Golitsyn, who worked in Vienna, was an amateur musician. Wolfgang Amadeus was often invited by him to the Russian embassy to play music. He thought at one time that he had a chance with a young Württemberg princess as a music teacher, when he applied for the position of music teacher to the Duchess Elisabeth of Württemberg, but unfortunately this was thwarted by the emperor, who wanted to offer the young duchess, who he also held in high esteem personally, the best person and teacher he had, and from his personal point of view that was his court music director, a classical composer, conductor and teacher, born in Legnago south of Verona, Antonio Salieri.

In the years that followed, Salieri would always get in the way of Wolfgang Amadeus. One cannot therefore speak of a rivalry in social life; the relationship between the two was too clear for that. However, a certain rivalry existed in the artistically sensitive, critical following and observing of the other's musical paths. When they met in person, Salieri behaved extremely jovially and confidently towards Wolfgang Amadeus. Salieri wasn't angry with Wolfgang Amadeus either, that he had chosen Lorenzo da Ponte – born Emanuele Conegliano – whom Salieri had once introduced to Emperor Joseph II as a court poet and libertarian, as his most important collaborator. Da Ponte was previously a Roman Catholic priest in Venice, but he led a dissolute life, taking a mistress with whom he had two children. In the year 1779 there was a trial, where he was charged with 'public concubinage' as well as 'abduction of a respectable woman' and it was alleged that he had been living in a brothel and organizing the entertainments there. He then was found guilty and banished for fifteen years from Venice and moved to Gorizia in Austria, then worked as a poet in Dresden, before moving as librettist to the Italian Theatre in Vienna.

The numerous visits by princes and the associated performances, during which the audience applauded Wolfgang Amadeus warmly and enthusiastically, also had private effects. Wolfgang Amadeus and his young wife planned to visit his father in Salzburg on his name day on 15 November and to finally seal a reconciliation with him personally. But because of the concert opportunities that were now offered to him in Vienna, he postponed this idea again. He really had great success as an artist in various entertainment academies. The crowd cheered him as soon as he touched the keys of a piano with his fingers or raised the conductor's baton. In March 1783, Emperor Joseph II attended concerts by Wolfgang Amadeus twice in a row. Since Wolfgang Amadeus was extremely busy with his various performances in Vienna until the summer, he was only able to go to Salzburg in July with Constanze – after the birth of their first child, Raimund Leopold, who had to stay in Vienna and died unfortunately there in mid-August. The two stayed with Leopold and Maria Anna until the end of October.

Constanze immersed herself in the social life of the people of Salzburg and experienced for the first time several weeks of astonishingly intense social life. She attended numerous invitations, participated in classic 'Bölzl-shootings' (shooting darts at decorated targets with an air gun) or she participated in playing music, or did long walks with the Mozart family and she also attended numerous theatre performances. The highlight of the Salzburg-trip took place at the end of the holidays, on 26 October, in the abbey church of the Benedictine Archabbey which was situated at the foot of the Mönchsberg. Wolfgang Amadeus had made a vow to compose a Mass after the successful birth of his first-born child. But after the death of his son, he stopped the work on the composition – precisely at the *Et incarnates est* which was one of his most beautiful and heartfelt moments, dealing with the topic of incarnation and birth. There, at the beautiful abbey church, Constanze got the big chance to appear as a soprano-soloist and sang the performance of the *C-Minor Mass*. You can't blame her for not having a particularly soprano voice. The *Kyrie*, *Gloria* and *Sanctus* were performed with the *Hosanna* and *Benedictus*, that is, all the fully-composed movements. This mass was the fulfilment of the vow of the previous year, when Wolfgang Amadeus had longed for the paternal blessing on his union with Constanze Weber. The next day, the couple left Salzburg to return to Vienna.

Everyone who was present during these holidays had honestly tried to get along due to the good will of Wolfgang Amadeus and Constanze – but this visit still remained only a simple visit. Nothing more. Wolfgang Amadeus and his wife got the impression of being safe and at home only in their hometown Vienna. And shockingly, Wolfgang Amadeus was never to set foot in Salzburg again and he also would never see his sister again.

One would assume that, due to the respect for those who remained in Vienna and the upcoming musical concert winter season, which was extremely important for Wolfgang Amadeus, the return trip would be quick. But that was far from the case. In fact, Wolfgang Amadeus, who was a connoisseur, really enjoyed the numerous stops during his trip back home, which included longer stays with friends. For example, three weeks in Upper Austria, where the Mozarts were guests at Count Johann Joseph Anton Thun-Hohenstein's castle in Linz. He was the stepfather of Countess Wilhelmine Thun in Vienna, he loved music and he had his own house band, which he also took with him when he was in his castle in Prague. But he was also a Freemason and with his help, Wolfgang Amadeus could soon also be a member of a lodge of Freemasons in Vienna. But for the moment, the two men did not talk about Freemasonry, but about several concerts as well as another music academy that Wolfgang Amadeus was about to give at the Linz theatre. This unprompted project got him massively into trouble, because he had not composed a single symphony, nor did he have any compositions with him. That is why he was therefore dependent on composing something entirely new in Upper Austria. The *Linz Symphony* (KV 425), was thence written in just a few days and under an extreme time pressure, but for his host Count Johann Joseph Anton Thun-Hohenstein. Finally he earned some precious money.

It was not until the end of November that Wolfgang Amadeus and Constanze returned to her beloved apartment in Vienna. But as soon as they arrived, the first problems fluttered into their house, as the saying goes. First, on their arrival, Wolfgang Amadeus was presented with the old Strasbourg bill of exchange from 1778; it was an amount of 132 guilders plus interest, that he had to repay. After five years, the banker wanted the money back – and interest on top of that. That is why Wolfgang Amadeus protested and was surprised that his father had not yet paid the amount for him. But Leopold was no longer willing to do this after his son married Constanze. He said it was now up to the Weber family to intercede for his son.

Wolfgang Amadeus experienced fist-hand how the emperor had suddenly lost interest in his German National Theatre and since the spring of 1783, had concentrated on Italian operas at the Burgtheatre. That is why the first opera was Antonio Salieri's *La scuola de'gelosi* which was performed for the opening. After this arrival of an Italian opera in Vienna, other Italian composers followed with their operas, which were favoured by the emperor – including Domenico Cimarosa, Giuseppe Sati and Giovanni Paisiello. Wolfgang Amadeus had to act, but for a while he was undecided on which genre to focus for the future direction of his career. He had great success with the Singspiel, and in February he had already worked on the German version of Carlo Goldoni's *Il servitore di due patron*. He then composed several interlude arias for Italian operas by his fellow composers to attract the attention of the music world.

This meant that since his arrival in Vienna, he had continued with intensive work and tremendous success. Week after week, between five and six concerts took place in the famous salons of the noble families, including the houses of Kaunitz, Galitzin, Esterhazy, Cobenzl, Thun, Palffy, Zichy, Ployer, Trattner and many more.

In the spring of 1783, Wolfgang Amadeus was in touch with Lorenzo da Ponte, who was his most important collaborator. But he discovered that da Ponte was working on one of his introductory works and a libretto for Antonio Salieri. Because of the latter, Wolfgang Amadeus was very upset. Ambassador Karl Heinrich Joseph, Count Sickingen zu Sickingen, the 'true connoisseur of musique', who in Paris in the year 1778 invited the brilliant Amadeus Mozart to come to him for several days and to study opera scores with him, showed up in Vienna and asked for Wolfgang Amadeus, who immediately ran to him with the libretto of the opera *Idomeneo* in his hand.

The soirees in the various palaces earned him between 300 and 500 guilders every week – if not more, apart from the public concerts, the imperial rolls of ducats, the van Swieten Baroque Sundays, the publisher's fees and his own sale of copies of scores, which again brought him some more money.

Towards the end of the year, Wolfgang Amadeus was again busy with plans for a Singspiel. Nevertheless, he kept thinking about further opera projects, but unfortunately there were no operas in the next two years. The dilemma between German and Italian opera – but possibly also the beginning of the rivalry between the Italian Salieri and the Austrian Wolfgang Amadeus – prompted Emperor Joseph II to combine the two, suddenly, out of the blue, into one more than cheerful event.

At the beginning of the Carnival in February 1786, he organized what he called a 'theatre on the theatre' as part of a spring festival on a winter day in honour of the governor general of the Netherlands, who was staying in Vienna, and for the amusement of the courtly society. In two concurrent short operas, an Italian one composed by Salieri called *Prima la Musica e poi le parole* and a German one composed by Wolfgang Amadeus called *Der Schauspieldirektor* – the well-known and usual excitement of theatre people was to become comedy.

Wolfgang Amadeus had chosen Gottlieb Stephanie as his librettist. In the meantime, he had found his personal solution to the conflict with his competitor Salieri by composing the opera *The Marriage of Figaro*.

In the months that followed, his great enthusiasm for work concentrated on completely new fields. Wolfgang Amadeus rose to more success in the years 1784 and 1785 and established himself as a fascinating figure in Viennese musical life. He had hardly ever earned so much money before or since. The choice of beautiful new apartments in the city centre of Vienna also spoke for his good economic circumstances – with the constant relocation. It's easy to explain where all that money really came from; although it was not due to opera productions or the publication of piano and chamber music-works. Rather, it came from the very intensive teaching activity and the many self-organized and co-organized concerts in which Wolfgang Amadeus was involved. For example, during the Lenten season in the year 1784, he performed at no fewer than twenty-two concerts within six weeks. This was of course an extreme case and didn't happen all the time.

Interestingly, there are now statistics that came about based on the subscription lists of his music academies and these statistics give a cross-section of the visitors and audience. It follows that the majority of his listeners and visitors to his concerts were members of the high aristocracy – they came from the families of counts and princes, as well as from the petty and financial nobility and from court officials, but also from the commoners. Wolfgang Amadeus thus played in front of Vienna's best society, which also had the necessary financial strength to afford his concerts and performances.

But not all of his performances were on a large scale; he also took part in smaller events, for example in a hall in the Trattnerhof, where he lived from the beginning of 1784 until 29 September of the same year. This can be documented in a letter from the musician and composer dated 10 February 1784 (addressed to his father). In it he gives details about his current address – 'In the Trattner house, second staircase, third floor'. Graben 29 and 29A together formed the Trattnerhof. A short alley bearing the same name and consisting only of these two houses separated them from each other. It created the connection between the Graben and the Goldschmiedgasse or the farmers' market. At Trattnerhof, Wolfgang Amadeus gave three concerts during the Lenten season in 1784; the price for all three was six guilders for each guest. These concerts took place in the upper room of the former house chapel, in which an intermediate ceiling had been installed above the ground floor.

Wolfgang Amadeus achieved the greatest recognition among the public and his patrons, above all with his piano concertos. With his immeasurable talent, he was virtually the creator of the modern piano concerto. In no other genre has a single composer had such a lasting influence on the entire development and created something as important as he has. In the course of just a few years, he succeeded in finally overcoming the level of conventional utility music and composing individually shaped works of art which, since they emerge from the historical process of becoming and passing away, require interpretation, and indeed constant reinterpretation.

Between 1784 and 1786 he wrote twelve piano concertos and presented them to the public for the most part in his own events, the so-called 'Academies'. Even before that, when he had just finished his first *Vienna Piano Concerto in A major* (KV 414), he explained the new concept to his father:

Mon trés cher Pére!

I must write in the greatest haste because it is already half past 5, and I have arranged for people to come here to make a little musique; – I have altogether so much to do that I often do not know if I am coming or going; – the whole morning, until 2 o'clock, goes past with teaching; – then we eat; – after the meal I must at least allow my poor stomach a brief hour for digestion; then – there is only the evening in which I can compose something – and that is not certain because I am often asked to attend concerts; – now 2 concertos are still needed for the concertos on subscription – the concertos are something precisely in the middle between too difficult and too easy – are a very brilliant – pleasant to the ear – without of course falling into fatuousness – here and there the knowledgeable alone can obtain satisfaction – yet in such a way – that those without knowledge will surely be content with it, without knowing why.[53]

In the first weeks of 1784, Wolfgang Amadeus Mozart performed in twenty-two different academy concerts on just thirty-eight days, and he mentioned in a letter to his father, 'Now you can easily imagine that I necessarily have to play new things – so one has to write about it.'[54]

Compared to today, the audience at that time was primarily interested in new music, and the 28-year-old Wolfgang Amadeus, who had been living in Vienna as a freelance artist now for three years, was able to skilfully combine his successes as a pianist with those as a composer.

Starting in the spring of 1784, he wrote six piano concertos which, despite their individual differences, were similar in terms of formal structure and instrumentation, especially for the wind instruments. Two more concertos were written in the autumn of the same year. That was his power and passion. From February of 1784, he also created a special index of all of his works. His confidence and the happiness he felt to be allowed to make music in this city, rose by the fact that he suddenly no longer felt the urge to travel to other cities and countries, as he had been used to do before, with his father as his mentor. Even without a permanent job, he remained a stable personality. This was certainly a premiere in his life and in the life of his devoted family in Salzburg.

The luck of a musician and the fortune of a ruler only have something to do with one another on the outside. Never on the inside. This is a chimera. But such an outward appearance can actually be very stimulating and cast a spell over the audience and the fans of a music personality such as Wolfgang Amadeus. While in the metropolis of Vienna, after the visit of Pope Pius VI in 1782, the basic mood of enlightened liberality increased. And Wolfgang Amadeus, with his inspiration, his alert mind and his love of music, immediately felt like an element in this trade – as a part of it. He lived in Vienna and he loved this city so much that he literally merged with it artistically.

Chapter 7

Mozart's Love for the Masonic Mindsets

It remained the enlightened liberality of 1784, as a basic position of political philosophy and historical and current movements, that increasingly strove for a free state, economic and social order in Austria and this new culture of conviviality – in which the commoners and the liberal nobility alike took part – helped to reduce many hostilities. One of these new meeting places was characterized by extremely strict admission rules; the lodge of the Freemasons. It was a special source of ethical exchange. Rituals and symbols were taken over by the medieval stonemasons, who were organized into building huts (Lodges). According to tradition, on 24 June 1717, the first four lodges founded a Grand Lodge in London – the founding act of Freemasonry. In the 1730s, Freemasonry spread across the European continent and adapted to the societies there, which were still heavily influenced by the nobility. It was mainly aristocratic diplomats, who expanded their networks in the lodges.

The first lodge in Vienna was founded in 1770. At the beginning of the 1780s there were already eight lodges in Vienna. Freemasonry flourished in Vienna as it did elsewhere in Europe, because it promoted values important to the age: free speech; tolerance; benevolence; and fraternity. Within the Temple, all of the brothers met as equals; identity was based in individual merit and achievement rather than birth-right, and each lodge was independently governed. As a cultural phenomenon, Freemasonry was international, reaching across the nations and the continents. It is interesting to see that many of the century's leaders, like Frederick the Great or George Washington or even Benjamin Franklin – were Masons, as were writers of various nations, like for example Goethe, Stendhal, Swift or Lessing, because Freemasonry flourished in the intellectual climate of the Enlightenment, which had finally gained a foothold in the Austrian lands.

In Austria, the Holy Roman Emperor Francis I, the future husband of Empress Maria Theresa, also belonged to the Masons for a short time. He was admitted as a Freemason in The Hague in 1731 and was soon promoted to Master in England at the Grand Lodge of England. Nothing more is known of his career as a Freemason. But the British people could now count among their number a powerful heir to the throne. Freemasonry was also promoted by Empress Maria Theresa's son, Emperor Joseph II at the time.

Wolfgang Amadeus's points of contact with Masonic ideas dated back to his youth; at the age of sixteen he wrote a *Hymn of praise to the celebratory St. John's Lodge* (KV 148). While at that time it was just an occasional work with no deeper connection to his views, many years later, during his time in Vienna, he consciously and out of conviction, turned himself with the time to Masonic ideas. Numerous public figures in Austria were Masons. There was a multitude of lodges in the city, and it was not uncommon for the members to change the lodge, if it was necessary.

Wolfgang Amadeus had many close associates already during his time in Salzburg and in other cities he had visited who were Freemasons and members of the Order of Illuminati – who were also all Freemasons. During his stays in Germany and France for example, he was befriended by prominent Masons and Illuminists including the diplomat and playwright Baron Otto Heinrich von Gemmingen, the conductor and composer Christian Cannabich, or the director of the Concert Spirituel, Joseph Legros.

Wolfgang Amadeus's personal and official engagement with Freemasonry in Vienna began on a special day, 5 December 1784. A visible sign of Wolfgang Amadeus's orientation was his admission as Apprentice Mason to the Viennese lodge *Zur Wohltätigkeit* ('To Charity') on 14 December. At that time there were about 600 to 800 Freemasons in the whole of Vienna. The diplomat, enlightenment writer and a friend Otto Freiherr von Gemmingen was the master of the lodge *Zur Wohltätigkeit* at the time. And as a great friend and supporter of the 28-year-old composer, he introduced him to the ideas of the Masonic mindsets of the lodge.

And his rise was rapid; on 7 January 1785, Wolfgang Amadeus was already promoted to the Fellow Craft degree and became a Master Mason soon thereafter. The lodge frequently engaged in charitable works and in the spring of 1784 had already raised 4184 florins for flood victims.

As many other members of the lodges in Vienna did, Wolfgang Amadeus often attended meetings of larger and more prominent lodges, for example at the lodge *Zur wahren Eintracht* ('True Concord'). And he then shifted his interests more and more to this lodge, where Ignaz von Born set the tone as master. Mozart was raised to the rank of journeyman here and soon thereafter achieved the degree of master. He was so enthusiastic about the Freemasons, that he even persuaded his friend the composer Joseph Haydn, as well as his own father, to join a lodge. As an indication of the compatibility of Freemasonry with a strictly Catholic view of the world and morals, the fact applies, that in April 1785, Wolfgang Amadeus also brought his very conservative father to the *Zur wahren Eintracht* lodge. On 11 February of the same year, Joseph Haydn was also admitted to this same lodge.

In general, none of this had much to do with the style and quality of the musical works that Wolfgang Amadeus was composing in those years. In an elaborate way, however, there may have been a connection between an image of man in balance between free individuality and yet sedentary and social framework conditions here and the individualization of voices and sound groups within the music industry and with the dramatization of the musical passage of time under genre specifications there.

Rather a conventionally favourable atmosphere emerged for Wolfgang Amadeus's compositional urge to explore, not just on the outside. The artistic liberality to which he was drawn was one of the inner discourses of the musical and theatrical genres, without giving up their framework function. The much-admired interrelationship between the piano concertos and the Lorenzo Da Ponte-operas at this time is just one station in a compositional trend that Wolfgang Amadeus had long been pursuing. A sublime, bold musical world arose here, which, apart from the attraction of the pianist Wolfgang Amadeus Mozart, not everyone understood.

It was all the more important for him to experience the social establishment, also respect and collegiality of musicians of high rank, which simply did not exist in Salzburg when he was a child or an adolescent. Such recognized artists were, for example, Gluck and Salieri – Wolfgang Amadeus may have mistrusted their politeness – as well as musicians with whom he worked in the Van Swieten circle. But this social establishment had many more facets than he currently knew.

Wolfgang Amadeus also composed incidental music of an operatic character for the playwright Baron Tobias Philip Gebler's quasi-Masonic play *Thamos, King of Egypt* between 1773-1780 (KV 345/336a). The ideals of Freemasons appealed to Wolfgang Amadeus, who had sent a letter to Padre Martini with the following words:

> We live in this World in order to learn industriously and by interchanging our ideas, to enlighten one another and this endeavor to promote the sciences and the fine arts. Oh, how often have I longed to be near you, most Reverend Father, so that I might be able to talk to and have discussions with you. For I live in a country, where music leads a struggling existence, though indeed apart from those who have left us, we still have excellent teachers and particularly composers of great wisdom.[55]

It is interesting to observe that many of Wolfgang Amadeus's Viennese friends and acquaintances were Freemasons, for example his brother in law Joseph Lange, the librettist Emanuel Schikaneder, the Moravian-

Austrian classical composer Paul Wranitzky and the textile merchant from Lower Austria, Michael von Puchberg. Wolfgang Amadeus enjoyed the camaraderie of fellow Masons at an eating lodge, where the brothers enjoyed not only good food, but also good discussions, good games and good music. Many important patrons of music also were Masons, like Count Karl Joseph Pálffy de Erdőd, Karl Johann Baptist, Prince of Dietrichstein or Count Johann Baptist Esterhazy of Galantha.

The best minds in Vienna, men of law, medicine, science as well as letters and the arts, were all members of Freemason-lodges. The leading figure of the Austrian enlightenment was perhaps the imperial adviser Joseph von Sonnenfels, an Austrian and German jurist and novelist who was also among the leaders of the Illuminati movement in Austria. He was a close friend of Wolfgang Amadeus and a patron.

No lodge was more firmly committed to working on behalf of Josephine reforms, than the lodge *Zur wahren Eintracht*. In fact, the lodge held meetings twice a week and frequently featured scholarly lectures, but also many presentations and sponsored publications, like *The Journal for Freemasons*, which was launched in 1784. The first issue featured an interesting essay, which dealt with the topic 'About the mysteries of the Egyptians', which stood at the beginning of a cooperation between the German impresario, dramatist, librettist, actor and composer Emmanuel Schikaneder and Wolfgang Amadeus Mozart. This topic might have influenced the two creative men in the conception of the opera *The Magic Flute*.

Several lodges met at the house of Baron Moser, which was situated in the centre of Vienna, at the Landskrongasse, on the second floor in a series of rooms that included a grand meeting hall preserved in a prominent painting of the time, under the title *Initiation Ceremony in a Viennese Masonic Lodge* (1785). To this day the painter has remained anonymous – although Ignaz Unterberger, who also engraved a title page for Mozart's *Maurerfreude*, could be a good candidate, as is also Achaz Gottlieb Raehmel. The painting is now housed at the Wien

Museum (*Museen der Stadt Wien*). The almost one metre wide and three quarters of metre high oil painting, shows a ceremony, at which a blindfolded initiate is about to, but has not yet seen the light. Masonic imagery is visible on the walls and in the clothing of the members. And Wolfgang Amadeus is thought to be the figure on the far right wearing his Masonic apron and square. This painting is seen as a help to understand the Masons of the time and to imagine Wolfgang Amadeus as an active member of the Craft.

Indeed, Wolfgang Amadeus developed a remarkable commitment, both in social and musical terms and dedicated a number of his works to the Freemasons, for example the journeyman's journey song *Lied zur Gesellenreise* (KV 468) – *Die ihr ein Neuen Grade* (KV 468) for a voice and piano or organ accompaniment was written on 26 March 1785. The text basis for the journeyman's journey song was penned by the Viennese writer Joseph Franz Ratschky and was published reprinted in 1785 in the *Journal für Freymaurer* in the version by the composer Johann Holzer. It is assumed that Wolfgang Amadeus had already heard Holzer's version of the song during his own promotion ritual to the journeyman's degree. The specific reason for Wolfgang Amadeus's composition is unclear. The journeyman's song was in fact one for the fellow Craft journey and might have been written in connection with his father's participation in that installation ceremony on 16 April 1785. Whether the song was actually dedicated to Wolfgang Amadeus's father is difficult to prove, given the sources. However, it is very likely that it was composed for a journeyman ritual.

The lodge songs of the Freemasons often had a ritual reference. They were sung at the opening and closing of the lodge or on special occasions. For example, a record of the influential Viennese lodge *Zur wahren Eintracht* shows that 'in journeyman work, vocal music should also be used in addition to instrumental music'. The singing of songs was therefore not uncommon in the Masonic ritual context. Lodge songs were mostly monophonic songs for male voices, sung a cappella or with simple accompaniment.

Wolfgang Amadeus also composed two Masonic songs, which are unfortunately lost, which were performed in August 1785 at *Zur wahren Eintracht* and which he entered in his thematic catalogue, the *Verzeichnis* (called the 'Köchel catalogue') in July. In November of this year his *Masonic Funeral Music* (KV 477) was performed at a lodge of sorrows given by Crowned Hope lodge to honour two recently departed Masons; the German nobleman, sailor and soldier Duke Georg Augustus of Mecklenburg and the Grand Master of the Masonic Lodge L'Orian, Count Franz Esterházy von Galántha. During this year, Wolfgang Amadeus provided music and participated in a number of concerts and performances serving as a kind of resident composer for his and for several other Lodges in Vienna.

At the turn of the year 1785-1786, Emperor Joseph II issued the Masonic Decree, which meant great restrictions and control and was rigorously implemented by the officials, like other patents. In the wake of the new Masonic Decree, two new lodges were established under the supervision of the Grand Master of the Austrian Masonry. The first new lodge *Zur Wahrheit* (To the Truth), which merged four Lodges, was established in January 1786 with Ignaz von Born as Grand Master. It had hundreds of members and seemed to be a success. But suddenly, the atmosphere changed and ill-feeling and dispute grew, so that the memberships dwindled over the following eight months. In addition, internal discord increased, which caused Ignaz von Born to give up his arrogant plans and to withdraw from the lodge work. Ignaz von Born even resigned in 1787 and the Lodge was disbanded two years later.

There was a second big Lodge, which merged four Lodges, which was established with playwright Baron Tobias Philip Gebler as Master in January 1786 with something around 116 members. Wolfgang Amadeus composed various songs for the opening and closing of the first meeting in 1785, for example *Flow this day, beloved brothers* (KV 483) as well as *You, our new leaders* (KV 484).

The composer was certainly among the most loyal members and he was one of only two brothers who maintained his membership from 1784 to 1791. He remained actively engaged after 1786 though he evidently had fewer opportunities to compose Masonic Music. It is important to mention that wherever Wolfgang Amadeus travelled in the next years, he sought out and was welcomed by Masons. For example, when he went to Prague, he was invited by the Lodge Truth and Union (*Zur Wahrheit und Einigkeit*). He also identified himself as a Freemason when he wrote a dedication for his composition for solo piano *Kleine Gigue in G* (KV 574), that he composed during his stay in Leipzig, Germany, in May 1789 and in the guest book of the Saxon court organist, composer and conductor Karl Immanuel Engel. While in Dresden in the same year, he met with fellow Freemason brother Johann Gottlieb Naumann, composer of the Masonic opera *Osiride* from 1781 – which is seen by music experts as a forerunner of Wolfgang Amadeus's own opera *The Magic Flute* – and a collection of Masonic songs *40 Masonic songs* (1782). Needless to say, when Wolfgang Amadeus needed financial assistance, he turned almost exclusively to his Masonic brothers for help. It was the Austrian jurist, Franz Hofdemel who worked at the Austrian Chancellery, Carl Prince Lichnowsky, fifth Prince and seventh Count Lichnowsky, a general of cavalry, and also the textile merchant Johann Michael von Puchberg who all helped him out, if necessary.

Wolfgang Amadeus Mozart even considered the idea of one day founding a secret society on his own, because he was dissatisfied with the existing masonic order. In fact, following Emperor Joseph II's decree, Wolfgang Amadeus was unwilling to come to terms with the decline of Freemasonry, so he intended to make a new start by founding a secret society called *Die Grotte* (The Grotto). After his death, Constanze sent his essay on this special topic to the publisher Breitkopf & Härtel.

In 1785, Wolfgang Amadeus started to compose a cantata *You, soul of the universe* (KV 429), based on the text of fellow Mason Lorenz Leopold Haschka, a Jesuit, poet and author of the words to *God receive Franz the Emperor*, which was Austria's national anthem until 1918.

This cantata was one of Wolfgang Amadeus's densest compositions. Probably created for a ritual celebration of the elevation to the master, it revolves around the confrontation with human mortality. It was intended for the Saint John's Feast in 1786 but has been left incomplete. In 1791 Wolfgang Amadeus was commissioned by Franz Heinrich Ziegenhagen, a merchant, social Utopian and Mason, to compose a cantata for him. It became a small German cantata for one part at the piano – *You who honour the creators of the immeasurable universe, etc* (KV 619).

Written for one voice with piano accompaniment, the cantata's proximity to the opera *The Magic Flute* is clearly noticeable. How the composition was commissioned has not been clarified with certainty, but it may have played a major role that the text contains, in addition to Ziegenhagen's enlightening thoughts, recognizable Masonic ideas and that both Ziegenhagen and Wolfgang Amadeus were Freemasons. Contrary to popular belief, the cantata is not 'Masonic music' in the narrower sense, because it was neither written for a lodge nor intended for use in Masonic lodges. Rather, Wolfgang Amadeus's setting was intended to disseminate Ziegenhagen's ground-breaking socio-political ideas, which found condensed expression in the cantata's text.

When writing the Singspiel *The Magic Flute* later, Wolfgang Amadeus and his librettist Emmanuel Schikaneder appear to have been influenced in a variety of ways by Masonic rituals and thinking, but these elements – for example the Egyptian setting, the role of the trials, the veiling of the initiates, the journey through darkness to light, the ritualized knocking represented in the music by the threefold chord first heard in the overture, and so on – were woven into the setting without any direct affiliation to the Masons. The Singspiel was indeed influenced by the Enlightenment philosophy and can be regarded as advocating enlightened absolutism. The Queen of the Night was often seen to represent a 'dangerous form of obscurantism'; to other music experts she 'represented the Roman Catholic Empress Maria Theresa, who banned the Freemasonry from

Austria'. Nevertheless, whenever we read about Wolfgang Amadeus's most famous opera being 'a Freemason instrument', we can be assured that it was simply not one of them, however it was only too often interpreted in connection with Freemasonry. Wolfgang Amadeus's final Masonic music composition *A Little Masonic Cantata* (KV 623), was composed by him for the inaugural meeting in the new premises of *New Crowned Hope Lodge* and premiered on 17 November with the composer himself conducting his own piece of music.

In 1789 there was only one lodge in Vienna to which Wolfgang Amadeus belonged. His music, throughout these years in Vienna, fostered a shared spirit of camaraderie, reverence and music-making, that was quite essential to the bonds of brotherhood. Wolfgang Amadeus's commitment to his allies, the Freemasons and the various Lodges he worked for, goes far beyond his music, it begins in his heart, goes along with his search for the right melody, then continues on the composition of the right piece and has been a strong commitment to him. He was – undoubtedly – a loving and caring composer and a wonderful dedicated brother to all of the members of the Lodges of Vienna.

Chapter 8

Mozart – The King of Love and Music

The social establishment, getting to know celebrities in the salons of high society, the opportunity to perform and organize concerts together with outstanding musicians from different genres, was a highlight in the short life of the now 28-year-old Wolfgang Amadeus Mozart. The truth is that he had already achieved everything that a musician and composer – in his, but also in our current time – could only dream of. He was not only well-known in Vienna, but in different European cities. He was popular, and gave endless concerts, which were not only attended by the high society, but also in large numbers by the citizens of Vienna. He had become a superstar and he was a music authority when it came to composing and collaborating with various artists. But – most of all – there was no doubt that his music was heavenly.

'Anyone who wants to understand the poet must go to the poet's country.' Goethe's sentence applies to Wolfgang Amadeus Mozart as it does to every creative genius. Wolfgang Amadeus's ascent to becoming the star of society began barely a year after his arrival in Vienna in 1781. He excelled as a composer and pianist, the aristocratic and bourgeois salons clamoured for him. He enjoyed the favour of the emperor, who attended most of his concerts and commissioned him to write operas. Praise also came from the composer Joseph Haydn. 'Your son is the greatest composer I know personally and by name,' he said to Leopold, 'he has taste, and the greatest knowledge of composition.' Wolfgang Amadeus's subscription concerts and academies were huge successes and his income in 1784 was estimated to be – at least – 10,000 guilders, which is around £213,000 today.

Everybody would have liked to imagine Wolfgang Amadeus was not only a 'King of Music' and a 'King of Pop', but also a handsome man, at least 6ft tall, beautiful as hell and a pure diplomat of music. But unfortunately, this was not the case. He is said to have been remarkably small, around 5ft, and rather unsightly. An oversized head sat on a slender body and he was pale, with a slightly pockmarked skin and a large and broad nose. In the paintings showcased in his birthplace in Salzburg, Wolfgang Amadeus's eye colour seemed to be different in each eye. The reason for this is that in the eighteenth century, artists liked to give their subjects blue eyes – which was a beauty ideal at the time. But Wolfgang Amadeus probably had dark-green or even brown eyes in reality. In Vienna they spoke of the 'enormously afflicted Mr. Mozart'. On the other hand, his eye was fiery, even if the gaze was often absent-minded.

He was constantly on the move and was a hyperactive person. His hands were beautiful and so was his hair, and he liked to dress exquisitely – with the help of his patrons in the Viennese society. His estate included coats made from Chinese and satin silk, fur coats and handkerchiefs made from lace. He dressed in fact like a chamberlain, but unfortunately his demeanour did not always match. He was considered cheerful, friendly, enormously helpful and – sometimes – also shockingly naive. He was no match for the hypocrisy and intrigues of the society around him. He was highly sensitive, irritable and he could get excited about trifles. Then he'd jump up like gunpowder or faint trembling.

But Wolfgang Amadeus had also another side, another face; he was notorious for his poisonous outbursts, his haughtiness towards colleagues. He knew he was better and he showed it to them with all his energy. Once he improvised so supernaturally on the piano in the salon of the writer and pianist Karoline Pichler that everyone held their breath. Pichler told friends, that:

Once when I was sitting at the grand piano and playing the *Non più andrai* from *Figaro*, Mozart, who was with us at the time, stepped up behind me and I had to please him, because he was growling along with the melody and beat the beat on my shoulders. Suddenly he pulled up a chair, sat down, asked me to continue playing the bass, and began to vary impromptu so beautifully that everyone listened with bated breath to the tones of the German Orpheus.

Suddenly, however, the thing became repugnant to him, he started up and, in his foolish mood, began, as he often did, 'to jump over the table and chair, meowing like a cat and doing somersaults'.

Wolfgang Amadeus's fans were even more disturbed by his lust for dirty things, his inexhaustible enthusiasm for 'shit, farts and dirt – oh sweet word'. According to the motto 'Everything smart makes a headache', he rhymed in the canon, '...good night, fuck the bed that's cracking; good night, sleep soundly and healthily and stretch your ass to your mouth.'

'Everything is already composed – but not yet written', Mozart once noted. He worked best when there was a party, people and hustle and bustle around him, even when bowling, in a carriage or playing billiards. Basically, he just put down on paper with flying pen what was already in his head. He almost always wrote it down right away, he hardly ever corrected anything, and sometimes he even came up with a new composition. Most of the time he had no time. He wrote the overture to *Don Giovanni* in Prague two nights before the premiere. The copyists hardly had time to copy them, the orchestra had to play *prima vista*, without having rehearsed beforehand.

What must his father – who was a respected composer, but also the author of a famous violin tutor-book and vice-kapellmeister of the prince-archbishop's court orchestra in Salzburg – have felt, when he suddenly realized, that a 'little, curious monster' was sitting at his table in Salzburg at No. 9 Getreidegasse. Incidentally, an amiable and noticeably needy child who climbed onto the piano stool at the age of three, received his first lessons at the age of four, learning incredibly quickly, and at the age of five banged his first composition into the keys.

However, in reality, only Wolfgang Amadeus's own utterances can inform us of the very core of his being. A lot of contemporary testimonies and observations about his personality are available, good and bad in a colourful mixture, much of it will even be correct if checked accordingly. One understands the impression that this extraordinary musical phenomenon made on ordinary people of the time and the frictions to which it was exposed in reality.

But the primary sources, letters and works, are also testimonies of the first rank, and only a few of them do not contain a piece of Mozartian individuality. But they were been written in one particular moment and are determined by the personalities of the recipients. Although Wolfgang Amadeus Mozart only very rarely entrusted his heart to the people to whom he wrote. The letter-writing Wolfgang Amadeus was fundamentally none other than the composer. On the contrary, it is the same forces that determine his external life and his artistic work. Nevertheless, one should not apply to him the standard of the ordinary mortal. His actual source of life was, and always remained, his artistic vision and work. He saturated his bourgeois existence, so that it was no longer understood by those around him. 'Apart from music, he was and always will be like a child,' his sister Maria Anna said later about him. His own sister felt the same way when she chose the term 'child' to describe his nature in a general way, and it was very popular with her contemporaries. This was in fact the statement that Wolfgang Amadeus's world was fundamentally different from that of ordinary people. He did not need any stimulus from outside, but he did not tolerate any arbitrary interruption either. Artistic creation was the true essence of Wolfgang Amadeus and thus also his destiny. It is known of other well-known musicians – including George Frederick Handel, Joseph Haydn and Ludwig van Beethoven – that they saw themselves as 'vessels of a higher power'. It was the expression of their own awareness that their creative power reached far beyond themselves. Although there exists no similar statement by Wolfgang Amadeus, this in no way precludes the possibility that this feeling of the 'demonic', as Goethe called it, was also present in him.

His father could compose, summon art and say goodbye whenever and as often as he pleased. But Wolfgang Amadeus's creativity did not allow him to be dictated to by any laws from the outside, but instead shaped his external life according to his own. One cannot separate this from his art; it is the same force at work here as there. Above all, Wolfgang Amadeus had a sharp intellect and was also completely free of aimless daydreaming in his work. But it was far from his intention to base his worldview on thinking as such, or even to strive for a complete system for this purpose. In this respect he was and remained an artist, a particularly sensuous person, whose world was that of views and feelings, but not that of concepts.

He did not measure life by a certain sum of cognitive principles, but he was much more inclined to measure these principles by life and he followed Goethe's wisdom – 'Because we depend on life and not on contemplation.'

Wolfgang Amadeus was a man of genuine, conscious morality, just as far removed from the amorality of so many stormers and pushers as from the over-morality of a certain and special modern art style known as Gypsyism, which was created by imitating and accentuating the found poetic and musical material. He owed a lot to the healthy atmosphere of his parents' home, so kindness and helpfulness were innate in him, but the morality that he gradually created for himself was not a categorical duty for him, as it was for Ludwig van Beethoven, the kindred spirit of Immanuel Kant and Friedrich von Schiller, but rather a duty which came simply from giving his nature free rein; he was morally out of inner need and therefore far removed from moral narrowness. With Leopold Mozart morality was rooted in rationalism, but with his son it was rooted in humanity. His conscience was extremely finely developed and revealed all the sensitivity of the eighteenth century.

The old saying that we are masters at the first step and servants at the second, was fulfilled in him. Such a conflict tends to drag down smaller natures to the point of complete mental insensitivity. Wolfgang Amadeus fought his way through, albeit in pain, without suffering any internal damage. How much that cost him, to go his own way to his highest goals, he also settled with his conscience alone and with real nobility of his soul fulfilled the duty to the end that the contrast between his world and his self-chosen marriage bond imposed on him.

It is particularly appealing to follow how Wolfgang Amadeus' humour developed from satire to irony the more he distanced himself from the Italians. Was the character of Osmin from the Singspiel *The Abduction from the Seraglio* essentially a satirical character? One did not get the impression that it was a piece of Wolfgang Amadeus's own nature, as if these character traits had bothered him internally? Later, however, one has the feeling that Wolfgang Amadeus himself felt the weaknesses and self-consciousness of his characters and only reproduced them from a standpoint superior to them. That is why the satire became that strangely warming irony that completely replaced a common kind of comedy.

It was sometimes almost as if the creator looked down on his own creations with satisfaction and a cheerful smile. Like no other in musical drama, Wolfgang Amadeus was able to live at the same time with the people of the moment and with the idealists, and at the same time to constantly measure the two opposites against one another.

In previous operas, both serious and comic, there were no surprises for the listener as far as mood and characterization were concerned, but with Wolfgang Amadeus he was never sure whether the seriousness was turning ridiculous or the ridiculous into seriousness, and yet never had the impression of the arbitrary and accidental, but of the most immediate life. It was a tremendous step from theatre to real drama, which opera owed to Wolfgang Amadeus Mozart. But this position towards man also determined his relationship to society and the state. Back then, society was incomparably more important for the individual than what is understood by it today, more important than the state. In the case of the artist in particular, it determined not only his external existence, but also and foremost his art.

With Wolfgang Amadeus, counts and nobleman-characters primarily moved sensual passion in a constant struggle with their self-confidence; their status as a count was only relevant insofar as it was the outward expression of that self-confidence, of that insistence on an old master's right.

In short, what was his primary aim was not the social, but the human. Accordingly, Wolfgang Amadeus attached almost no importance to the external environment etc. Man binds him only as an independent personality, not as a result of factual circumstances and relationships. That's why he was never a politician, because the state was far less important to him than society as a primary experience, and political theories belonged entirely to him in the realm of the abstract, removed from sensual perception, with which he did not know what to do.

Here again there was a wide chasm between him and his father, who thought and acted with an eye to politics. The son, on the other hand, was fairly indifferent to political principles, he only felt for the people who represented them and therefore never allowed himself to be determined by political considerations in his choice of associates.

Wolfgang Amadeus had a soul that was particularly receptive to friendship. As he closed himself to the world without hate, so he looked throughout his life for a friend with whom he could have shared his innermost being. It was not just the joy of harmless sociability that drove him again and again to people, but the drive to work from person to person, to let his own nature continue to work in others and in return to gain enrichment and relief from them. The stronger the ideal of humanity lit up in him, the more vividly the urge awoke in him to put the principle of universal human brotherhood into practice.

In addition, there was an innate goodness of heart and that is why he was always ready to help his fellow human beings in all external and internal needs. And yet he never imposed himself on people. On the contrary, he had the strange gift, again flowing from his observation, of immediately instinctively examining every person who turned to him, for what he himself had to offer him.

Love played an even more important role than friendship in Wolfgang Amadeus's experience and it had accompanied him throughout his life since his youth. That is why the urge to love was always alive in Wolfgang Amadeus. He in particular was never destined to see his dream realized, as was the case with Robert Schumann through his union with his Clara.

With Aloysia Weber, the sister of his wife Constanze, whom he greatly admired and loved, he was close to it for a long time. A later trace points to Maria Theresa von Trattner, his first piano student in Vienna. With his wife Constanze, on the other hand, he saw himself further than ever far away from that goal, and so he was forced – both artistically and personally – to make do with what he got.

This renunciation did not touch the slumbering urge to love. On the contrary, it appeared more and more as a driving force in his dramatic art. It is rightly emphasized again and again in music circles, that the basic theme of Wolfgang Amadeus's operatic art, was love. In the older sense, as gallantry, he understood love only in his youthful operas, where, for lack of real experience, he was dependent on his role models. For the mature Wolfgang Amadeus, on the other hand, it was something completely different, a primal and natural force that, depending on how it met other inner forces, elevated or humiliated, liberated or crushed the human being, but under all circumstances became his fate.

In the face of such a primal phenomenon there is, of course, again no moral standard, no difference between good and evil. Wolfgang Amadeus knew love neither as a sin nor as a redeemer. He certainly did not exclude love based on morality, for it too was one of the realities of life for him, but it was not an ideal against which everything else could be measured.

Yes, Wolfgang Amadeus was particularly fond of juxtaposing these different forms in the same drama. In him we encounter a force of nature in the most varied expressions; as a demonic life instinct, as passion in its various degrees, as a moral power and as a dull natural instinct together with its caricature, lust. In the versatility of his ability to experience love and to present it artistically, Wolfgang Amadeus had no equal in the history of opera.

Several sources show that Wolfgang was also an outspoken animal lover. Domestic animals, dogs and birds, feature prominently in his letters. The Mozart family didn't keep hamsters or goldfish in their apartment on Makartplatz, but they had songbirds. In addition, they also had a dog, a fox terrier, with the name of Pimperl. This dog was adored by the whole family and amusingly had the run of the household. When Wolfgang Amadeus lived in Vienna, he also had several birds, including a starling. He even dedicated a poem to the bird upon its passing: *Poem to a Dead Starling* 1787.

At times he also had a close relationship with horses, for during his years in Vienna we hear of daily morning rides which he had to undertake on medical advice. However, he never became a passionate rider, because he never got rid of a certain fearfulness on horseback. Although his attitude towards religion was determined to a large extent by his external environment and especially by his upbringing, it developed entirely in accordance with his other nature. Given the nature of his father, it goes without saying that he was brought up in the strictest Catholic dogma. He thus also shared his point of view in relation to other confessions, albeit to a lesser extent.

In this way, he strictly separated the Lutheran composers from other composers, and in 1778 he particularly wished to be employed in a Catholic place. In fact, he remained a faithful follower of the Catholic Church to the end, even when he began to be more critical of its dogmas.

Chapter 9

Mozart's Collaboration with Musical Partner Haydn

For the social establishment, important facets of getting to know each other between celebrities were given in the stunning high-level salons of high society in Vienna. Wolfgang Amadeus Mozart knew these salons from his youth, where the entire power of intellectuality was concentrated in just one place. At the same time, it gave the opportunity to organize concerts together with outstanding musicians, concerts of different genres and – perhaps most importantly – they gave him the same intensifying contact with the Austrian composer and expert for chamber music, such as string quartet and piano trio, Joseph Hadyn.

In a series of string quartets dedicated to him and published, Wolfgang Amadeus always was extremely respectful towards his friend. He even called Haydn '*Padre*', '*Guido*' and '*Amico mio*' in the preface. This designation seemed important, because in Haydn – who, at the time, was without any doubt the leading composer in Europe – Wolfgang Amadeus found a very special musical partner, who also took him seriously. Because Haydn had a keen sense of the level of Wolfgang Amadeus's artistic creativity, their discourses took place over the years in many cool conversations, in the form of making music together and – what was particularly fruitful – in composing together. Their works – specifically Joseph Haydn's *Op. 33 String Quartets* and subsequently his *Six Haydn String Quartets* (KV 387, KV 421/417b, KV 428/421b, KV 458, KV 464, KV 465) dedicated by Wolfgang Amadeus in 1785 to Joseph Haydn in admiration of his op 33, something that is now referred to as 'intertextuality' – are a great pleasure to trace for anyone interested in music. The *Six Haydn*

String Quartets contain some of Wolfgang Amadeus's most memorable melodic compositions as well as refined compositional ideas.

In fact, Joseph Haydn heard the six quartets for the very first time at two invitations to Wolfgang Amadeus's house – on 15 January and 12 February 1785. After hearing the music of his fellow composer, he was so enthusiastic that he made a well-known remark about Wolfgang Amadeus to Leopold, who was visiting Vienna at the time, 'I say to you before God, as an honest man, your son is the greatest composer that I know in both person and name: he has taste, and beyond that the greatest knowledge of composition.'[56]

This praise from Joseph Haydn was passed on in a letter that Leopold Mozart wrote to his daughter on 16 February of the same year. One difference between the two composers was that Wolfgang Amadeus was very fixed on Vienna, while Joseph Haydn fulfilled and enjoyed composition commissions and performances abroad.

However, Wolfgang Amadeus was settled in Vienna. Another son, Carl Thomas was born to him and his wife Constanze in September. The two of them were over the moon. The previous summer, Wolfgang Amadeus' sister Maria Anna had met the magistrate Johann Baptist Franz von Berchtold zu Sonnenburg and on 23 August had married him, settling with him in Saint Gilgen, a village in Austria about 29 km east of the Mozart family home in Salzburg. While in the summer of 1783 she had developed a relationship with Franz d'Ippold, who was a captain and private tutor, unfortunately this relationship did not evolve into a marriage. Von Berchtold zu Sonnenburg was twice a widower and had five children from his two previous marriages, whom Maria Anna helped to bring up. However, she continued to see herself as a pianist, practising three hours a day and continuing to teach the piano. As a brother with experience in marriage, Wolfgang Amadeus wrote her a lovingly suggestive and also self-deprecating poem from his 'poetic brain box'. And he continued to maintain a close relationship with his father. That is why he suggested Leopold Mozart move to Vienna in the summer of 1784 and even asked his sister to help him convince his father. Because of her marriage, Wolfgang Amadeus worried that his father might become lonely in their apartment in Salzburg.

Leopold visited Munich in February 1785 and then went to Vienna to spend two and a half months with his son. The father observed exactly how his son was doing in married life and accepted that Wolfgang Amadeus introduced him to Viennese society and concert life. During this time, he also applied for admission to the Masonic lodge *To Charity*, enjoyed life in Vienna, the social evenings and – most of all – making music with his son on the occasion of social invitations. He was also deeply delighted, as soon as he listened to his son at his concerts. Leopold Mozart met many famous personalities, but over time it became too much for him and news also came from Salzburg, where the court chamber threatened him that, if he did not return to Salzburg by mid-May, they would stop paying him. That is why he packed his bags and left Vienna on 25 April. Constanze and Wolfgang Amadeus accompanied him as far as a village outside Vienna with the name of Purkersdorf. They ate with him one last time a good dinner and then he got into his carriage. Leopold Mozart drove back to Salzburg via Linz and Munich with his travel companion, the violinist Heinrich Marchand. In Munich, Leopold even indulged in social life and enjoyed it again, before finally returning to his beloved Salzburg.

In the meantime, Wolfgang Amadeus was working on a new opera. Four years had passed since his last full-length opera *The Abduction from the Seraglio*. During this time, he had mastered his skills with ground-breaking compositions, especially in the field of the piano concerto and the string quartet.

Lorenzo da Ponte, who was valued by Emperor Joseph II, worked together with Antonio Salieri, the court music director at the time, but their opera *Un ricco d'un giorno* unfortunately had little success. Salieri was furious and accused Lorenzo da Ponte of having failed and then turned to his rival Giovanni Battista Casti. Da Ponte was now able to join forces with his colleague Wolfgang Amadeus. Giovanni Paisiello's opera

Il Barbiere di Siviglia was a popular example which succeeded in Vienna and so both men decided to write and compose a sequel to Paisiello's opera. Da Ponte wrote that he personally said to Emperor Joseph II, that the opera could be performed in contrast to the theatrical version. Among other things, Mozart played a few numbers for the emperor. Objections from the court theatre director Franz Xaver Wolfgang von Orsini-Rosenberg and his favourite Giambattista Casti were finally overcome. Compared to the original, Da Ponte softened many morally questionable passages and left out some details, that would hardly have been understood in Vienna. On the other hand, he left the political tensions largely unchanged. The language is less rhetorical, on the other hand more emotional and sensual, the action easier to understand than Beaumarchais. Da Ponte noted that the piece was completed in six weeks. *Le Nozze di Figaro* did not tie in with the plot of *The Barbier of Sevilla*, but did contain a number of typical plot elements that could be found in Italian operas previously performed in Vienna.

The opera's libretto was written by Lorenzo Da Ponte and was based on the 1778 comedy *La Folle Journée ou le Mariage de Figaro* by Pierre Augustin Caron de Beaumarchais. In February 1785, it was listed by the theatre troupe of Emanuel Schikaneder and Hubert Kumpfs at Vienna's Theatre am Kärntnertor, which was later named Theatre an der Wien. The scandalous play provoked problems with the censors. The rule of the nobility was openly criticized, the count's immorality was drastically painted, while the third estate, represented by the servants Figaro and Susanna, was upgraded. Censors banned the planned performance but allowed the play to be printed.

The political injunctions demanded by Emperor Joseph II were made by da Ponte in his libretto for Mozart. This lessened the explosive nature and brought it closer to the genre of an *opera buffa*. This is probably the unspectacular reason why the premiere of *Le Nozze de Figaro* took place on 1 May 1786 at the *Burgtheatre* did not cause a sensation, although the best singers available in Vienna at the time were hired. Unfortunately, while other theatrical events were discussed at length, *Figaro* was largely ignored and it had only moderate success with the public. But the actual explosiveness brought only Wolfgang Amadeus's music to the piece. His lack of great success with *Figaro* expressed his old dilemma, namely, the balance he was striving for between his delight in musical imagination on the one hand and his work on the other hand, making the social place of a musical genre compatible with the public.

Piano chamber music and the string quartet, which had become just as popular in the 1780s, were initially two important genres for house concerts, but pieces that could hardly be used in public concerts. They should rather be adapted to the abilities of a good dilettante. What was considered acceptable by a composer like Joseph Haydn, because of his international popularity and fame, was in fact ingenious in compositions by Wolfgang Amadeus Mozart, but then felt 'a bit overdone'. This was even true of the six string quartets that Wolfgang Amadeus composed which were dedicated to Joseph Haydn for promotional purposes.

The *Magazine of Music* published in Hamburg (later in Copenhagen) by Carl Friedrich Cramer, was critical, saying that Wolfgang Amadeus's 'artificial and really beautiful movement' was recognized, but in this Wolfgang Amadeus 'has set himself *much* too high'. And the critic goes on to say in derogatory terms, 'Everything is probably too heavily seasoned – and what palate can endure that for a long time.'

Nevertheless, in *Figaro* and in the six *Haydn quartets*, Wolfgang Amadeus found his personal answers as a composer to the challenge of finding the right music genre. What drove him as a composer to place his music in a tense relationship with conventional expectations, can be formulated retrospectively from the point of view of idealism and in the words of the philosopher Hegel as 'Mozart's success'. Especially in this phase of his life, he was a happy player in a society that wanted to be challenged by his works.

This historical situation had something oriented towards unrealistic expectations. Wolfgang Amadeus tried to overcome his grief – due to the discord within some Masonic lodges in Vienna which really affected him, because he took his calling in the lodges extremely seriously – with his exciting artistic life. A wonderful experience came to his aid, that he had never expected. For the moderate success of the opera *Le Nozze di Figaro* in Vienna became an incomparably special one with its neighbours in Prague. In 1786, his opera was performed again and again. Needless to say, the economic conditions of the Czech opera company improved considerably.

Unlike in Vienna, Italian opera had been introduced and continuously cultivated in Prague for decades. In addition, there was an extremely positive atmosphere in the city of Prague itself. The Austrian Emperor Joseph II was particularly fond of the rich Bohemian lands. He promoted cultural life and especially Czech literature.

At the beginning of 1787, the circle of music lovers invited Wolfgang Amadeus to Prague and published a poem in his homage. He was so overwhelmed that he sent the poem to his father in Salzburg, then he answered them very quickly and drove to Prague with his wife, a servant and nine musician friends, where they arrived on 11 January 1787. He lived with his wife and his nine colleagues in the palace of Count Johann Joseph Franz Graf von Thun-Hohenstein. The next evening, they attended a ball together and immersed themselves in the bliss of the hustle and bustle of society in the Czech capital. Wherever he was in Prague, Wolfgang Amadeus kept hearing melodies from his *Figaro*. On 15 January he wrote to his friend, the composer, musician and civil servant Gottfried von Jacquin, with whom he had a very close and heartfelt friendship:

Dearest friend! –

At last I have found a moment to write to you, sir; – I was resolved to write easily four letters to Vienna on arriving, but in vain! ...

...for here they are talking about nothing except – Figaro; nothing is played, tooted, sung and whistled except – Figaro: no-one goes to any opera except – Figaro and eternally Figaro; certainly a great honour for me.

But now Wolfgang Amadeus Mozart, the composer of the opera, was right there in Prague and the whole city revolved around him. He was celebrated. A good moment to perform his *Prague D major symphony* (KV 504). Whoever pays close attention, will hear some familiar sounds that can also be heard in *Le Nozze de Figaro*. That is why the theatre salesman and opera singer from Bruneck in Italy, impresario Pasquale Bondini, immediately met with and then ordered a new opera from Wolfgang Amadeus for the next autumn season. Well acquainted with Prague and the wonderful and respectful Prague theatre scene, the Mozarts left for Vienna after one month.

Amidst the wonderful high spirits of Wolfgang Amadeus's family, concern suddenly arose about the state of health of his father. In February 1787, Leopold Mozart attended the Munich carnival. Afterwards, as soon as he was back in Salzburg, he received exciting guests, who were sent to him by his son. Nancy Storace, accompanied by her brother Stephen, mother Elizabeth, the singer Michael O'Kelly and Wolfgang Amadeus's composition student Thomas Atwood, were returning to London from Vienna, where Attwood wanted to explore the possibility of an opera contract and the possibility of organizing a concert. And in Salzburg they met with Leopold Mozart. But in mid-March, Leopold Mozart suddenly fell ill. His daughter Maria Anna came to Salzburg to take care of him. She was worried about her beloved father and by 14 April he was seriously ill.

Meanwhile, Wolfgang Amadeus was once again thinking about the path of his career; he was active and had his head full of plans. He toyed with the idea of travelling to England, even taking English lessons, while his friend and colleague Joseph Haydn was currently negotiating with an English impresario. On 4 April, Wolfgang

Amadeus wrote a letter to Leopold. He was alarmed by the news from Maria Anna, although he did not travel to Salzburg to see him. In this last letter, Wolfgang Amadeus described death as 'life's true end' and its 'true, best friend'. When Leopold Mozart finally died on 28 May, little information is available on how Wolfgang Amadeus took his father's death. The postscript that he included in a letter to his good friend in Vienna, Gottfried von Jacquin suggested that – despite all the quarrels and the partial estrangement the two men had during Leopold's lifetime – Wolfgang Amadeus's father's death was definitely a great shock to his son. 'I inform you that on returning home today I received the sad news of my most beloved father's death. You can imagine the state I am in.'[57]

Unfortunately, Wolfgang Amadeus was unable to attend the funeral, because travelling to Salzburg would take too much time and he had important music obligations in Vienna. He later wrote a letter to his sister Maria Anna on 2 June, ruthlessly and coldly, in which he stated that he agreed to the public sale of his father's estate.

On 1 October he travelled to Prague with his wife, leaving their 3-year-old son Carl in a Viennese educational institution. Officially, he remained distant from the death of his father, but what it looked like inside Wolfgang Amadeus was probably completely different and was never made public. However, it remained a fact that his work, the composing, distracted him. In the meantime, he had developed and composed the opera *Don Giovanni* and was now in his artistic bliss. Undoubtedly, in this new opera the expectations of an *opera buffa* seem shifted. The excitement before the end of the opera work and the success of the first series of performances, which started on 29 October, gave Wolfgang Amadeus hardly any time to ponder more deeply. Especially the furioso of joie de vivre in the famous 'champagne aria' of the opera is only a momentary counterpoint to the state in which the staring seducer finds himself throughout the opera's plot. Don Giovanni is in fact always the loser in everything he undertakes, and he is always on the run. Yet, it is not a caricature of its claim. The librettist da Ponte and also Wolfgang Amadeus as a composer have both extremely strongly emphasized the moral component in *Don Giovanni*, more so than other dramatists did in operas of this period.

The divine judgment in Don Giovanni's descent into hell breaks through all earlier ambiguities. The constant fading from serious to cheerful offended the audience from the start – although at that time the mixture of *opera seria* and *opera buffa* was not common. The approach of Wolfgang Amadeus and da Pontes repeatedly challenged profound interpretations.

Interestingly, both men followed a tradition of Spanish and Portuguese comedy in which the mixture between comedy and tragedy was inherent in the genre. The intensity of their musical implementation by Wolfgang Amadeus meant a great moment of humanity, to have been a part of it was a wonderful experience for da Ponte – at least that's how he described it in his autobiography written in New York.

The world was just wonderful and his stay in Prague was a real treat. When Wolfgang Amadeus and Constanze were finally on their way back to their home in Vienna, Christoph Willibald Gluck died on 15 November. Three weeks later, Emperor Joseph II appointed Wolfgang Amadeus as chamber composer and as Gluck's successor. From then on, he earned 800 guilders. An honourable office, but unfortunately not what Wolfgang Amadeus had dreamed of. His father would have been so proud of him – but regrettably he was already dead. Meanwhile, Wolfgang Amadeus's operas *Le Nozze de Figaro* and *Don Giovanni* were performed more often in German-speaking countries – albeit only in German versions – but sadly rarely performed in Italy. In Vienna, unfortunately, *Don Giovanni* had only a moderate success.

The concise judgment of Joseph II, which he wrote to his theatre director Count Rosenberg-Orsini, is indicative of the assessment of even well-meaning people – '*La Musique de Mozard est bien trop difficile pour le chant*'. And although the assessment that the music was 'too difficult to sing' was later to be spectacularly refuted, a German critic summed up the reactions of many people towards the end of the 1780s when he wrote 'The beautiful, the great and the noble in music to the Don Juan will always only be obvious to a small bunch of chosen ones. It's not music for everyone's taste that just tickles the ear and starves the heart.'

New commissions for operas did not arise immediately, not even in Prague, and the number of Wolfgang Amadeus's concert appearances also fell significantly. Something crept in that threatened to hurt his artistic euphoria at its base, despite the fact, that he had just achieved courtly security. Viennese society was not bored with the attraction of the pianist and composer Wolfgang Amadeus, of course they were already very used to it, which always made people careless. But the decisive, hard-to-grasp reason was the change in the atmosphere in Vienna and one thing above all; namely the general political climate.

Although Emperor Joseph II's work had shown lasting advances in the fields of education, science, and public health, those in economic, fiscal, and ecclesiastical policies were of dubious use, and what's more, they offended deep-rooted customs among subjects. The emperor's contempt for the institutions of the Estates proved to be more dangerous. In 1787, rebellions against centralist efforts began in Belgium. Although this restricted his freedom of action, he embarked on his second trip to Russia to meet Tsarina Catherine II. The Ottoman Empire felt increasingly encircled and declared war on Russia, with whom Emperor Joseph II had settled at the end of the year, despite all other difficulties in a declaration of war allies in turn. And so, to everyone's displeasure, a little successful Turkish war began. All of this drew forces, means and interest from the cultural life of the metropolis of Vienna. The emperor's absence for the whole of 1788 also proved unpopular. He only returned from the field towards the end of the year and attended – how could it be otherwise – a performance of *Don Giovanni*.

Meanwhile, Wolfgang Amadeus evolved as the emperor's court composer, for example, by generating new ways of composing music and by developing new sounds. As court composer he had to generate dance music for many dazzling events in the Redoutensaal – in this case, it was music that had a broad impact.

He also tried to place less demanding genres – such as piano music for young pianists – with publishers of scores. But the pressure of demanding chamber music did not find many interested parties. The plan to organize academies at the casino could not be realized either. The subscription concerts, which used to be very successful, met with very little interest from the public. His piano teaching activity also no longer flourished. And therefore, he had to realize that the really lucrative musicians' businesses were declining significantly. Added to this were his worries about Constanze, who was constantly ill after her pregnancies and that also cost a lot of money. The income fell, but a fixed salary of 800 guilders per year was earned. Still, he wasn't poor. He was lucky that in 1787 he received 1,000 guilders from his father's estate, as well as another 1,000 guilders for a concert in Prague and then another 450 guilders for *Don Giovanni*. A middle-class life – even in Vienna, which was so expensive – would actually be easy to deny.

But the bitter reality was different. Wolfgang Amadeus Mozart was in debt. His lodge brother Michael von Puchberg was constantly harassed by him with humiliating begging letters until 1791. Since the spring of 1788, Wolfgang Amadeus had been in debt to him under the given circumstances, however, this was quite incomprehensible. Nonetheless, he was not left unscathed. He was visibly offended that the success he knew for such a long time, as a child, then as a teenager and last as 20-year-old, suddenly failed to materialize. The numerous commissions that he had easily got before also ceased to exist. What kind of world was that? Wolfgang Amadeus fell into a deep depression during the summer of 1788, writing in letters to Michael von Puchberg about his 'black thoughts':

> Come and visit me; I'm always at home; – I worked more in the 10 days that I live here than the 2 months in other lodgings, and if I didn't have such black thoughts (which I have to shake off with violence) I would be doing even better than I live pleasantly, – comfortably – and – cheaply. – I don't want to keep her any longer with my babble, but keep quiet and hope.

Forever her bonded servant true friend & O.B. WA Mozart.[58]

It has been suggested that he may have had a cyclothymic personality, which caused emotional ups and downs and was linked with manic depressive tendencies, which could explain not only his depression, but also other aspects of his behaviour, including his spells of hectic creativity. But one thing was absolutely sure; during this period his musical performance slowly declined.

One gets also the impression that he had slipped between a 'conflict between appearance and being' – or between his artistic and the social urge to develop and a darkening hopelessness in the late phase of the reign of Joseph II. Wolfgang Amadeus was no longer able to find a balance for himself in his very special tightrope act. Suddenly, he fell back into a behavioural pattern of a typical escape attempt with these fictional circumstances that had shaped his life before the Vienna period. It started with a whole bar of lawsuits against Vienna.

But as always, he did not give up, but instead he continued to fight with all his strength for his existence as a music artist. He sat down and in the summer of 1788 he composed the *Triad of symphonies in E flat major, G minor and C major*, which represented the pinnacle of his symphonic life. He worked intensively for the influential Dutch-born

Austrian diplomat, librarian and government official Baron Gottfried van Swieten as an arranger and performer of Handel's oratorios. But all this remained an external stop for a deep irritation; it also speaks of the suppression of old family ties from his life. Wolfgang Amadeus still did not travel to Salzburg to view his father's grave. Instead, he wrote a letter to Maria Anna on 12 August 1788, sending her his 'latest piano pieces'. It would be his last letter to his sister. He dismissed her in this way from his field of attention.

Wolfgang Amadeus was now 33 years old. And as it always is, things may happen suddenly, but they happen. For example, a tour of three countries. His decision to spontaneously seize an opportunity that arose at the beginning of April 1789 to accompany Prince Karl Lichnowsky – who was a fellow Mason and his student – on a trip to Berlin, also fitted into this picture and became one of his adulthood journeys to a series of cities between Austria, Czechoslovakia and Germany. This journey, which was full of nostalgia on Wolfgang Amadeus's side, took place during a difficult time in his life.

In fact, it was mortifying for him to admit, but it was at a time, when Wolfgang Amadeus was not earning what he expected from the concerts he gave. Not enough for him and his family that he had to support. This tour-trip lasted almost two months; Lichnowsky had offered him the ride. The programme was very tight, but the trip to Berlin did not bring in much money at all. It looked more like a disaster trip for the creative composer.

Although he was negotiating a new opera with the Italian tenor singer, producer and impresario Domenico Guardasoni in Prague, he was also giving concerts in Dresden at the court of Frederick Augustus I of Saxony, who reigned as the last Elector of Saxony from 1763 to 1806 as Frederick Augustus III in the Holy Roman Empire.

In Saxony, under Elector Frederick Augustus III, up until the 1870s, one rarely had the opportunity to become acquainted with his music. The after-effects of the Seven Years' War were still very noticeable. But cultural life slowly began to flourish again and became an important part of a self-confident bourgeoisie. Compared to Vienna, Salzburg, Mannheim, Paris, Prague and Berlin, the Saxon residences seemed to have to take a step back.

And when Wolfgang Amadeus embarked on his new concert tour from Vienna via Prague in 1789, the goal was not the hope of much honour and fame in Dresden, but in Prussian Berlin. The fact that the trip – after the rather casually planned encounters – experienced its particularly noteworthy significance in Dresden and Leipzig testified to an open-minded, art-loving climate in the country.

But Wolfgang Amadeus was not unknown; traveling theatre companies like the Electoral Saxon Privileged German Actors who performed the opera *The Abduction from the Seraglio* for the first time in Dresden in 1785 at the Redoutensaal, the Theatre Troupe Abel Seyler or the Guardasonische Gesellschaft of Italian Operavirtuoso with their performances of his musico-dramatic works, had prepared the ground for a warm welcome for Wolfgang Amadeus in Saxony.

It is true that he had been connected to the electoral family since 14 October 1787, when – in honour of the marriage of Archduchess Maria Theresa of Tuscany, a daughter of the later Emperor Leopold II, to the brother of the Elector, Prince Anton Clemens Theodor of Saxony (he himself became king in 1827) – he conducted a performance of *Le Nozze di Figaro* in Prague. The Elector had been interested in his instrumental works for a long time, he had brought in from Vienna what was available and he even played them in arrangements himself.

That is why it seemed quite normal that Wolfgang Amadeus received an invitation to a court concert at the Residenzschloss immediately after his arrival in Dresden on Easter Sunday, 12 April 1789, which he followed two days later.

In the Electress' Room, which was located on the first floor of the west wing, where the court concerts usually took place, he played his *Concerto for Piano and Orchestra in D major* (KV 537), which later became popular as the *Coronation Concerto*.

After a successful concert at the Elector's on 14 April, which brought in Mozart 'a very nice box' – whether it contained 100 ducats has unfortunately not been documented – the Hofkirche then witnessed a veritable organ competition the next day with the Erfurt organist Johann Wilhelm Hässler, who was a grand-pupil of Johann Sebastian Bach.

Here, as in the house of the Russian ambassador Prince Alexander Mikhailovich Beloselski-Beloserki on Neustadt's Kohlmarkt, where the competition on the fortepiano continued, Wolfgang Amadeus Mozart left the place as the winner.

As was usually the case during his travels, Wolfgang Amadeus cultivated old and new contacts. On the same evening, he attended a performance of an opera by Cimarosas at the Dresden Italian Opera House, which he found 'truly miserable', and celebrated a reunion with his 1775 first Sandrina from *La Finta Giardiniera*, Rosa Manservisi.

He met some new people and discussed with them possible composing-projects. For example, Mozart used the last two days of his stay in Dresden, on the Thursday and Friday after Easter, primarily to visit the Körnerhaus before leaving on 18 April. There he continued his journey with the lawyer Christian Gottfried Körner. Körner loved to organize literary and musical salons at his home. At Körner's house, Wolfgang Amadeus was not only attracted by the prospect of excellent cuisine, for which he provided the table music after long improvisations, but above all by the sister-in-law of the householder, Dora Stock. She was a well-known and popular Dresden painter and she made one of the most authentic depictions of the composer today, the well-known silverpoint drawing-portrait of Wolfgang Amadeus, which she probably had the opportunity to make because of his extended table music. All in all, Mozart was able to book his visit to Dresden as a complete success, because he was celebrated alike by the nobility and the bourgeoisie.

In the city of Leipzig in Germany, on the evening of his arrival, Wolfgang Amadeus met the secretary of the Secret War Council,

Johann Leopold Neumann at Schloßstraße 36 – certainly not just to meet the outstanding soprano of the Classical era, Josepha Duschek, because Neumann's pianist wife Natalie Bassemann was considered the soul of the people who had been there since 1777, held academies – the so-called 'Bassemann concerts' – with the participation of the court orchestra. The contact was soon made, the next day they visited the Hofkirche together to hear a mass by the Dresden composer Johann Gottlieb Naumann and got together in the afternoon for a private concert.

Then, Wolfgang Amadeus improvised on the organ and gave a concert on 12 May in the Gewandhaus Concert Hall. The concert program consisted of the piano concertos KV 456 and KV 503, as well as two scenes for soprano (KV 505, KV 528), the fantasy for piano solo (KV 475) and two unknown symphonies. He then reported to his wife on the failure of his concert. This concert, organized at really short notice, apparently was not well attended, which must have been frustrating for the Austrian composer who was used to having crowds of fans waiting for him. In a letter to his wife, he tried to explain the situation to her, presumably to get her sympathy:

Dearest, most treasured little wife of my heart!

What? – Still in Leiptzig! – Although I said in my last letter, of the 8th or 9th, that I would already be leaving again at 2 o'clock that night, my friends' numerous requests moved me not to cause affront to Leiptzig: just because of the mistakes of one or two persons: but to give a concert on Tuesday the 12th. – On the one hand it was splendid enough as far as applause and honour were concerned, but on the other hand all the more beggarly as far as takings are concerned.[59]

While Prince Lichnowsky decided to drive home, Wolfgang Amadeus remained in Leipzig until 17 May because of his desire – as he later related in a letter to Constanze – to remain in the company of 'a group of friends who were also visiting the city'; he specifically spoke of Johann Leopold Neumann, his pianist wife Natalie and Josepha Duschek. His departure then was delayed again, so he tried to explain this to his wife by arguing that there weren't enough horses available for the trip. Behind the scenes it was more credible that Wolfgang Amadeus had incurred financial debts with Lichnowsky during this trip. The amount of the debt was in fact 1,415 guilders, for which the prince would successfully sue him in October 1791.

But Wolfgang Amadeus continued his way on to the Prussian court in Berlin and on 19 May – which was the night he arrived in Berlin – he attended a performance of his own opera *The Abduction from the Seraglio* incognito at the Royal Opera House, which is today the Lindenoper. Nevertheless, local newspapers did never report his presence. It was recorded much later – not until 1856 in the posthumously published memoirs of the German poet, fiction-writer, translator and critic Ludwig Tieck. At the time, Ludwig Tieck was 16 years old:

Ludwig's appreciation for Mozart was to be rewarded in surprising ways. One evening in 1789, when he entered the dimly lit and still empty auditorium, as usual, long before the start of the performance, he saw a man he did not know in the orchestra pit. He was small, agile, restless, and had a silly expression on his face: a nondescript figure in a grey cloak. He walked from one music stand to the next, seemingly examining the music on them carefully. Ludwig immediately struck up a conversation. They spoke of the orchestra, of the theatre, of the opera, of the taste of the public. He expressed himself openly, but spoke with the deepest admiration of Mozart's operas. 'So you often listen to Mozart's operas and like them?' 'That's very kind of you, young man,' the stranger asked. They continued talking for some time, the hall slowly filled, and finally the stranger was called away by someone on the stage. Ludwig was strangely moved by his words; he asked. It was Mozart himself, the great master, who spoke to him and expressed his appreciation.

On 26 May, Wolfgang Amadeus directed the performance himself, in the presence of the king and the queen. The atmosphere was excellent. The orchestra, he praised afterwards, saying that they were 'the best gathering of virtuosos in the whole world, which of course could be even better if the gentlemen played together'. He would never become a 'Berliner', although he was offered four times the annual salary compared to Vienna. But the people remained fond of him in Berlin. He later reported on receiving an award of 800 guilders as well as commissions from the king for six string quartets and a set of six easy piano sonatas for Princess Frederica Charlotte of Prussia.

Wolfgang Amadeus left Berlin on 28 May. He then travelled via Dresden to Prague, where he stayed till 2 June and finally arrived in Vienna at noon on 4 June. As he returned to his family, he found a sick Constanze in his apartment. In the summer she travelled for the first time to Baden near Vienna for a special cure. During her marriage to Wolfgang Amadeus, Constanze Mozart was pregnant six times in the nine years together, which exhausted her strength so that she was bedridden again and again. Added to this were frequent moves and the lack of money in recent years. All of this always weighed heavily on her and as a result, Wolfgang Amadeus repeatedly sent his wife to Baden for cures, with a friend, the choir director Anton Stoll, helping the two of them to find a suitable accommodation for her. It is said that she had problems with her feet. With time, it turned out that Constanze's foot ailment seemed to lead to a therapeutically complicated and dangerous clinical picture. This also resulted in high doctor and pharmacy bills, to which there were also added the constant spa stays in Baden. In June and July 1791, Constanze also visited the 'Antonienbad', which was particularly expensive and was therefore 'only visited by patients of a higher rank', as reported in a contemporary description. It is said, that Constanze aged quickly during all of her stays in Baden, because of the intense cures she got there.

Wolfgang Amadeus visited his wife repeatedly during her times at the cure and – on this occasion – performed several works in the Baden parish church together with Anton Stoll, who was responsible for church music there as choirmaster. Wolfgang Amadeus composed especially for Anton Stoll on 17 and 18 June 1791 in Baden one of his most famous sacred works, the *Ave verum* (KV 618), which had its world premiere on Corpus Christi Day of the same year – 23 June – in the Baden parish church.

Whenever Constanze took a cure in Baden and was separated from her husband, Wolfgang Amadeus wrote her. There were a total of sixty letters and notes that he wrote to her in the summer and autumn of 1791 and sent to Baden. Unfortunately, not all of them are preserved today, just twenty-one pieces. At least one letter every day, in which the loving husband outlines a great deal about what he does, how he does it and how he advances in his career. He writes about his love for her, that he misses her infinitely and that he longs for letters from her. But she is very reluctant to write back to him. In his letters that he mostly started with a salutation in French (*Ma très chère* épouse), before unexpectedly switching into German, even if sometimes he used a combination of other languages like Italian, his writing had more a funny narrative character and was, in fact, full of love.

It might be a fact, that Constanze Mozart had an affair with a very young man, at a time when she was pregnant for the last time. Officially, of course, her husband seemed to be the father of this new child in their life. After Constanze had alienated Wolfgang Amadeus from his father and sister, ruined him and socially isolated him, it becomes more and more clear, that she sought some distraction from this marriage with the 'child prodigy' in the elegant city of Baden, while her husband was in despair, officially still happily set about raising money for his dear family through his compositions.

One can follow closely in Wolfgang Amadeus's letters that he only found mockery of the crudest kind for her young companion, whose name was Franz Xaver Süssmayr. Süssmayr strove to be at the centre of musical life, which was making waves in the imperial city of Vienna at the time. And he quickly pulled it off. He was 25 years old, and she used to refer to him as Wolfgang Amadeus's 'student', since he had known him since 1788, because in a letter dated 26 August 1797, Franz Xaver Süssmayr mentions to the Abbot of Lambach that his operetta *Der rauschige Hans*, which he dated 6 March 1788, was written 'under the direction of the blessed, immortal Mozart'.

Franz Xaver Süssmayr was originally a student of Antonio Salieri. According to a statement by Constanze, however, Süssmayr then became a student of her husband in 1790. However, according to lore, this man was introduced to everybody as a music copyist and a family friend. Süssmayr also prepared the voice excerpts and copies of a composition for his master that was about to be created in Vienna and he is said to have assisted Wolfgang Amadeus in composing the secco recitatives in *La clemenza di Tito*.

In Wolfgang Amadeus Mozart's letters, the mockery towards Franz Xaver Süssmayr reads something like this –

I shall answer Süssmayer when we meet – it is a pity to waste the paper. (25 June 1791).

I would ask you to tell Süssmayer, that clumsy boy, that he should send me my score of the first act, from the introduction to the finale, so I can do the instrumentation. (2 July 1791)

They wanted to make the acquaintance of Süssmayer, that Great Man, and only called on me in order to ask where he lives, because they had heard that I am fortunate enough to carry some weight with him. – I said they should go to The Hungarian Crown and wait there until he comes back from Baaden! – Snaï! – They want to engage him as a candle trimmer. (same letter as before!)

Give <Süssmayr> a clip round the ears, and say you had to swat a fly which I had seen! – farewell Catch! - Catch! – – sm – sm – sm smacking little kisses, sugar-sweet, are flying towards you! (6 July 1791)

Süssmayr also became the accompanist of the heavily pregnant Constanze Mozart in Baden, where he made the parts and copies of the opera *Die Zauberflöte*, written in Vienna, for his 'master' Wolfgang Amadeus Mozart. As already written, he had a love affair with Constanze and from this the last son, Franz Xaver Wolfgang Mozart, born on 26 July 1791, is said to have resulted. The first names Franz Xaver are perhaps not real proof of paternity, because they were common male first names in the Alpine republic of Austria at that time. Several friends of Wolfgang Amadeus even have the first name Franz.

It is also interesting to note that Constanze, together with her later second husband, the diplomat Georg Nikolaus von Nissen, often deleted the name 'Süssmayr' from Wolfgang Amadeus's letters. The depiction of one of Wolfgang Amadeus Mozart's ears, with the indication that his son Franz Xaver has the same unusual, atavistic ear shape, seems a bit strange considering that there is nothing special in the portraits that exist of Wolfgang Amadeus regarding his ears.

Should Franz Xaver Mozart nevertheless be a legitimate child, then he could well have been born prematurely, because Wolfgang Amadeus was not in Vienna until mid-November 1790, but was travelling. Another question that historians keep asking is whether Franz Xaver Süssmayr was a possible composing blockade for Wolfgang Amadeus for almost a year – between January and December 1790? And was Franz Xaver the reason why the letters from Constanze and Wolfgang Amadeus Mozart were already in Baden in the summer of 1790?

Not to mention the psychological aspect; historians are right to ask how Wolfgang Amadeus was able to endure his wife's relationship with Süssmayr.

In letters to the textile merchant Michael von Puchberg, Wolfgang Amadeus complained about everything – he seemed extremely dissatisfied with his life and his work. In mid-November 1789 he became again a father, but his baby daughter Anna Maria did not survive.

Concerning politics, there was a change too. An era came to an end, because on 14 July the French Revolution began with the storming of the Bastille in Paris and on 20 February 1790, Emperor Joseph II died in Vienna. Austria was not threatened with revolution; after this great reformer on the throne the pendulum swung in the direction of restorative efforts. The death of his emperor came very inconveniently for Wolfgang Amadeus. In January 1790 he had entered the *opera buffa Così fan tutte, ossia La scuola degli amanti*, which means 'All Women do it, or The School for Lovers', in his Köchel catalogue under KV 588.

This opera dealt with the two friends, Ferrando and Guglielmo, who were working as officers, and who expressed certainty that their fiancées Dorabella and Fiordiligi, will be eternally faithful. But the old philosopher Don Alfonso was sceptical and laid a wager with the two officers, claiming that he could prove in a day's time that those two, like all women, were fickle.

The premiere of Mozart's setting took place on 26 January 1790 at the Burgtheatre in Vienna. The opera was successful; it was performed five times before its run was suddenly halted by the death of Emperor Joseph II and the resulting time of court mourning. It was performed twice in June 1790, with the composer conducting the second performance, and then again in July (twice) and performed (once) in August. But after that, it was unfortunately never performed again in Vienna during Wolfgang Amadeus Mozart's lifetime.

Today, the psychologically daring and abysmal experiment of this opera fascinates in an incomparable way. Experts think that *Così fan tutte* was da Ponte's best libretto. But the refinements lie in a literary parody technique. Da Ponte played with a knowledge of poetry such as Ovid's *Metamorphoses*, Ariost's *Orlando furioso* or the dramas of Pierre de Marivaux, which was anticipated for the time. Pierre Choderlos de Laclos' epistolary novel *Les Liaisons Dangereuses* was also highly topical.

In reality, *Cosi fan tutte* was a mixture of irony and seriousness, as well as of masquerade and unmasking. In addition, there is music that does not clarify the text statements in the difficult action situations of the stage characters, but rather undermines the expectation that is aimed at it with calculation, and with a charming smile, so to speak.

Three weeks after the death of Emperor Joseph II, his brother Leopold II, previously Grand Duke of Tuscany, moved to Vienna and became his successor. He was immediately crowned king and half a year later he was also crowned Emperor in Frankfurt. For Austria, this man was something of a stroke of luck; as a regent, he saw his task as serving for the well-being of the people, but he was also committed to their approval. He was efficient and straightforward – and he made progress compared to other rulers of the time. During his two-year reign, he moderated his brother's reforms without abandoning them. He distanced himself from Russia so that a reconciliation of interests with Prussia became possible. He also acted extremely cautiously despite the historically existing alliance with France; between the expectations of his brother-in-law Louis XVI and the hot events of the French Revolution.

Leopold II was a prudent and sober Realpolitiker, not a frivolous person, but unfortunately, he could only spend little of his time on culture and cultural topics – music, theatre and art. Nevertheless, changes were to come. During his years in Florence, Italian taste in music had become his taste. These were not favourable conditions for Wolfgang Amadeus nor for the Imperial conductor Antonio Salieri – although the new emperor had experienced the child prodigy performances at the imperial court. In addition, Gottfried von Swieten lost his influence and his position at the imperial court.

Unfortunately, Wolfgang Amadeus's attempts to get a second court music director position through a connection that he had with Leopold's son, Archduke Francis II had no chance from the start.

In 1790, Wolfgang Amadeus's position was obviously the most critical of his time in Vienna. His efforts to get major concert appearances, to attract well-heeled students and to position his compositions well in the international music publishing industry had had absolutely no effect. In any case, far too little to offset his debts.

Every week he asked his friend Michael von Puchberg for money and this was probably difficult for him – all in all – to bear. Being in debt and constantly begging others for money can't do you any good in the long run. Despite an income of 1,500 guilders in 1790, which was more than a doctor or a university professor earned at the time, he lived much too lavishly. He had a soft spot for luxurious apartments in downtown Vienna.

In his flat at the Rauhensteingasse, which cost him 300 guilders a year, he had a lot of space for him and his family, but also a music room, a study room and a billiard room. In addition, he was a vain man who always wanted to be well perfumed and well dressed and so he spent enormous amounts of money on this. In his household he employed a cook, a maid and a servant. He also owned a riding horse with modern equipment. Overall, the danger in his actions was of losing touch with concrete reality.

As a young man he was secure because he had his father, who watched over him and warned him if he took things too far, because Leopold simply wanted his son to do well. But after that he lived out his time as a musician in Vienna and no longer had any critical confidants as his wife did not take over this function.

Wolfgang Amadeus travelled once more, to Frankfurt. On the same day that Leopold II left for Frankfurt to be crowned – 23 September 1790 – Wolfgang Amadeus left for the same city accompanied by his brother-in-law and a servant. He travelled in a single carriage at lightning speed on a previously unknown route via Regensburg,

Nuremberg, Würzburg and reached Frankfurt unharmed on 28 September. There he once again met some former acquaintances and hoped that he could possibly get commissions for compositions or maybe even a position at court.

When the emperor arrived on 4 October, Wolfgang Amadeus believed that the Churmainz Actors' Society would put on *Don Giovanni* in his honour. But things turned out very differently and *Die Liebe im Narrenhause* by Karl von Dittersdorf was performed. At the coronation of the emperor, nothing by Wolfgang Amadeus was performed either, but a festive mass by Vicenzo Righini and the *Te Deum* by Antonio Salieri. Wolfgang Amadeus was very sad about it.

But a few days later, *The Abduction from the Seraglio* was unexpectedly performed by an acting company from the Electorate of Trier. This gave him a boost again. Nothing was lost yet. The hope for further pieces triumphed, because on 15 October he was allowed to give a big academy at the theatre – unfortunately at lunchtime, whereas Antonio Salieri was allowed to perform his operatic *dramma tragicomico Axur, re d'Ormus* in return. In the second week, Wolfgang Amadeus travelled to Mainz to bring in a considerable fee with a concert for the elector there.

On the same day as the emperor, Wolfgang Amadeus also left the Rhine-Main area to return to Vienna. In his frustration, however, he reacted even more strangely, for he demanded that the coachman take the same route that Wolfgang Amadeus had first travelled west from Salzburg with his family twenty-seven years ago, as a child. Again, he stopped everywhere. In Mannheim, he watched *Le Nozze di Figaro*, he visited the garden and the castle of Schwertzingen, in Augsburg and in Munich he visited many old friends, including Cannabich, Marchant and Ramm. He also took part in a court academy in the Munich Residence in honour of King Ferdinand IV of Naples and his wife – both of whom were also returning from Frankfurt.

After that, however, the journey was delayed; because the return journey from Mainz to Vienna took a total of three weeks, much longer than the outward journey. However, Wolfgang Amadeus avoided a stop in Salzburg and also a stop in Sankt Gilgen with his sister Maria Anna. One still wondered whether this could be a world farewell trip? Why did he delay returning home for so long?

Another blow came when his long-time friend Joseph Haydn took a job in London and left via England in December. During Haydn's absence, Wolfgang Amadeus received an offer from his manager in England linked to an opera contract. However, it is still unclear whether he ever reacted to this offer. The actual life with worries about his wife and children as well as the preparation for the carnival season of 1791 and with plans and activities, caught up with the composer and brought him back to earth. The mountains of debt had to be dealt with. As he had done several times before, the 34-year-old Wolfgang Amadeus shook off a hint of an approaching depression and turned to the continuation of his career.

In mid-1790, Wolfgang Amadeus Mozart took a creative break while he had to recover personally from the anxiety about his financial situation. After completing the opera *Cosi fan tutte* in January 1790, he entered a string quartet in May and then nothing more until December 1790. Only then, in December of 1790, did he compose the *String quartet in D-Major* (KV 593), which was a viola concert, again written down in his Köchel catalogue.

Chapter 10

1791 – Mozart's Last Year and his Controversial Death

The year was 1791 and it seemed that since January, a rich and continuous production of music in Wolfgang Amadeus Mozart's Köchel catalogue took its course. It was a kind of magic. On one hand, Wolfgang Amadeus started to compose a large number of works for everyday use, such as; dances, songs, piano variations, pieces for mechanical musical instruments and interludes for operas by various composers. But this new year 1791 turned out to be extremely successful and promising. Unfortunately, the old cliché that has been polished over and over again about Wolfgang Amadeus Mozart, being 'lonely, rejected by society, desperate and plagued by premonitions of death' was simply wrong. Instead, he found a new meaning in his life and career and, at the same time, a perspective of completely new opportunities and successes developed for him.

And, more importantly, for the first time, he assessed this situation realistically; therefore, it was clear, that he couldn't expect much from the imperial court right now. However, his contacts in Prague offered him the chance, together with the Italian impresario Domenico Guardasoni, to contractually fix a long-discussed opera plan for a festival opera for the coronation of Leopold II as King of Bohemia. There was also reason for hope for Wolfgang Amadeus in the field of church music, because the strict Josephine church policy had suddenly been relaxed. In the spring of 1791, he decided to submit his application to the Vienna magistrate for the position of 'assistant to the cathedral conductor'. He knew that this job was not paid, but it contained the promise of being able to succeed Leopold

Hofmann as cathedral conductor, who was 53 years old at this time. The compositions by Wolfgang Amadeus of the *Ave verum* and then of the *Requiem* should also be viewed from this point of view.

But the year 1791 was also a tough one, because the new emperor fired Wolfgang Amadeus's colleague Lorenzo Da Ponte as opera librettist, due to intrigues. Da Ponte received no support from the new emperor and Antonio Salieri resigned from the directorship of the Italian-language opera in Vienna. Wolfgang Amadeus thought about it, but from this point of view, he saw no chance for a successful further production of an *opera buffa* in Vienna. Even in the difficult year of 1790, *Le Nozze di Figaro* and *Don Giovanni* were performed several times at the Burgtheatre. And so, after several years, Wolfgang Amadeus decided to turn back to the German Singspiel because, in this area, he was considered an undisputed compositional great ever since the huge success of *The Abduction from the Seraglio*. The Singspiel was no longer cultivated at the Burgtheatre, so it made sense for him to look elsewhere.

The best impresario and librettist at that time was irrevocably Emmanuel Schikaneder and his resident theatre troupe at the Theatre an der Wieden, run by his ex-wife, the actress and singer Eleonore and the Austrian journalist, actor and poet Johann Friedel. But when Friedel died in March 1789, he left his estate to Eleonore and the theatre was closed. Eleonore managed to get her ex-husband back to Vienna and they reopened the theatre again. The new company was financed by a Masonic friend of Wolfgang Amadeus, Josef von Bauernfeld.

Since 1790, Wolfgang Amadeus had attended several performances on Schikaneder's stage and also composed interludes for him. The two men knew each other from Salzburg in the 1770s, when Schikaneder's troupe made extended stays in Salzburg and when he befriended the Mozart family.

Wolfgang Amadeus had suddenly reoriented himself 180 degrees; he gave up his previously occasionally desperate efforts to organize large academies. His last public appearance as a pianist was in March

1791. As part of a concert by one of the first internationally famous clarinet virtuosos, Johann Joseph Beer in the hall on the first floor of the court traiteur, court chef and restaurant operator, Ignaz Jahn, situated in the Himmelpfortgasse number 6 (where the Café Frauenhuber is today). In the 1790s, this hall developed into a very successful concert venue in downtown Vienna. Here, Wolfgang Amadeus played his last concert on 4 March 1791, which was a solo part, the *Piano Concerto in B flat major* (KV 595). After that, he concentrated almost exclusively on compositional production.

For example, on 15 November he entered *A small Masonic Cantata in C-Major* (KV 623) in his Köchel catalogue. Then, there were also masterpieces such as the *B flat major Piano Concerto*, the *Clarinet Concert for Anton Stadler* (KV 622), *The String Quintet no. 6 in E-flat major* (KV 614) or the motet *Ave verum corpus* (KV 618). But the central works in this fabulous year were – without any doubt – the two famous operas as well as his unfinished *Requiem* (KV 626). Wolfgang Amadeus was clearly in a very special creative euphoria in this new year, which was mainly expressed in his letters – except for those to his friend Michael von Puchberg.

A letter to his wife in October 1791 shows how exact and focused he was all the year through – and it reads like that:

> This morning I composed so assiduously that I finished late, at ½ past 1 – therefore ran to Hofer's in the greatest haste: simply so as not to eat alone: where I also met Mama. Immediately after the meal I went back home again and composed [until] it was time for the opera.[60]

While the letters to his wife, when he was in Frankfurt, sounded more depressed – you could almost say depressive. But now, in the year 1791, the challenged, motivated and happy Wolfgang Amadeus reappeared again. And he was working like hell on his career and especially on his commissions.

Although the evidence is still inconclusive despite research, it seemed that wealthy patrons in Hungary and Amsterdam pledged annual donations to Wolfgang Amadeus in return for occasional compositions. He is believed to have profited from the sale of dance music written in his role as Imperial Chamber Composer. He no longer borrowed large sums from Michael von Puchberg and suddenly began to pay off his debts, which was very reassuring.

A special aura has formed around Wolfgang Amadeus Mozart's last great works. Each of them was received differently by the public. Together, however, they are genius par excellence. His opera *La Clemenza di Tito* was a completely different *opera seria* than *Idomeneo*. It was planned as a festival opera and premiered on the day of Leopold II's coronation on 6 September 1791. The commission came from the impresario Domenico Guardasoni, who lived in Prague and who had been charged by the Estates of Bohemia with providing a new work to celebrate the occasion. Guardasoni had been approached about the opera in June and he wanted to realize it with Wolfgang Amadeus. No opera of his was more clearly pressed into the service of a political agenda than *La Clemenza di Tito*, in this case to promote the reactionary political and social policies of an aristocratic elite.

From April 1791, however, Wolfgang Amadeus Mozart had another new project he became completely taken up with; he was very busy composing a new opera under the title *The Magic Flute*. After *The Abduction from the Serail*, *The Magic Flute* was Wolfgang Amadeus's second major challenge to a German Singspiel, which was a popular form during the time, that included both singing and spoken dialogue. The sources for this work fell into – at least – four categories: works of literature; earlier productions of Schikaneder's theatre company; Freemasonry; and the eighteenth-century tradition of popular theatre in Vienna. Like the opera itself, its practical and theoretical interpretation was extremely multifaceted. Brought to one formula, *The Magic Flute* fascinates as a popular and – at the same time – as an enigmatic work. It premiered on 30 September 1791 at Schikaneder's new installed theatre, the Freihaus-Theatre auf der Wieden, located on the northern edge of the Wiedner suburb, separated from the city centre by the Glacis – the ring of open ground that surrounded the interior of the city of Vienna for military defence purposes.

The public success of some of his works, in particular *The Magic Flute* – which had been performed several times in the short time between its premiere and the death of Wolfgang Amadeus – and the *Little Masonic Cantata* (KV 623), which premiered on 17 November 1791, gave him enormous pleasure.

An aura of mystery surrounds Wolfgang Amadeus's *Requiem mass* (KV 626). The romantic appeal of a fragment combined with fantasies of decoding kept the debate about this work alive for decades.

The discreet awarding of orders came about through the eccentric Count Franz Walsegg zu Stuppach, who was a passionate lover of music and the theatre, following the death of his twenty-year-old wife Anna. The grieving count, only 28 himself at the time, would never remarry. A Freemason and amateur musician, Walsegg zu Stuppach had a penchant for commissioning works from composers of the day and passing them off as his own – though a sense of copyright was not as highly developed then as it is today. In this particular case, Walsegg zu Stuppach commissioned the *Requiem mass* anonymously through intermediaries and Wolfgang Amadeus received only half of the advance payment.

Details of the work's history have been critically examined again and again, and the question of which text passages and text words Wolfgang Amadeus composed last tempts burlesque speculation that has nothing to do with serious source criticism. It is said that the Austrian composer and good friend of Wolfgang Amadeus, Joseph Leopold Edler von Eybler, may have been one of the first composers to be asked to complete the score before he soon gave up and returned the manuscript to Constanze Mozart. The task might have then been given to another Austrian composer. It is the one who was first a student and became then composing assistant of Wolfgang Amadeus

– Franz Xaver Süssmayr. After that, some other, maybe younger composers, could have helped Süssmayr to finish the mass.

However, to die over the composition of a *Requiem* is an extraordinary fate and coincidence. Historians, medical historians as well as conspiracy theorists at home and abroad had for a long time many many questions about Wolfgang Amadeus's death and the connections between the funeral mass and the death of the composer. The most prominent question was: Was Wolfgang Amadeus Mozart killed? Preceeded by: Did Wolfgang Amadeus really want to compose and write his own requiem mass? Very early on there was repeated talk of a certain 'grey messenger' and of a possible poisoning of Wolfgang Amadeus by Salieri or another musical adversary.

There is a plethora of more than 150 theories and speculations from a wide variety of sources: some are less credible, while others seem believable. There are also a certain number of different hypotheses. It is amazing and disturbing at the same time. By reading and approaching them, one gets into the depth of the conspiracies.

When Wolfgang Amadeus Mozart died shortly after midnight on 5 December 1791 in Vienna and was buried in the next days without a ceremony, in a multiply documented shaft grave, no one was apparently thinking of murder. It was not until a week later that the *Musikalisches Wochenblatt* magazine from Berlin expressed the suspicion that Wolfgang Amadeus had been poisoned 'because his body swelled up after death'. He himself is said to have said in his final days that he was convinced he had been poisoned.

This theory was later supported by an alleged confession by the well-known director of the Vienna Court Opera, Antonio Salieri. He is said to have admitted to having poisoned Wolfgang Amadeus Mozart before his own death when he was taken to a psychiatric facility. Why was this a topic? Well, because one gave him greatest jealousy of Wolfgang Amadeus's successes.

However, this odd suspicion had a big catch, confirms the historical expert at the Salzburg Mozarteum, Ulrich Leisinger. Salieri was a highly respected musician of his time until the end of his life. He had a very good position at the court of the emperor and he was also very successful. That is why he had no good reason to murder Wolfgang Amadeus out of jealousy, mainly because Wolfgang Amadeus's fame was very limited during his lifetime. Furthermore, Antonio Salieri eventually retracted that claim. There are independent traditions and the fact that Salieri retracted his statement was often ignored. Only after Salieri had been largely exonerated by witnesses, expert opinions and recognized biographers were other personalities included in the group of suspects. This included not only believers, students, librettists, Freemasons, Jesuits and Jews, but also his wife Constanze as an accomplice in a conspiracy.

In addition, other rumours and assumptions about the background to his death have surfaced over the years; syphillis, lead, food, drink and organic as well as mercury poisoning and other murder theories involving other perpetrators.

Another theory by the Viennese Germanist Franz Forster adheres to the murder theory by the Viennese cloth dealer Johann Michael Puchberg. Forster expresses the suspicion that Wolfgang Amadeus was absolutely not as impoverished as is constantly claimed. For this reason, Johann Michael Puchberg poisoned him in order to get hold of his fortune – possibly even with the help of his wife Constanze Mozart.

According to another murder variant, the Austrian composer is said to have been a victim of the Freemasons. He had a close connection to the secret society and also dedicated many pieces to it. According to this murder theory, he allegedly gave away far too much information about the Freemasons in the opera *The Magic Flute*. Because of the betrayal, a lodge brother poisoned him. But *The Magic Flute* is not a purely Masonic opera, the composition is based on a fairy tale. In addition, according to this theory, the lyricist Schikaneder should have been killed much sooner than Mozart. Poisoning can therefore be ruled out.

There are several locks of Mozart's hair that have been analysed. The investigations showed that the death was not due to severe metal or lead poisoning. The anecdote with Mozart's statement that he had been poisoned cannot be proven either. This claim only surfaced ten years after his death.

Although one of Mozart's treating physicians was a chief physician of a Viennese hospital, there was no admission to a hospital. A hospital in the modern sense did not exist at that time and patients were usually treated at home, though only those who could afford it.

Shortly after Wolfgang Amadeus Mozart's death, Viennese newspapers in particular spread the claim that he had died of 'heart or chest dropsy'. Apologists who suspect genuine heart decompensation or who associate acute heart failure with other theories have referred to this.

The claim that Mozart had suffered from an overactive thyroid since 1782 and ultimately died of it, is based on descriptions by relatives and well-known portraits, in particular on the silverpoint drawing by Dorothea Stock in which the 'goggle eyes' are attributed to hyperthyroidism.

Pictures are apparently stronger than sober words. The ancient saying of the 'young dead are the darlings of the gods' has not yet lost its fascination. Again-and-again it tempts researchers, physicians, doctors, pathologists with changing results, which are then published and discussed in all the media worldwide. Unfortunately, we learn relatively little about the last weeks of his life from well-known and reliable sources.

But the facts are there; in the first half of October 1791, Constanze Mozart was back in Baden with her youngest child for her cure. In mid-October she brought Wolfgang Amadeus and their son Carl back home to the Rauhensteingasse. In the same month there were twenty-four performances of *The Magic Flute*. Then Constanze left again for Baden, this time accompanied by Franz Xaver Süssmayr. The 7-year-old Carl Mozart was at boarding school, but she took baby Franz Xaver and her younger sister Sophie to Baden with her.

Wolfgang Amadeus, alone in Vienna, first composed the *Clarinet Concerto in A major* (KV 622) for his friend, the clarinet and basset horn player Anton Paul Stadler. This concerto was the final major work he completed. It is the composer's last instrumental work and is seen as his last great completed work of any kind. Experts also call it Mozart's swan song. But he also worked – as already mentioned – on the *Requiem mass*.

His last surviving letter is dated 14 October 1791, to Constanze, and it ends as follows:

> Yesterday the journey to Bernstorf cost me the whole day, which is why I could not write – but for you not to write to me for 2 days is unforgivable, but today I firmly hope to receive news from you, and tomorrow to speak to you face to face, and to kiss you from the heart.

> Farewell, eternally your Mozart

> I kiss Sophie a thousand times, with X.Y. (Süssmayr) do what you want. Adieu.[61]

Wolfgang Amadeus's last entry in his Köchel catalogue is from 15 November; *A little freemason cantata* (KV 623). On 17 November he conducted the *Little Masonic Cantata* (KV 623) that he had finished two days before, in the lodge *To the Newly Crowned Hope* to mark the inauguration of a new temple.

His final notes are a few bars of the *Lacrimosa* in the *Requiem mass*. On 20 November, however, he fell ill and had to stay in bed. He developed a high fever, abdominal pain and extremely swollen arms and legs. The composer remained in his right mind, but he was so miserable that he even had his beloved canary taken out of the room, because he could no longer endure its trilling.

His doctors, from the First Vienna Medical School, prescribed him salts of mercury, antimony or arsenic in addition to some drugs. From the point of view of that time, most medications were plausible and understandable. However, according to our current knowledge, one could also explain the traditional symptoms of the disease with undesirable effects from these medications.

It did not get better. In the second week of illness, Wolfgang Amadeus also suffered from vomiting and diarrhoea. His body was so swollen that his clothes did not fit him any more. On 28 November, the two doctors treating him, Dr Thomas Franz Closset and Dr Matthias von Sallaba held a consultation on the course of his illness. They had helped him again and again with medicines and bloodletting, but also with cooling compresses.

On 4 December, Wolfgang was visited by Antonio Salieri who in mid-October had still been enthusiastic about the performance of his opera *The Magic Flute*. And, as his friend the composer and tenor of the Classical Era, Benedikt Emanuel Schack noted:

> On the eve of his death he had the score of the requiem taken to his bed (it was two o'clock in the afternoon) and sang the alto part himself. Schack, the friend of the house, sang, as he had always done before, the soprano part, Hofer, Mozart's brother-in-law, the tenor, gerl, later bass player at the Mannheim theatre, the bass. You were on the first bars of the *Lacrymosa* when Mozart began to cry profusely, put the score aside, and passed away eleven hours later, at one o'clock in the morning....[62]

Then, Wolfgang Amadeus fell into a coma. He died on 5 December. Contemporary specialist literature and the correspondence of the Mozart family clearly show how common bloodletting was at the time. The aim was to remove the 'matter that causes illness' from the body and restore the inner balance of fluids. The bloodletting, which was carried out on Wolfgang Amadeus shortly before his death because of acute complaints, apparently had fatal consequences.

His doctor, Dr Thomas Franz Closset, who was responsible for the procedure and was very familiar with the technique, the indications and the risks, was surprised by the quick end of his patient. At the end, his two doctors stated – and it is also in the book of the dead of St. Stephen's Church – that their patient had died of 'hot Friesel fever'. Today one would speak of an acute rheumatic fever caused by a strain of streptococcus.

The following day his corpse was laid out in a small chapel of St. Stephen's Cathedral in Vienna called the Crucifix chapel – he was also blessed. The blessing took place in the presence of his relatives and friends. After that, in the evening, his body was buried in a grave in the Sankt Marx cemetery. At that time, transfers and funerals were usually carried out without the accompaniment of relatives. There was also no right of ownership or continued existence of graves. A marking of the burial site would have been permitted, but was not carried out in Wolfgang Amadeus's case.

However, it remains incomprehensible why Constanze Mozart did not visit her husband's grave once after the funeral and apparently also did not have a gravestone laid. A funeral mass was held on 10 December in the parish church of Saint Michael and there his *Requiem Mass* was played. Whether his death was medically justifiable or unforeseen remains a mystery, despite the strenuous efforts of doctors around the world to delve into the mystery. Relatively reliable information about Wolfgang Amadeus Mozart's illnesses and their treatment are provided today by the family correspondence, which was kept in a diary up to 1787. On the other hand, only Constanze Mozart and her sister Sophie Haibel as well as a few biographers were asked about the course of the disease that led to his death, mostly only after decades. The resulting, unfortunately unavoidable, gaps in memory, contradictions and amateur descriptions of illnesses, as well as misleading translations, have had an adverse effect on the medical-historical interpretation, as have the destruction or the embellishment of records – especially those by Wolfgang Amadeus's widow Constanze and her second husband.

The most reliable source today are Wolfgang Amadeus's surviving autographs, which could not be manipulated or interpreted in a biased manner. Since numerous letters from Wolfgang Amadeus have been preserved and since he wrote his *Requiem* without any graphomotor disorders until a few hours before his death, retrospective statements about alleged impairments to his health in the course and at the end of his life are unlikely. The hypotheses discussed so far about the circumstances of Wolfgang Amadeus's death contain at most assumptions about which illness could have tied him to his bed in his last two weeks. The cause of the sudden end cannot be proven with the information available either, but a drug interaction during bloodletting seems at least obvious and has never been disputed.

All that is known is that he actually died at a time when he had regained the courage to get his career and his life under control and was still looking to his personal future with a stunning great confidence. His true fame, similar to musicians of the twentieth and twenty-first centuries – either it was hippie icon Janis Joplin, Doors frontman Jim Morrison, guitar legend Jimmy Hendrix, reggae inventor Bob Marley, Nirvana frontman Kurt Cobain, R&B hope Aaliyah or the British blues singer Amy Winehouse – only came posthumously.

Wolfgang Amadeus's adult career in Vienna was determined by many changes in the musical environments that occurred between the ten years he lived there, notably from the year 1781 till the year 1791. In terms of scope and extent, these changes in the city of Vienna presumably heralded one of the most culturally exciting but also one of the most eventful musical decades of the eighteenth century. And the always bright and enthusiastic composer Wolfgang Amadeus had to navigate this very special time very carefully and react and act constantly attentively and diplomatically to new, changing and traditional things in patronage, concert life, opera life, church music and the music trade. The changing dynamics of these elements created a cultural environment that was unique in its challenge and that suddenly produced a musical variety in his work that was unmatched by any other Viennese composer of the time and even today.

The way Wolfgang Amadeus had lived, had everything geared towards producing music – and above all himself. It wasn't just the upbringing of his parents – especially his strict father – that led him to this, but also his own experiences from childhood, his naive outbursts of the expectations placed on him into the overwhelming experience – 'Challenge me, I can do anything.' His ability to perform and compose complex pieces of music at an age at which most of the children struggle to read books, messes with the mind and is astonishing. According to eyewitnesses, Wolfgang Amadeus could improvise astoundingly well at the same age, playing his own material for hours on end. When he was a teenager, he could listen to a single performance of a piece and write down the music from memory. And what is amazing is that half of the symphonies he wrote were composed between the age of 8 and 19.

He was driven to constantly ignore his urge to explore and its limits, difficulties that arose were marginalized and so he was then able to rise again like a phoenix from the ashes. He was a sovereign artist; in order to assess how right Wolfgang Amadeus was in his self-esteem, his opponents were usually not sovereign enough and he himself seemed arrogant to them. In dealing with his fellow musicians, he was an astute critic, but unlike his role model and friend Joseph Haydn, who always expressed himself in a friendly and appreciative manner in public, he never held back his opinion.

It is interesting to observe that the many global Mozart experts, based on analyses of his letters and passages from his scores, have interpreted him in a wide variety of directions; on the one hand, he is associated with Austrian patriotism, as well as with cosmopolitanism, the German Nationalism, the liberality of tolerance or Freemasonry, as well as bourgeois sentiment and humanistic classicism.

But in reality, the Austrian musician Wolfgang Amadeus Mozart was more than a simple artist; he was after all a brilliant musician, an eclectic composer, a highly accomplished piano virtuoso, a 'King of Pop' even of his time – solely because of his enormous self-confidence. The reason for that was, that he already knew, that art and culture opened up world dimensions. This is also proved his meteoric rise soon after his death, all over Europe – and with the time one can say all over the world.

His most brilliant and solid glory was founded on his unique talent as a melodist and songwriter, whose purity of soul was untarnished. Wolfgang Amadeus Mozart was a multi-talented composer who was at ease, with a very special musical charm, a jolly temperament and therefore the beautiful products designed by his spirit will always stand the test of time.

Bibliography

VON ARNETH, Alfred Ritter, *Briefe der Kaiserin Maria Theresa an ihre Kinder und Freunde*, Verlag Wilhelm Braumüller, 1881

BERNSTEIN, Leonhard, *The Infinite Variety of Music*, (Leonhard Bernstein Masterclass in Venice on November 22, 1959), Amadeus Press, 2007.

BÖTTGER, Dirk, *Wolfgang Amadeus Mozart*, DTV Portrait, 2003

GRUBER, Gernot, *Mozart – Leben und Werk in Texten und Bildern*, Insel Taschenbuch, 1995.

GRUBER, Gernot, *Wolfgang Amadeus Mozart*, C.H. BECK Wissen in der Besck'schen Reihe, C.H. BECK Verlag, 2006.

KEEFE, Simon P., *Mozart in Context*, Cambridge University Press, 2019.

KEEFE, Simon P., *Mozart in Vienna – the Final decade*, Cambridge University Press, 2017/3rd printing 2019.

KLICKSTEIN, Gerald, *The Musician's Way: A Guide to Practice, Performance, and Wellness*, Oxford University Press; 1. Edition (3. September 2009).

LEONHART, Dorothea, *Mozart – Eine Biographie von Dorothea Leonhart*, Diogenes Verlag AG, 1996.

Mozart – The Years in Vienna - Guidebook about Mozarthaus Vienna, Metroverlag Vienna, 2018.

TENSCHERT, Dr Roland, *Mozart. Ein Künstlerleben in Bildern und Dokumenten* Mozart. Leipzig, Amsterdam, 1931.

WOLFF, Christoph *Mozart at the Gateway to his Fortune – Serving the Emperor 1788-1791*, W.W. Norton & Company Inc., 2012.

Wolfgang Amadeus Mozart Briefe – adieu, tausend küsse, und dem lacci bacci tausend Ohrfeigen, MarixVerlag GmbH, 3. Auflage 2011.

Notes

1. *Mozart Letters and Documents - Online Edition*, Stiftung Mozarteum Salzburg, Letter from 1791-06-11; Author: Mozart, Wolfgang Amadeus; Bauer/Deutsch No. 1160 (Bd.4, S.136-137); Source: Salzburg (AT), Internationale Stiftung Mozarteum, Bibliotheca Mozartiana. Addressee: Mozart, Constanze. The text is reproduced according to the *Mozartiana*. Edited from found manuscripts by Gustav Nottebohm, Leipzig 1880, pp. 46-47. The dating follows the information in the complete edition, vol. 4., p. 136.

2. Ibid. Letter from 1756-02-09, Author: Mozart, Leopold, Bauer/Deutsch No. 22 (Bd.1, S33-34); Source: Augsburg (DE), city archive. Addressee: Lotter, Johann Jakob. The note in someone else's hand "NB." on the first page refers to Leopold Mozart's notification of the birth of his son Joannes Chrisostomus, Wolfgang, Gottlieb on 27 January 1756.

3. Ibid. Letter from 1762-10-11 and 1762-10-16; Author: Mozart, Leopold, Bauer/Deutsch No. 34 (Bd.1, S.50-53); Source: Salzburg (AT). Addressee: Hagenauer, Johann Lorenz (1712-1792).

4. From *Mozart – sein Leben und Schaffen* by Karl Storck, via Projekt Gutenberg: https://www.projekt- gutenberg.org/storck/mozart/chap004.html

5. *Mozart Letters and Documents - Online Edition*. Letter from 1764-02-01 and 1764-02-03; Author: Mozart, Leopold; Bauer/Deutsch No. 80 (Bd.1, S.121-128); Source: Salzburg (AT). Addressee: Hagenauer, Maria Theresa.

6. *A Dutch report on Mozart in London* (addendum), from the *Nederlandsch Mengel-Nieuws*, Comprising all the most remarkable happenings inside and outside the Republicq, from the month of July 1764 to July 1765 [...], vol. 2, Amsterdam: 1765. This article from the second volume of *Nederlandsch Mengel-Nieuws* is a variant of one printed in the *Oprechte Haerlemse Courant*

on 16 Feb 1765 (Dokumente, 41–42, Dutch original 512). When the article appeared in the Haarlem paper, the Mozarts were still in England.

7. *Nice to meet You, Glenn!* Documentary, *How Mozart became a Bad Composer* – from Glenn Gould Magazine by Kevin Bezzana, Fall 2008 Issue (Vol.13/NO.2).

8. Glen Gould explains why Mozart was a bad composer in a controversial Public TV Show in 1968, via Open Culture.com, 22 October 2020.

9. *The Infinite Variety of Music*, Leonard Bernstein, Amadeus Press, New York, 2007, Leonhard Bernstein Masterclass in Venice on 22 November 1959.

10. *Bernstein on Teaching and Learning – Bernstein on Elvis, Mozart, and Brahms: How Notes and Ideas Blossom into Beautiful Music (Video)*, produced by Roger Englander and directed by Charles S. Dubin, What Makes Music Symphonic? was originally broadcast on the CBS Television Network on 13 December 1958, via: https://bernstein.classical.org/features/bernstein-on-mozart-presley-and-brahms-how-ideas-blossom-into-beautiful-music/

11. *The Infinite Variety of Music*, Bernstein.

12. Ibid.

13. Ibid.

14. *Mozart Letters and Documents - Online Edition*. Letter from 1762-10-11 and 1762-10- 16; Author: Mozart, Leopold; Bauer/Deutsch No. 34 (Bd.1, S.50-53); Source: Salzburg (AT). Addressee: Hagenauer, Johann Lorenz.

15. Ibid. Letter from 1764–06-28; Author: Mozart, Leopold; Bauer/Deutsch No. 90 (Bd.1, S.154-160); Source: Salzburg (AT). Addressee: Hagenauer, Johann Lorenz.

16. Quoted in *The Musician's Way: A Guide to Practice, Performance, and Wellness*, Gerald Klickstein, Oxford University Press; 1. Edition (3 September 2009), p. 4.

17. *VIII.Account of a very remarkable young musician. In a letter from the Honourable Daines Barrington, F.R.S. to Mathew Maty, M.D. Sec. R. S, Daines Barrington*, 15 February 1770 https://royalsocietypublishing.org/doi/abs/10.1098/rstl.1770.0008?_ga=2.162293628.1322840070.16467565 42- 1340956995.1646756542

18. Ibid., 1 January 1771.

19. *Mozart: Compiled and explained by Dr. Roland Tenschert*. Leipzig, Amsterdam [1931], p. 49., Johann Adolph Hasse on Mozart, from a letter from Hasse to Abbate G.M., Vienna (?), 23 March 1771.

20. Quoted in *The Musician's Way*, Klickstein.

21. Leopold Mozart in a letter to his wife, Verona, 7 January 1770.

22. *Mozart Letters and Documents - Online Edition*. Letter from 1770-01-11; Author: Mozart, Leopold; Bauer/Deutsch No. 155 (Bd.1, S.303-304); Source: Salzburg (AT). Addressee: Mozart, Anna Maria Walpurga.

23. Ibid. Letter from 1770-04-21; Author: Mozart, Leopold and Mozart, Wolfgang Amadeus; Bauer/Deutsch No. 177 (Bd.1, S.333-336); Source: Rome, Internationale Stiftung Mozarteum, Bibliotheca Mozartiana. Addressee: Mozart, Anna Maria Walpurga, Mozart, Maria Anna.

24. Ibid. Letter from 1770-04-14; Author: Mozart, Leopold and Mozart, Wolfgang Amadeus; Bauer/Deutsch No. 176 (Bd.1, S.337-340); Source: Rome. Addressee: Mozart, Anna Maria Walpurga.

25. Deiters, Arneth Alfred Ritter von (Hrsg.), *Letters from Empress Maria Theresia to her children and friends*, Vol. I, p. 92.

26. Böttger, Dirk, *Wolfgang Amadeus Mozart*, DTV Portrait, Munich/Germany 2003, p. 81.

27. *Mozart Letters and Documents - Online Edition*. Letter from 1777-10-25; Author: Mozart, Wolfgang Amadeus; Bauer/Deutsch No. 356 (Bd.2, S.86); Source: Augsburg. Addressee: Mozart, Maria Anna Thekla.

28. Ibid. Letter from 1777-11-13; Author: Mozart, Wolfgang Amadeus; Bauer/Deutsch No. 371 (Bd.2, S.121-123); Source: Augsburg. Addressee: Mozart, Maria Anna Thekla. Also *Wolfgang Amadeus Mozart Briefe – Adieu, Tausend Küsse, und dem Lacci Bacci tausend Ohrfeigen*, Marix Verlag GmbH, Wiesbaden, 3. Auflage, 2011, p. 16.

29. Ibid. Letter from 1778-02-28; Author: Mozart, Wolfgang Amadeus; Bauer/Deutsch No. 432 (Bd.2, S.307-310); Source: Augsburg. Addressee: Mozart, Maria Anna Thekla. Also *Wolfgang Amadeus Mozart Briefe* p.19.

30. Ibid. Letter from 1777-12-11; Author: Mozart, Leopold; Bauer/Deutsch No. 389 (Bd.2, S.181-185); Source: Salzburg. Addressee: Mozart, Wolfgang Amadeus and Mozart, Maria Anna Walpurga.

31. Ibid. Letter from 1777-12-20; Author: Mozart, Wolfgang Amadeus; Bauer/Deutsch No. 394 (Bd.2, S.197-200); Source: Salzburg. Addressee: Mozart, Leopold; Mozart, Joly; Maria Anna Rosalia Walpurga and Mozart, Maria Anna.

32. According to the German musicologist and lecturer Christoph-Hellmut Mahling, in: Mahling, Christoph-Hellmut (1996), *Junia's aria in Lucio Silla*. In Stanley Sadie (ed.). *Wolfgang Amadé Mozart: Essays on His Life and Music*, Oxford: Clarendon Press.

33. *Mozart Letters and Documents - Online Edition*, Letter from 1777-12-20; Author: Mozart, Leopold, Bauer/Deutsch No. 422 (Bd.2, S.272-279); Source: Salzburg. Addressee: Mozart, Wolfgang Amadeus.

34. Ibid. Letter from 1778-07-03; Author: Mozart, Wolfgang Amadeus, Bauer/Deutsch No. 459 (Bd.2, S.390-391); Source: Salzburg. Addressee: Bullinger, Joseph.

35. Ibid. Bauer/Deutsch No. 458 (Bd.2, S.387-390); Source: Salzburg. Addressee: Mozart, Leopold.

36. Ibid. Letter from 1778-09-11; Author: Mozart, Wolfgang Amadeus; Bauer/Deutsch No. 487 (Bd.2, S.472-478); Source: Salzburg. Addressee: Mozart, Leopold.

37. Ibid. Letter from 1778-07-09; Author: Mozart, Wolfgang Amadeus; Bauer/Deutsch No. 462 (Bd.2, S.393-399); Source: Salzburg. Addressee: Mozart, Leopold.

38. Ibid. Letter from 1779-01-08; Author: Mozart, Wolfgang Amadeus; Bauer/Deutsch No. 520 (Bd.2, S.536-538); Source: Salzburg. Addressee: Mozart, Leopold.

39. Ibid. Letter from 1780-12-16; Author: Mozart, Wolfgang Amadeus; Bauer/Deutsch No. 563 (Bd.3, S.59-61); Source: Salzburg. Addressee: Mozart, Leopold.

40. Ibid.

41. Ibid. Bauer/Deutsch No. 569 (Bd.3, S.69-71); Source: Salzburg. Addressee: Mozart, Wolfgang Amadeus.

42. Ibid. Letter from 1780-11-29; Author: Mozart, Wolfgang Amadéus; Bauer/Deutsch No. 545 (Bd.3, S.34-35); Source: Salzburg. Addressee: Mozart, Leopold.

43. Ibid. Letter from 1781-01-03; Author: Mozart, Wolfgang Amadeus; Bauer/Deutsch No. 574 (Bd.3, S.79-80); Source: Salzburg. Addressee: Mozart, Leopold.

44. Ibid. Letter from 1780-11-29; Author: Mozart, Wolfgang Amadeus; Bauer/Deutsch No. 545 (Bd.3, S.34-35); Source: Salzburg. Addressee: Mozart, Leopold.

45. Ibid. Letter from 1781-03-17; Author: Mozart, Wolfgang Amadeus; Bauer/Deutsch No. 563 (Bd.3, S.93-95); Source: Salzburg. Addressee: Mozart, Leopold.

46. Ibid. Letter from 1781-04-04; Author: Mozart, Wolfgang Amadeus; Bauer/Deutsch No. 586 (Bd.3, S.101-103); Source: Salzburg. Addressee: Mozart, Leopold.

47. Ibid. Letter from 1781-05-09; Author: Mozart, Wolfgang Amadeus; Bauer/Deutsch No. 592 (Bd.3, S.110-112); Source: Salzburg. Addressee: Mozart, Leopold.

48. Ibid. Letter from 1781-05-12; Author: Mozart, Wolfgang Amadeus; Bauer/Deutsch No. 593 (Bd.3, S.112-114); Source: Salzburg. Addressee: Mozart, Leopold.

49. Ibid. Letter from 1781-12-15; Author: Mozart, Wolfgang Amadeus; Bauer/Deutsch No. 648 (Bd.3, S.179-182); Source: Salzburg. Addressee: Mozart, Leopold.

50. Ibid. Letter from 1782-08-07; Author: Mozart, Wolfgang Amadeus; Bauer/Deutsch No. 684 (Bd.3, S.218-219); Source: Salzburg. Addressee: Mozart, Leopold.

51. Ibid. Letter from 1781-06-02; Author: Mozart, Wolfgang Amadeus; Bauer/Deutsch No. 602 (Bd.3, S.124-125); Source: Salzburg. Addressee: Mozart, Leopold.

52. Ibid. Letter from 1781-03-24; Author: Mozart, Wolfgang Amadeus; Bauer/Deutsch No. 585 (Bd.3, S.97-101); Source: Salzburg. Addressee: Mozart, Leopold.

53. Ibid. Letter from 1782-12-28l; Author: Mozart, Wolfgang Amadeus; Bauer/Deutsch No. 715 (Bd.3, S.245-246); Source: Salzburg. Addressee: Mozart, Leopold.

54. Ludwig Schiedermair, *The Letters of W.A. Mozart and his family*, *Letter to Michael von Puchberg*, Vienna, 27 June 1788.

55. *The Letters of Mozart and his Family*, Emily Anderson (ed), *Letter from Mozart in Salzburg to Padre Martini in Bologna*, 4 September 1776, Palgrave Macmillan, 1966.

56. *Mozart Letters and Documents - Online Edition*, Letter from 1782-02-16; Author: Mozart, Leopold; Bauer/Deutsch No. 847 (Bd.3, S.372-374); Source: Salzburg. Addressee: Berchtold zu Sonnenburg, Maria Anna.

57. Anderson, *Letter from Mozart in Salzburg to Padre Martini in Bologna*, 4 September 1776, Palgrave Macmillan, 1966.

58. *Mozart Letters and Documents - Online Edition*. Letter from 1789-05-16; Author: Mozart, Wolfgang Amadeus; Bauer/Deutsch No. 1099 (Bd.4, S.86-87); Source: Salzburg. Addressee: Mozart, Constanze.

59. Ibid. Letter from 1791-10-08; Author: Mozart, Wolfgang Amadeus; Bauer/Deutsch No. 1195 (Bd.4, S.159-161); Source: Salzburg. Addressee: Mozart, Constanze.

60. Ibid. Letter from 1791-10-14; Author: Mozart, Wolfgang Amadeus; Bauer/Deutsch No. 1196 (Bd.4, S.161-163); Source: Salzburg. Addressee: Mozart, Constanze.

61. Ibid.

62. Deutsch (1965, pp. 536–7). The obituary appeared in the Allgemeine musikalische Zeitung, 25 July 1827 (36 years after Wolfgang Amadeus Mozart's death) and probably reflects a story told to the author by the composer, tenor and close friend of Mozart, Benedikt Emanuel Schack.

Index of People